Ex Líbrís

KAREN ADIRIM

D1091495

frederick's
OF HOLLYWOOD
1947 - 1973
26 Years of Mail Order Seduction

Edited by Laura & Janusz Gottwald

CASTLE BOOKS / NEW JERSEY

New York

Since this book is a collection of fashions from
1947—1973, most of the styles, unfortunately,
are no longer available, nor are the prices
applicable.

Cover Illustration: Patrick Ball
Cover Design: Jon Scherff
Design: Amperzand Design, Inc.
This Edition published by
arrangement with Strawberry Hill, Inc.

Published in 1973 by
Drake Publishers Inc.
381 Park Avenue South
New York, New York 10016

© Strawberry Hill, Inc., 1973

ISBN 0-87749-582-3

LCCCN 73-17466

Printed in the United States of America

Don't look INSIDE unless you love daring Hollywood Fashions!

Don't Get Caught

WITH NOTHING TO WEAR!

STOCK UP NOW WITH LOTS OF NEW, SMART HOLLYWOOD ORIGINALS!

STYLES THAT WILL BRING YOU

★ Hollywood Glamour & Allure
★ Many Flattering Compliments
★ Thrilling New Romance
★ Dreams Come True!

Contents

Introduction

by Frederick N. Mellinger

Recently, I received the following letter. It's just a sample of the thousands of such letters we receive each year:

> Dear Mr. Frederick:
>
> What's *she* got that *I* don't? Last night I went with my boyfriend to our favorite steak place. And you know what happened . . . after all these months of going together he saw another girl and he started ignoring me.
>
> Now, Mr. Frederick, I am not all that bad. I've got the kind of bumps most men like and I thought they were in the right places. And so did George. Until last night. Well this gal was sitting with another guy and she was in a top that looked like two G strings tied together over a long skirt with a slit way up to her thigh. George flipped. Well, I was wearing my new pantsuit and I thought I looked great. George sat and stared and when her guy went to pay the check, George went over and talked to her. I nearly threw a pitcher at him and started yelling. George finally came back with a red face and a stupid look. You know what he did? He said, "Well I got it." And I said, "What, her phone number, you miserable slob, I never want to . . ." And George leaned over and kissed me right in front of everybody and gave me . . . a Frederick's catalog.
>
> Dear Mr. Frederick: What is the hottest number you have got? What did you do to make that girl look so good? Your new customer,
>
> Marion S.
> Riverside, California

I personally answered her letter and told her that *fashion* does not always enhance a woman if her *under*fashions are not doing the right job.

The girl who doesn't know about Frederick's figure balancing act can be at a disadvantage. Just like the woman who wrote that letter to me. You know, we *do* have a figure balancing act! We can bring up a droopy bust, suppress the stomach, pull the waist in to achieve proportion in a woman's figure. If a woman is short, we can add 5 inch heels, put a dome on her head under a wig, and re-distribute her figure so that she looks taller, slimmer, more in balance. Our experts will tell you . . . there is no "perfect" woman, but a perfectly proportioned woman with a balanced figure is a real attention-getter.

A woman can buy what should be the curviest, clingiest, jersey dress and when she turns her back, disappoint a male admirer. Why??? Because her rear end is flat or saggy, and the dress then becomes baggy over her derriere. Our Fanny Padders or "Living End" girdles do extremely well, and we introduce new versions whenever we feel a fashion trend in the air.

At Frederick's we always have something new in our balancing act, from four way switchable-strap bras to sculptured leg pads for skinny (or malformed) legs. You wouldn't, think leg pads would be a popular item, but we sell thousands every year. With *fashion* trends always in mind, we know that the popular long skirts slit to about the knee emphasize a woman's leg . . . and that leg better be nicely curved or a man can lose interest.

I love women. I love their curves. I love looking. That's how it all started in 1946.

Where were the satin and lace nightgowns and slips that went with every mental picture I'd had of girls, who *did* turn me on when I was in the Army?

I was working for a mail order firm as a buyer. I suggested changes to my bosses. The changes were sneered at.

I moved to Hollywood. Started a mail order catalog business in one tiny room, near the Main Post Office. A very unfancy neighborhood. But I had one thing in mind. I wanted to help make ANY woman her most feminine, alluring, sexy self. I studied anatomy. Why breasts drooped. Why fannies or hips were flat. Why waists were thick. Why legs were "piano legs." I knew there *had* to be ways to reproportion women and give *every* lovable one of them EQUAL OPPORTUNITY in the eyes of men!

Here, in this book, you'll see why Frederick's of Hollywood fashions have become famous! That Frederick's Catalog look has always been *consistent*. Always SEXY. Always FEMININE. Always ALLURING. Always aimed at MEN! Yes. I have always believed that a woman should dress to please the MAN in her life.

Popular demand over the years made our first retail stores happen. I started small, with just a couple of stores in the Hollywood area in 1952. There are over 68 Frederick's of Hollywood stores coast to coast, now, each specializing in the most. The most alluring, body-hugging, figure-enhancing outer fashions and body-sculpture foundations I can discover.

I believe that a woman's body should NEVER be a VEHICLE for a designer's fashions. Rather – a designer should FASHION his clothes to ENHANCE a WOMAN'S BODY.

I BELIEVE I OWE IT TO ALL WOMEN . . . to help them proportion and reproportion their bodies so that their appearance in our *fashions* is perfect and in proportion.

DUMB FASHION TRENDS ARE NOT FOR US, OR OUR CUSTOMERS. The tent, trapeze, the square "Mandarin" look, the "sack" had no place in *our* catalog OR on our customers!

WE CHANGE FASHIONS for the BETTER . . . to DO MORE for a woman! THE DIFFERENCE is for *one purpose*. To glorify and re-glorify a woman's figure.

Yes, Frederick's of Hollywood *is* different. We have *never* sold fashions that aren't basically *sexy*.

For 27 years we've been helping women "keep the life in their love . . . and the love in their lives."

On that score, we're not going to change.

We've celebrated "la difference" for 27 years . . . why break up the party now?

"Come Up and See Our Gorgeous Glamour Hollywood Store when you are in Hollywood"

Editors' Note

These are the clothes that fulfilled and helped define the American woman's dream from the mid 1940's to the early 1970's. We've tried to capture some of this dream in our selections from the Frederick's collections.

All of the copy and fashion illustrations are directly photographed from the Frederick's of Hollywood catalogs. We have also tried to preserve the feeling and texture of the original catalogs in the design of this book.

In compiling these materials we encountered some difficulties. All the original artwork had been lost or destroyed. A number of catalogs were also lost (most notably the years 1959 through 1962). And, all of the existing catalogs were poorly preserved, thereby forcing from the book many items which couldn't be salvaged or reproduced.

However, the less-than-perfect quality of some of the reproductions is far outweighed by both their authenticity and the design of the fashions themselves.

September 1973

Flats Fixed Here

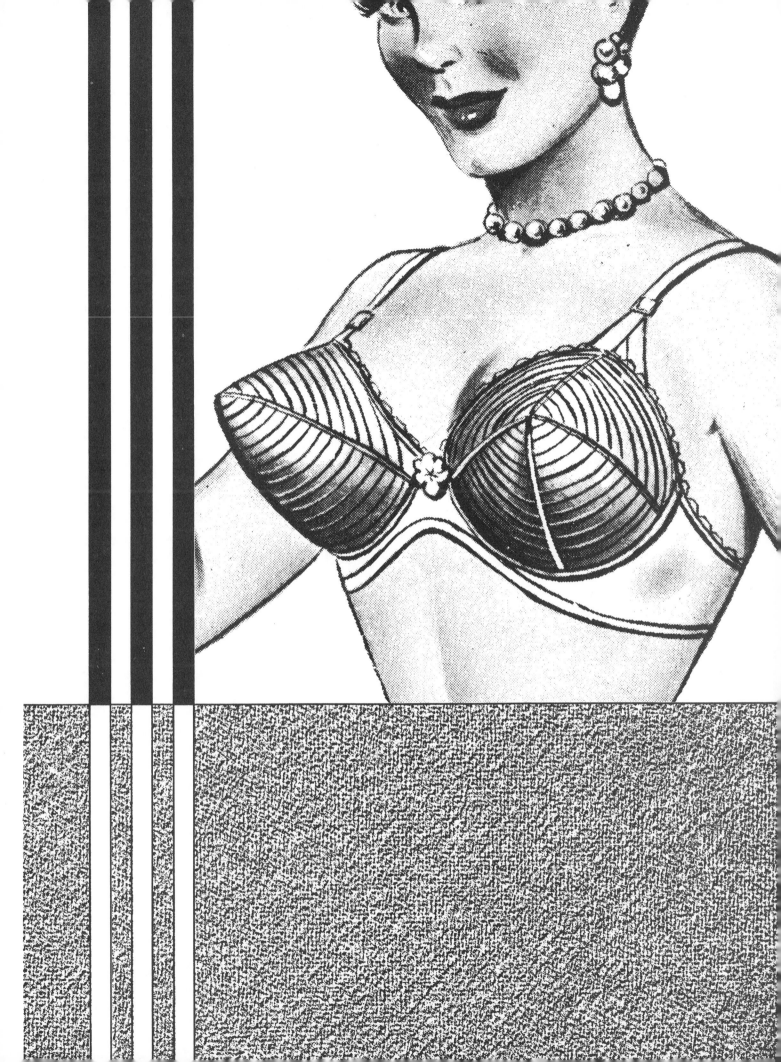

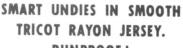

SMART UNDIES IN SMOOTH TRICOT RAYON JERSEY. RUNPROOF!

$1⁸⁹ ea.

HALF SLIP

Longer length. Elastic waist, lace trim. White or Tearose. Small, Medium, Large.
STYLE NO. 4-A   3 for $5⁵⁵

HOLLYWOOD → BRIEFS

Full-cut! Elastic legs and waist band. Double crotch. White or Tearose. Small, Medium, Large.
3 for $1²²
STYLE NO. 4-B

FLARED PANTY

← Full-cut; fine quality rayon;
TEAROSE
Size 6-(38 hips)
Size 7-(40 hips)
3 for $1⁸⁹
EXTRA SIZES:
Size 8-(42 hips)
Size 9-(44 hips)
STYLE NO. 4-C   3 for $2¹⁹

Just a MERE WHISPER of SHEER, SHEER *Nylon*

"Bare Illusion" Panties

To wear under your prettiest things when you want to feel extra alluring and just a little naughty, too! Adorable "sweet nothings" of 100% nylon diamond-net that wears like mad, because it's RUNPROOF . . . dries in a split second! Bridal White, Black, Flesh Pink. Sizes: Small (22 inch waist); Medium (24-26 inch waist); Large (28-30 inch waist).

Style No. 114 — ONLY $1⁹⁸

3 Pairs for $5.79
(Better Get THREE!)

Radiant PLUNGING BRA
by CHARMFIT of Hollywood

Just the bra you need for all the stunning low-necked styles you buy from FREDERICK'S! Gently wired for firm separation; stitched cups give alluring young bustline. WHITE rayon satin.
A Cup, Sizes 32 to 36
B Cup, 32 to 38 $3⁵⁰
STYLE NO. 116

BUY AT LEAST TWO!

"SLIP SENSATION"

Precious pure NYLON with 6-gore, fitted princess lines; trimmed with wide bands of dreamy NYLON LACE: Bust sizes: 32 to 40. White, Pink, Black.
Style No. 708
← $6⁹⁸

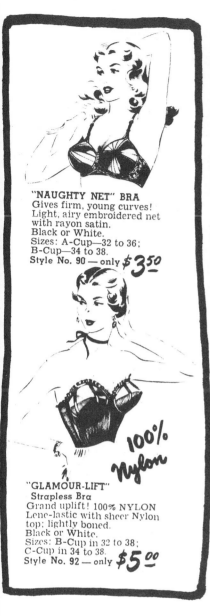

"NAUGHTY NET" BRA
Gives firm, young curves!
Light, airy embroidered net
with rayon satin.
Black or White.
Sizes: A-Cup—32 to 36;
B-Cup—34 to 38.
Style No. 90 — only $3⁵⁰

"GLAMOUR-LIFT"
Strapless Bra
Grand uplift! 100% NYLON
Lene-lastic with sheer Nylon
top; lightly boned.
Black or White.
Sizes: B-Cup in 32 to 38;
C-Cup in 34 to 38.
Style No. 92 — only $5⁰⁰

100% Nylon

"FANCY PANTS" in PLASTIC GIFT KIT
Seven pairs of panties—each a different shade
with embroidered names of days of week & cute
designs. Darling plastic gift kit can be used for
knitting, beach, sewing, etc.
Sizes: 24 to 30 inch waist. Gorgeous rayon
jersey—
Style No. 88
only $6⁴⁹ for 7 pairs in gift kit.

100% NYLON

"HOLLYWOOD SCANDALS" GARTER-PANTY
Sheer, sheer NYLON tricot. Elastic waist,
perfect fit, detachable garters, runproof.
White, Shy Pink, Black.
Sizes: 22 to 30 inch waist measure.
Style No. 128—only $2⁸⁹

"GAY PAREE" CHEMISE
Shorter, barer, sexier than a slip—and
perfect under sheer-top styles! Smooth
SATIN* hugs each curve. Lace bra-top and
trim for that French look. Button-crotch;
adjustable straps. Bust sizes: 32 to 40.
Paris-Pink, Black.
Style No. 714—SALE PRICE $5²⁸

Hollywood Glamour !

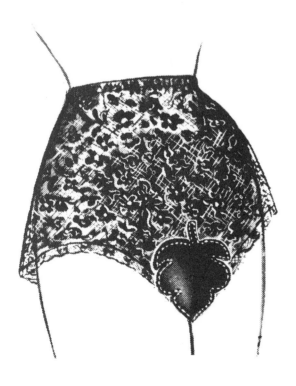

"SWEET NOTHINGS"
Bikini-Style Panties
Scandalously sheer lace—
fit perfectly—look SO cute.
Black or White. Waist
measure: 22 to 30 inches.
Style No. 706—
only $1.98 each

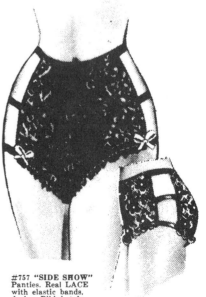

"ADAM-and-EVE" Panties
Naughty & new! Real
FRENCH LACE with
daring appliqued fig leaf
of satin. Black only-
Style No. 124 **$3.49**

#757 "SIDE SHOW"
Panties. Real LACE
with elastic bands,
daring Bikini-style
bare slit sides.
Black, White.
22-30" waist.
3 pairs $5.89

16

GIFT PANTIES

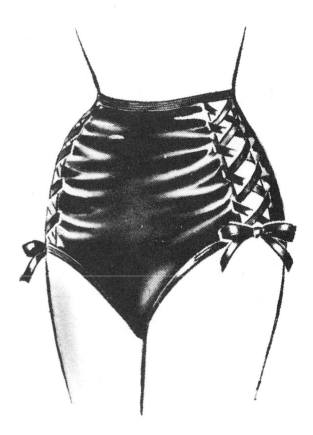

"SIDE-SHOW" Panties
Openwork design on sides
lets bare skin peek through!
Smooth BLACK rayon
satin; 2 tantalizing bows.

Style No. 126 **$2⁸⁸**

#773—"BABY PANTS"
100% NYLON brief beauties
with inset of pleats at each
side; lace trim.
White, Black, Blue.
22 to 30" waist. **3 pairs**
$5⁹⁹

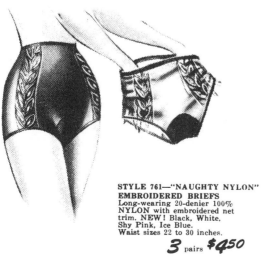

STYLE 761—"NAUGHTY NYLON"
EMBROIDERED BRIEFS
Long-wearing 20-denier 100%
NYLON with embroidered net
trim. NEW! Black, White,
Shy Pink, Ice Blue.
Waist sizes 22 to 30 inches.

3 pairs $4⁵⁰

7 SENSATIONAL PAIRS 7
NEW GIFT-BOXED NYLON PANTIES

#822 "PANTIES OF THE WEEK"
Thrilling gift! 100% Nylon panties for every
day of the week! Shockingly sheer form-fitting
panties come in 7 luscious shades . . . from
pastels to spicy Black, each embroidered for
a different day of the week. Exciting Gift Box
is yours at no extra cost! Waist sizes 22 to 30
inches.

7 pairs only . $9⁴⁹

#145—"PARIS PICTURE"
Wired 5/8 bra plus snug waist-cincher . . . AND a garter-belt all in one fabulous style. Glamorous NYLON LACE and NYLON NET; firm Satin Lastex support. Sizes 32-38, B-Cup; 34-38, C-Cup. **$9⁹⁵**

#146—"BRA-MAGIC"
New longer lines for added uplift and support. Magic "U" wire; daring low-cut for plunge-neck dresses. NYLON LACE over net with Satin Lastex. Sizes 32-38, B-Cup; 34-38, C-Cup. **$7⁹⁵**

#147—"HALF-ANGEL"
Adorable 5/8 bra to wear under low cut and strapless dresses. U-shaped padded wiring gives gorgeous separation. NYLON LACE and NET with Satin Lastex in wide band for firm support. Sizes 32 to 36. A or B-Cup. **$5⁰⁰**

#132—"SWEET 'N' LOW"
100% NYLON Plunge-Bra. Sweetest uplift, lowest plunge; lace lined with net. Wide NYLON elastic band makes it so comfortable. White 32 to 38 B-Cup; 34 to 40 C-Cup; Black, 32 to 38 B-Cup. **$4⁵⁰**

#130—"SHEER MAGIC"
Pretty HALF-BRA with sheer NYLON net top that may be folded under to make it still lower. Wired for perfect support. Rayon-Satin with power net. Sizes 32 to 36. A or B-Cup. **$4⁵⁰**

#105—"BARE FACTS" Nylon!
Lowest plunge ever for deep-neck dresses. U-shaped wire separates; new cross-over back and wired cups hold you, mold you firmly. Lined embroidered NYLON. 32 to 38 B-Cup. 34 to 40 C-Cup. **$5⁹⁵**

#104—"MY SECRET"–Padded
100% NYLON Bra. Wired cups with stitched-in foam rubber pads. Sizes 32 to 36. A or B Cups. White or Black. **$4⁵⁰**

#784—"FRENCH FOLLIES"
Chemise—Alluring, Paris-inspired, flatterer of smooth Rayon Satin with flesh-color inset of Rayon Sheer, criss-crossed lacing. Bra-fit lace top. Black with Flesh-Pink or All-Pink. Sizes 32 to 40. **$6⁹⁸**

FILMLAND'S FAVORITE BRAS

#145 NYLON $9.95

#146 NYLON $7.95

#147 NYLON $5.00

All Bras on this page in Black or White

#132 NYLON $4.50

#130 $4.50 NYLON

NYLON #105 $5.95

#784 $6.98

PADDED

100% NYLON

#104 Padded $4.50

BEFORE   AFTER

DON'T BE FLAT-CHESTED! Wear Frederick's WONDERFUL PADDED BRAS

THEY LOOK AND FEEL LIKE THE REAL THING! Springy foam rubber padding in these bras is sculptured into natural-looking curves. They look so beautiful and feel so real you'll be an alluring NEW gal! See how much smarter clothes look!

OUR PADDED BRAS ARE STYLED JUST LIKE REGULAR BRAS—AND THEY COST NO MORE!!

Don't wear dowdy, unflattering styles that shout "padded"! Frederick's padded bras are pretty as can be—look like regular bras . . . your best friends won't know you wear them!

#151 "BOSOM FRIEND" Padded Bra
Gives you adorable curves—really makes you look like a movie star! Rich Orlon Satin . . . with stitched cups and gorgeous trim of real Nylon Lace. Elastic back holds it firmly in place. White only. Sizes 32 to 36, A or B. **$5⁰⁰**

**STYLE 770—"RIOT SQUAD"
BIKINI BRA-and-PANTIE SET**
For daring gals with pretty
curves! Frederick himself
designs a pocket-size dance-set
of smooth NYLON crepe. Bra
has stitched cup and halter-tie
of elastic to wear under low-cut
styles. Bow-tied panties have
slit sides, held with elastic.
Black, White $5⁹⁸

"HOLLYWOOD FLIR-TEASE"
FRENCH LACE diaper-wrap
chemise-cute, comfy, pretty under
everything you own!
French-Pink or Paris-Black.
Sizes: 32 to 40.
Style No. 734 $ 8⁹⁸

all this Glamour for only .

#78
NYLON
$3.50

DOUBLE UPLIFT

#117
Nylon
$3.50

#117
1. Freedom from shoulder strap strain.
2. Freedom from pinching or binding.
3. Freedom from underarm wrinkles.
4. Freedom from midriff tension.

#97
REDUCED
$3.50

#96
Center of cup forms point for young natural look.
Circular stitching lifts bust up and out

$3.50 EACH

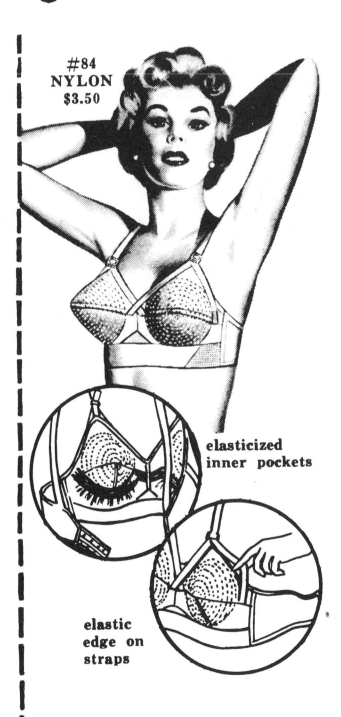

#84
NYLON
$3.50

elasticized
inner pockets

elastic
edge on
straps

#78 "DOUBLE UPLIFT" Nylon
Adjustable band under each cup assures uplift from underneath. No strain on shoulders! Lifts and separates each breast by itself; does away with droop and sagging to the side; puts you way out in front!! New and really different! White. Sizes 32 to 38, B-cup. 34 to 40, C-cup. **$3.50**

#117 "SHEER SORCERY" Nylon
Dainty Nylon net with embroidery shapes you into delicious curves! Nylon leno elastic back and band for firm uplift, lightly boned, too. Deep-plunge back and front. Black or White. Sizes 32 to 38, B; 34 to 40, C-cup. **$3.50**

#84 "STRAP MAGIC"
Lifts, separates, beautifies bust. Patented straps are elasticized to "breathe" with body and encircle bust for firm support; elasticized inner pockets end sagging. White, Black. Sizes 32 to 38, B; 34 to 40, C-cup. **$3.50**

#97 "CURVE APPEAL"
100% Nylon bra with cushioned under-cup and wide band of foam rubber. White or Black. Sizes 32 to 38, B-cup; 34 to 40, C-cup. Reduced! **$3.50**

#96 "UP AND OUT" Nylon
Filmy stitched Nylon crepe is designed to give youthful, pointed uplift to sagging breasts—wear it under sweaters and snug dresses. Black or White. Sizes 32 to 38, B; Sizes 34 to 40, C-cup. **$3.50**

PIN-UP HITS

#186 "TREASURE CHEST"
Show your pretty bosom off in Nylon-net-and-satin creation! Comfy foam rubber cushion under-cup and wide band. Black, White. Sizes 32 to 38, B; 34 to 40, C. **Reduced!** **$350**

#186
New Low Price
$3.50

#745 "PANTY PARADE" Boxed
Set of 7 pairs in 7 COLORS
Brief rayon beauties in six pastel shades with one black pair for Saturday night! Embroidered with different designs for each day of the week. Snug elastic waist, 22 to 30" waist.
7 pairs only . . . **$4²⁹**

#130
NYLON
$4.50

#130 "SHEER MAGIC" Wired
Satin with Nylon net half-bra
Top folds under for daring nude effect! Perfect for low-cut or strapless styles. Jet Black or White. Sizes 32 to 36, A or B cups— **$450**

#95 "FRENCH ACCENT" Nylon
Daring "Push-up" Lacy half-bra
Embroidered Nylon net with flirty "Can Can" ruffles. Hidden push-up insets; double wiring for divine separation. Black or White Ice. Sizes 32 to 36, A-cup; Sizes 32 to 38, B-cup. **$500**

#95
NYLON
$5.00

#111
$4.50

#111 "FRENCH SCANDAL"
WEAR IT IF YOU DARE!!
Nylon Lace cut-out cups are SO daring, so revealing . . . but give perfect uplift and support, too. White or Flirt Black. Sizes 32 to 38, B-cup. **$450**

#101 "DREAM-BRA" Nylon
Lacy, Low-Cut Half-Bra
Perfect uplift and separation! Wired to stay firmly in place. White, Black. 32 to 38, B-cup; 34 to 38, C-cup. **$500**

1954

SHAPE MAKERS

NEW OFF-SHOULDER STRAPS!

#124 "SHOULDER SHOW" New!
You can show off pretty shoulders and still have perfect uplift and support! Off-shoulder straps of light elastic stay in place—give you undreamed of freedom. Nylon lace over Nylon net with satin; light wires and insets under cups are plush-cushioned. Angel White, Black. Sizes 32 to 38, B; Sizes 34 to 38, C-cup. **$450**

#79 "STRAP STORY" Nylon
No more shoulder-strap strain! New wide-set straps of elastic power net are light and pliable—for perfect freedom and comfort. A must for scoop necks! Wired separation and insets under bust are cushioned with plush. Nylon net; net-lined. White or Black Mist. Sizes 32 to 38, B. 34 to 38, C-cup. **$350**

#169 "TWO TIMER" Nylon
2-in-one bra to wear as a regular bra or as a halter. (Detachable straps.) White only. 32 to 38, B-cup; 34 to 38, C-cup. **$295**

- So comfortable!
- Straps encircle bust.
- Added uplift, too.

- Stitched 5/8 cup
- Wired under-cup
- Wide-set straps

#115 "LACE VENUS" Nylon
Magical uplift and support . . . marvelous comfort! Straps are designed to encircle bust; and they're attached to elastic tab to stretch as you move. Dainty Nylon lace over Nylon net. So pretty you'll wish it showed! Black Mist or Gardenia White. (Buy one in each pretty color!) Sizes 32 to 38, B; Sizes 34 to 40, C. **$500**

#119 "LOW NOTE" Nylon
At last! The perfect 5/8 bra to wear with low or scoop necklines! Wide-set straps won't peep out to annoy you! Sweetheart-shape neck shows a lot of you; wired undercups are all-over stitched to give a young, firm line. Nylon lace over Nylon net with gay ribbon trim. White, Black. Sizes 32 to 34, A; Sizes 32 to 38, B-cup; Sizes 34 to 38, C-cup— **$395**

IT'S LATER THAN YOU THINK!

HOLLYWOOD

BUST

LINES

#72 "MAGIC CIRCLES"
Beautifies small or sagging bust!
Satin undercup gives sexy pointed
look! Nylon net top. White, Black.
Sizes 32 to 38, B-cup;
Sizes 34 to 40, C-cup. **$3.95**

#108 "SATIN ALLURE"
Rayon Satin cups are stitched
in 5 sections for pointed uplift
and firm youthful support. French!
Sizes 32 to 38, B-cup;
Sizes 34 to 38, C-cup.
Black or White. **$3.50**

#190 "OUT IN FRONT"
Magical Satin circle molds the
breasts . . . holds them high. 100%
Nylon lace over net; Satin trim.
Black, White, 32 to 38,
B-cup; 34 to 38, C-cup. **$4.50**

#81 "EVER-LIFT"
Nylon bra is Pellon-lined to stay
shapely forever! Magical free-
form cup molds bust and never lets
you down! Embroidered trim. White.
Try it and feel the difference!
Sizes 32 to 38, B;
32 to 38, C-cup. **$3.95**

$5.00 VALUE PEARLS FREE
SEE ORDER BLANKS P. 47

Satin circles
mold bust
"up and out"

Satin

#72
$3.95

#108
$3.50

#190
$4.50

For small or
sagging busts

PELLON-
Lined

#81
$3.95

4-WAY WONDER

Wear it
strapless

Wide-set
straps for
scoop necks

Tie as
a halter

#60 "BARE SHOULDERS"
Nylon 4-Way Wonder Bra with
Detachable wide-set straps. New!
Gently wired; lacy Nylon cuff—
and it ends strap problems. Wear:
(1) Strapless; (2) tied as halter;
(3) criss-cross straps; (4) add detachable wide-set straps for your
scoop necks. White, Black.
Sizes 32 to 36, B-cup. **$5.00**

BEAUTY AND THE BUST

24

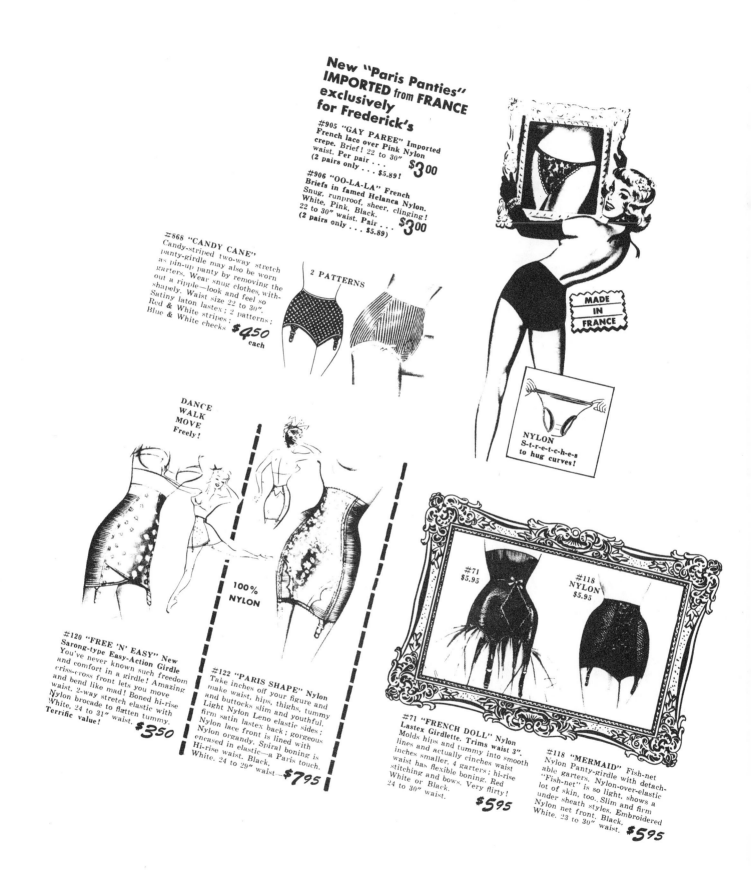

New "Paris Panties" IMPORTED from FRANCE exclusively for Frederick's

#905 "GAY PAREE" Imported French lace over Pink Nylon crepe. Brief! 22 to 30" waist. Per pair . . . **$3.00** (2 pairs only . . . $5.89!

#906 "OO-LA-LA" French Briefs in famed Helanca Nylon. Snug, runproof, sheer, clinging! White, Pink, Black. 22 to 30" waist. Pair . . . **$3.00** (2 pairs only . . . $5.89)

#868 "CANDY CANE" Candy-striped two-way stretch panty-girdle may also be worn as pin-up panty by removing the garters. Wear snug clothes, without a ripple—look and feel so shapely. Waist size 22 to 30". Satiny laton lastex; 2 patterns; Red & White stripes; Blue & White checks **$4.50 each**

2 PATTERNS

MADE IN FRANCE

NYLON S-t-r-e-t-c-h-e-s to hug curves!

DANCE WALK MOVE Freely!

100% NYLON

#120 "FREE 'N' EASY" New Sarong-type Easy-Action Girdle You've never known such freedom and comfort in a girdle! Amazing criss-cross front lets you move and bend like mad! Boned hi-rise waist. 2-way stretch elastic with Nylon brocade to flatten tummy. White, 24 to 31" waist. **Terrific value! $3.50**

#122 "PARIS SHAPE" Nylon Take inches off your figure and make waist, hips, thighs, tummy and buttocks slim and youthful. Light Nylon Leno elastic sides; firm satin lastex back; gorgeous Nylon lace front is lined with Nylon organdy. Spiral boning is encased in elastic—a Paris touch. Hi-rise waist. Black, White. 24 to 29" waist. **$7.95**

#71 $5.95   #118 NYLON $5.95

#71 "FRENCH DOLL" Nylon Lastex Girdlette. Trims waist 3". Molds hips and tummy into smooth lines and actually cinches waist inches smaller. 4 garters; hi-rise waist has flexible boning. Red stitching and bows. Very flirty! White or Black. 24 to 30" waist. **$5.95**

#118 "MERMAID" Fish-net Nylon Panty-girdle with detachable garters. Nylon-over-elastic "Fish-net" is so light, shows a lot of skin, too.. Slim and firm under sheath styles. Embroidered Nylon net front. Black. White. 23 to 30" waist. **$5.95**

PADDED PUSH-UP bras *

#150 "CURVE ALLURE" Exotic
Nylon lace, lined in Nylon jersey;
stitched-in push-up pads; elastic
band, stitched cups. Adds inches
to small B-cups. Black, White. **$5**⁹⁵
Sizes 32 to 36, B cup only.

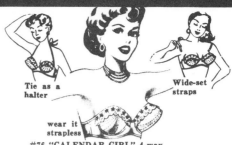

Tie as a
halter

wear it
strapless

Wide-set
straps

#76 "CALENDAR GIRL" 4-way
Nylon bra has stitched-in push-up
pads for full curves and cleavage.
Frilly lace cuff adds glamour. Wear
straps 4 ways. Black, White. **$6**⁵⁰
Sizes 32 to 36, A or B cup.

PADDED SENSATIONS

SATIN
& LACE

#177 "FRENCH FLIRT" Orlon
Satin bra; Nylon lace trim. Copy
of a French import raises and rounds
and looks like YOU! Fully padded
cups. All-white; Blue with **$5**⁰⁰
White. 32 to 36, A or B.

Inflatable
insets add
inches to bust
in seconds.
Foolproof!

#147 "AIR BORNE" Inflatable
plastic insets give any size bust
you want! Strapless embroidered
Nylon net; elastic sides and back.
White. Sizes 32 to 36,
A or B cups. **Fabulous!** **$5**⁹⁵

for PLUNGE or

#149 "DOUBLE DIPPER"
Low-cut Nylon net bra with
daisy trim, wired, stitched
undercup; wide-set straps.
White. 32 to 36, A; **$5**⁰⁰
32 to 38, B-cup.

DEEP WIRED
PLUNGE NECK

#143 "PRETTY PLUNGE"
Nylon net with plunge neck
and low-cut back. Wired under-
cup and separation. Wear straps
off-shoulder, too. Black with
Pink. White. 32-38, B; 34-38, C. **$3**⁵⁰

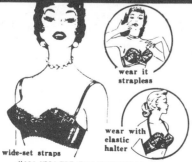

wear it
strapless

wear with
elastic
halter

wide-set straps

#136 "MAGIC CHANGE" Nylon Lace
and Dacron Elastic 5-way bra. Wear
shown or dip net cuffs to 5/8 or ½-
bra. Boned. White, Black. Sizes:
32 to 38, B; 34 to 38, C. **$5**⁰⁰

#136-P Same style—PADDED.
32 to 36, A cup; 32 to 38, B. **$5**

Adjustable
elastic strap
dips low in
back; hooks
in front.

#170 "EVENING GLORY" New
French look date-bra. Imported
Nylon lace over taffeta lifts bust
2" without bones or wires. Elastic
strap bares back for dates. Black
over Pink; All-White. **$5**⁰⁰
Sizes 32 to 36, B-cup

26

NOW HAVE **FULL CURVES & CLEAVAGE**

you are pushed up to here

padding to here only

before   after

AFTER

NEW FASHIONS DEMAND A PADDED PUSH-UP BRA! Stitched in push-up pads give you the full, high rounded bustline and tantalizing high "cleavage" that you've always longed for. Now you can have a real Movie Star bosom!

BEFORE

#145 "HOLLYWOOD PUSH-UP" Nylon crepe bra has push-up pads stitched in lower half of cup so you show thru sheer net top. Lacy daisy trim. White, Black Sizes 32-34, A; 32 to 36, B **$5.00**

#94 "AIRESS" Inflatable! Builds you up with just the size bust you want. Looks and feels so natural—and it's light as air, too. Plastic inserts fit into Nylon crepe fully-lined cups; elastic band holds it firmly in place—no

riding up. It's really magic—jus FEEL the difference! White. Sizes 32 to 36, A or B-cups. **$3.95**

Push-up pad in lower cup.

NEW, IMPROVED, INFLATABLE PADS ADD INCHES TO BUST! AIR ALONE . . . gives full, firm natural-looking curves that will make all eyes turn your way. Light plastic insets inflate to ANY size bust you wish in seconds— and they stay inflated. Foolproof!

#164 "HOLLYWOOD SECRET" Nylon lace with push-up pads in lower cup; regular padding above. Boned, wired; elastic back keeps it firmly in place. White. Sizes 32 to 36, A or B. **$8.50**

#179 "EYES FRONT" Nylon 5-in-one Shape-Maker. PADDED version of #180 has long smooth lines. Nylon crepe with lace and elastic. Black, White. Sizes: 32-36, A; 32-38, B-cup. **$7.50**

SCOOP necks

COPY OF A $50 IMPORT

#151 "PARISIAN PRIZE" Nylon satin & net. U-shaped wire separates, lifts and supports the fuller bust. Lace trim. White. Sizes 32-38, B; 34-40, C; 36 to 42, D. **$6.95**

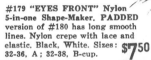

Wear strapless

Attach wide-set straps

Elastic-edged halter strap

#165 "TRIPLE PLAY" 3-way straps plus satin drawstring that adjusts to A, B, C cups. Contour-padded, boned; wired undercup, low back. Nylon crepe. White, Black. Sizes 32-38, **$5.00**

NATIONALLY ADVERTISED PERMA-LIFT "MAGIC INSET"

#171 "MAGIC INSET" Embroidered Nylon Net 5/8 strapless bra with famous magic insets in wired cups to support from below and keep bra shapely. Lightly boned; inner elastic band keeps it firmly in place for active gals! White, Black. 32 to 38, B or C. **$5.95**

#159 "NEW LOOK" Nylon Crepe and embroidered Nylon net, shaped to give firm pointed uplift, plus real separation. Stitched undercup supports bust; elastic goes all around to keep it from shifting or sliding. White. Sizes 32 to 38, B; Sizes 34 to 38, C-cup. **$5.00**

Hollywood's top figure specialist

Walter Winchell In New York and Hollywood

In interesting Jobs section: Frederick of Hollywood (he designs those scandalous scanties for the Hollywood-be-stars) does the "measuring" himself...

Earl Wilson

...Frederick of Hollywood, the underwear designer, returned from Europe and announced, "The under-all picture there is good."

FREDERICK IS FEATURED IN NEWSPAPER STORIES BOTH AT HOME AND ABROAD.

Lend me your Ears
By SAM'L STEINMAN
...Frederick of Hollywood, who's been in ladies lingerie for 20 years is writing a histoire of unmentionables through the ages, titled "Inside." (howzabout "The Undieworld"?)...

On the Broadway Scene
...Frederick of Hollywood, king of the undieworld (he makes scanties for the stars' home use) just came back from Paris shocked because they were shocked at his very peek-a-boo-ish line...

Abendzeitung
Von Frederick aus Hollywood

detachable straps

detachable garters

Nylon

#173

#175

#197

#92 "CONTROLLED CURVES"
Wired bra inflates easily—gives gorgeous curves! Slims inches off waist, hips, tummy, too. Boning in back and front; detachable garters. Embroidered Nylon net with elastic insets. White. Amazing! Sizes 32 to 36, A or B. **$10.95**

#173 "MOLDED TORSO"
4-in-one Magic Figure-Maker Uplift bra, waist-cincher, garter belt. Lifts bust, hides rolls of fat, trims hips and waist. 4 detachable garters. Black or White. In Sizes 32 to 38, B; Sizes 34 to 40, C. **$6.95**

#175 "MOVIE STAR SHAPE"
Strapless garment trims waist and flattens tummy, buttocks, thighs. Wired bra has net cuffs; side-zip closing. 2-way stretch satin lastex back with Nylon power net for comfort and control. Embroidered net front is Nylon. Black, White. Sizes 32 to 38, B or C cups. **$13.50**

#197 "HOUR GLASS"
Nylon elastic long line dips 6½" below waist for smooth control. Net-lined embroidered bra and center panel. Velvet straps detach; wear wide-set or halter, too. It's low-priced but looks like $$ more! Boned; has built-in waist-cinch. White or Black. 32-38, B; 34-38, C. **$13.50**

PULL IN THOSE INCHES!

#180 "HOLD ME" Nylon
Lacy 5/8 bra combines with gently boned Nylon crepe and airy elastic insets. Wired undercups; 4 detachable garters. Trims waist, tummy. Marvelous value, too! Black, White. Sizes 32 to 38, B; Sizes 34 to 38, C.
$5⁹⁵

BRA SLIP

#3024 SLIP-SLEEK
It's a slip — it's a Torsolette — it's a padded bra, too! Magic "all-in-one" nylon bra-slip has lightly padded bra for lovely hi curves, a long torsolette for sleek "under sheath" slimness, and beautiful slip with gorgeous lace flounce, which can be cut off to shorten as desired. Adjustable 5-way shoulder straps, light boning in torsolette, non-wrinkle zip-front, hidden detachable garters. This one garment gives you **everything!** A must for your fall wardrobe! White or Black. Sizes 32 to 36 A cup
32 to 38 B cup
$8⁹⁵

NAUGHTY FRENCH FLIRTY

Lucky Finds in VACATION LINGERIE

#106 "BUTTERFLY" Nylon
Very daring . . . Very French! Favorite of Paris beauties and it will be yours, too! Daring Butterfly-effect of firm, stitched Satin adds spice to sheer Nylon cup. Gives POINTED uplift and perfect separation. As dainty as a moonlight mist. Black or White. Sizes 32 to 38, B-cup. **$3.50**

#107 "FRENCH LINES"
Satin Siren with "Butterfly" Stitching! Extra-firm rayon Satin gives firmness and support. It's designed to really POINT up a gal's charms! Plunging V-front; fully-lined cups. It's a beauty! White or Black. Sizes: 32 to 38, B-cup; 34 to 38, C-cup. **$3.95**

#102 "OO-LA-LA"
French Nylon Creation
Sheer NYLON net with "Tulip" under-cup of Satin gives you those "Paris Model" curves! Daring and glamorous for wear under sheerest dresses and blouses . . . wonderful for plunging necklines! Lifts and separates breasts lightly, but firmly. White or Black. NEW! **$3.50** Sizes 32 to 38, B-cup.

#850 "NEXT TO NOTHING"
French Dance Set. NYLON!
Embroidered sheer Nylon net forms the daintiest, most daring wisps of undies ever seen! Cut-out bra is just big enough to lift gently and give perfect freedom. Matching "pocket-size" net Bikini panties. Just like wearing nothing! Rich Satin trim. Black or White. Sizes 32 to 36. **$7.98**

FREDERICK IN PARIS!
With him, a top, high-fashion French model in one of his own creations. (Our Style #248.) Background is famous Tuileries.

Detachable hoops roll up and pack with petticoat in case.

AMAZING "PETTI-PAK"

#914 "SWISH 'N' SWIRL"
Nylon jersey molds torso and swishes into a flounce of striped Nylon taffeta, bow-trimmed. Elastic at waist. 24-30" waist. White with Red; White with Blue. **$6.98**

#916 "PETTI-PAK" Nylon
Dotted Swiss Petticoat and Case. 2 light, detachable hoops fit into slits at hem of this bouffant petticoat. Slide 'em out, roll up, and they fit into tiny case along with petticoat. A vacation must! White or Black. 24-30 inch waist. **$4.98**

#918 "LEOPARD ALLURE"
Imagine! A form-fitting six-gore slip in cool Nylon jersey, with a daring leopard print. The bust section is lined for long wear. Easy to wash and pack, needs no ironing. Sizes 32 to 38. Tawny leopard tones. **$8.98**

30

Let's Be Brief!

#875 LOVE LACE
Nylon lace gift Bikini. New!
Hanky-size panties in White Frost
or spicy Black Pearl. Ultra-tiny
22 to 30" waist. Each $2.98
2 pairs.............only **$5⁸⁹**

#766 POODLE PANTS
Sheerest nylon jersey bikini has
cute hand painted poodles. A real
lift for your lingerie wardrobe!
Poodle Black, Fire Plug Red,
Snowy White.
Sizes 22 to 30". Only **$2⁹⁸**

#898 SPIDER WEB
Hand-painted nylon with spider
web design, ruffled trim. Red,
White, Black. 24 to 30" waist.
Pair $2.79
2 pairs............only **$5²⁹**

#942 BURLESQUE
Days of the week embroidered
rayon panties. 7 pairs in 7 colors
in a quilted satin hosiery box.
Really different gift! 22 to 30"
waist.
7 Pair only **$4⁹⁵**

#932 ZIG ZAG
Sheer nylon panties add zig-zag
insets of nylon lace to accent a
pretty hipline. Sunset Gold,
Devil Red, Black, White.
22 to 30" waist.
2 Pair only **$3⁵⁰**

#924 CAPTIVATION
Nylon tricot "Can Can" panty.
Lace and ruffle trim. French and
flirty! Black, Coral Red.
24 to 30" waist. **$3⁹⁸**
Pair only

#927 TUMMY HUG
Wear as glamour-panty or garter-
panty! Detachable garters give
this pert scanty a double life.
Nylon lastex insets flatten tummy!
Smooth nylon jersey hugs hips.
Perfect for active gals. Black or
White with plaid trim.
22 to 30" waist. **$3⁹⁵**

New!
#3756
SET OF 3
3 for **$3⁹⁸**

#3756 GLITTERAMA
Another Frederick's find — a trio of
lurex lovelies to luxuriate in 'neath your
dressiest dress. Glitter-up right down
to your panties! Washable, non-
tarnishing. Black, White or Red,
with Lurex. Sizes 22 inch to
28 inch waist. **3** for **$3⁹⁸**

#821 "BLACK SPICE"
100% Nylon Lace Step-ins
Daring flared style with
side slits. Black.
24 to 30" waist. **$4⁹⁸**

Glory in Padded Push-Ups!

You're pushed up to here

Sea shell embroidery over sheer

Increases your bust one full size.

Lightly padded

Padded push-up shelf

Wired Undercup

Leno Elastic

HEAVEN'S HELPER
Frederick's newest padded push-up will increase your bosom one full cup size, and give you glorious high curves you dream of! Bust section is exquisite embroidered Nylon lace with expertly wired undercup. Interchangeable shoulder straps for fashion's varied neckline—or wear strapless. Marvelous, firm Leno elastic at inset between bust and in broad back band gives superb support and comfort. Angel White or Exciting Black. **$5.00** Sizes 32 to 36, A or B-cup.

SCENE 1

AFTER

DON'T have a droopy aging bust!

BEFORE

Heavenly assistance for the small busted gal. Adds one full glamorous cup size. Light shell padded cups with padded push-up from beneath.

picture YOU in a PADDED bra

HOLLYWOOD HIGH-DIVE
Starting out high and diving to low deep plunge, this bra is cut to reveal lots of glorious curves created by specially designed cup. Bust section is Nylon net above, Nylon lace below, with Nylon marquisette lining. Remainder in sheer Dacron elastic. Not padded but invisible under-cup wiring assures curve glory. Tiniest bones at side and center keep it up—and you up. Newest shoulder straps can be worn wide or halter style. Perfect for youthful decollete fashions. White only. Sizes 32 to 36, A or 32 to 38, B; **$3.95**

2 for $7.77

More of You.

Hi-Dive angle for Hi-Rise Curves.

Set-in elastic for strap variation.

Light Boning

Invisible Wiring

Dacron Elastic

NEW! "BOOSTER" bras with sensational PUSH-UP PADS

You're pushed up to here
Pads to here only

AFTER

HERE'S HOW PUSH-UP PADS CAN GIVE YOU A MOVIE STAR BOSOM:

BEFORE

Stitched-in pads in lower half of cup BOOST your bust into high, gloriously full curves that look so natural. And you'll have that hi-rise cleavage that's so alluring. Try a "Booster" bra today!

SHOP AWAY FROM PRYING EYES — ORDER PADDED BRAS BY MAIL!!

32

Your new glamour curves are simply superb in a Hollywood-created Frederick's Push-up bra. Stitched-in push-up padding makes the magic difference—adds inches of curves—gives thrilling cleavage! Now you can have a real movie star bosom, and wear the same bras that the stars pay $50 or $75 for!

✳ **PADDED PUSH-UP SENSATIONS**

you are pushed up to here

padding to here only

BEFORE **AFTER**

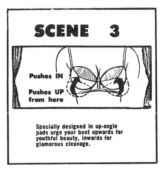

SCENE 3

Pushes IN

Pushes UP from here

Specially designed in up-angle pads urge your bust upwards for youthful beauty, inwards for glamorous cleavage.

SCENE 4

AFTER

DON'T have a droopy aging bust!

BEFORE

To give a higher bustline, plus glamorous cleavage to the small to average bosom . . . these wonder-workers feature stitched-in push-up pads.

SCENE 2

"IN-UP" Pad

Light shell padding to make your bust more voluptuous, plus extra side push-up pads for the cleavage you love. Ideal for the small busted figure.

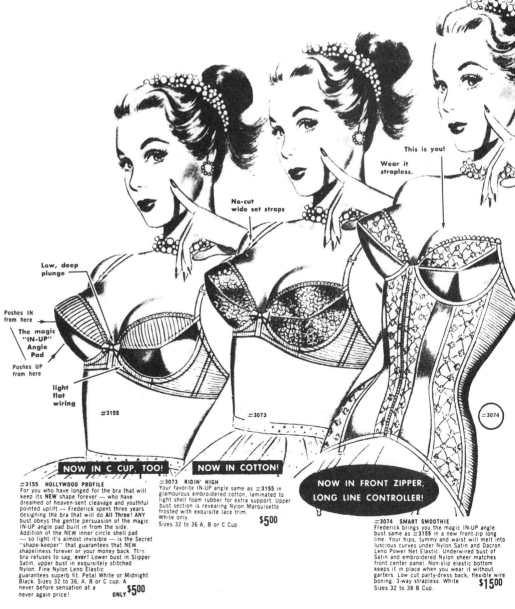

Low, deep plunge

Pushes IN from here

The magic "IN-UP" Angle Pad

Pushes UP from here

light flat wiring

No-cut wide set straps

This is you!

Wear it strapless.

#3155

#3073

#3074

NOW IN C CUP, TOO!

NOW IN COTTON!

NOW IN FRONT ZIPPER, LONG LINE CONTROLLER!

#3155 HOLLYWOOD PROFILE
For you who have longed for the bra that will keep its **NEW** shape forever — who have dreamed of heaven-sent cleavage and youthful pointed uplift — Frederick spent three years designing the bra that will do **All Three**! ANY bust obeys the gentle persuasion of the magic IN-UP angle pad built in from the side. Addition of the NEW inner circle shell pad — so light it's almost invisible — is the Secret "shape-keeper" that guarantees that NEW shapeliness forever or your money back. This bra refuses to sag, **ever**! Lower bust in Slipper Satin, upper bust in exquisitely stitched Nylon. Fine Nylon Leno Elastic guarantees superb fit. Petal White or Midnight Black. Sizes 32 to 36, A, B or C cup. A never before sensation at a never again price!
ONLY **$5.00**

#3073 RIDIN' HIGH
Your favorite IN-UP angle same as #3155 in glamourous embroidered cotton, laminated to light shell foam rubber for extra support. Upper bust section is revealing Nylon Marquisette frosted with exquisite lace trim. White only.
Sizes 32 to 36 A, B or C Cup.
$5.00

#3074 SMART SMOOTHIE
Frederick brings you the magic IN-UP angle bust same as #3155 in a new front-zip long line. Your hips, tummy and waist will melt into luscious curves under Nylon Satin and Dacron Leno Power Net Elastic. Underwired bust of Satin and embroidered Nylon sheer matches front center panel. Non-slip elastic bottom keeps it in place when you wear it without garters. Low cut party-dress back, flexible wire boning. 3-way strapless. White Sizes 32 to 38 B Cup.
$15.00

Youth Insurance

LOVING CUPS

MEMORY CUPS NEVER LET YOU DOWN

#3233

STITCH CUPS
because . . .
Round and round the stitching goes to make sure that every bit of bosom really lifts and shows! Never can you lose this curvaceous shape — the stitched-in magic gives you youthful pointing that makes 'em gape!

#3052

NEW! Extra High Uplift and Extra Low Back . . .

VICTORY CUPS

ELASTIC BRAS
because . . .
Every bosom has its own special beauty — elastic really does quadruple duty: lifts and points **each** bust, gives **out**standing support, prevents bulges, b-r-e-a-t-h-e-s as you play and sport. Buy it — and feel eighteen again!

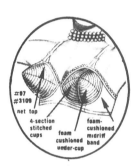

#108
Satin 5-Section Cups!

Circular stitching lifts bust up and out.

#97
#3109
net top

4-section stitched cups

foam cushioned under-cup

foam-cushioned midriff band

#3256
SPECIAL UPLIFT!

#3250

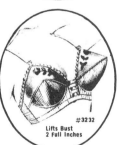

#3232
Lifts Bust 2 Full Inches

#3090
Lifts You a Full 2" Higher Than Ordinary Bras

#3124
Dacron Elastic

B-C AND D CUPS

#3263

FABULOUS NEW FIBER "K" FIRST AT FREDERICK'S!

#3281 EMPIRE LINE
Give yourself a new lift for the new Empire Look with this special youth-up shaped cup. Triple-tiered stitched satin gently urges bust towards center and separates. Wide elastic band beneath cups holds a flat smooth line. Gleaming Nylon lace over sheer. Lightly boned sides. White or Black. Sizes 32 to 40 B or C Cup. **$3 95**
Sizes 32 to 40 D Cup, $5.00

#108 DANGER CURVES
French look bra has stitched 5-section cups for that glamorous pointed uplift. Rayon satin is net-lined for firm support. In Jet Black or Gardenia White. Priced so low.
Sizes 32 to 38B, 34 to 38C cup **$3 50**

#97 CHORUS CURVE
100% Nylon crepe sensation! Frederick's famous 4 features for comfort, uplift and fit. The most comfortable bra ever, and a Hollywood favorite. Priced so you can buy 2. White or Black. Sizes 32 to 36A, **$3 50**
32 to 38B, 34 to 40C cup.

#3109.
Same style and figure flattering features as #97 but in fine quality Cotton. White only.
Sizes 32 to 36A; 32 to 38B; **$3 00**
34 to 40 C cup.

#3233 BUILD-UP
Get extra build-up with Frederick's special, undercover friend. 4 section cotton broadcloth cup has porous elastic rising diagonally from under center bust—parts and lifts you for pointed beauty. Back is beautifully crafted for perfect low or high styling. White. **$3 95**
Sizes 32 to 36A or B, 34 to 38C Cup.

#3256 BOSOM FRIEND
Build your own curves to dramatic new fullness with this magic molding cup pocket! Four sections of stitched nylon sheer point and lift, Rayon satin underlay with elastic insert supports UPlift. Floating movement straps, elastic at sides mean sure action-comfort. Pearl White. **$3 95**
Sizes 32 to 38B or 34 to 40C cup.

#3250 BOSOM FLOWER
The UPlifting construction of this bra's so sensational, it's been patented! Nylon lace knit cups are over and underlayed with Nylon satin-boosting your bosom **without wiring!** Bias cut under cups opening on top of bust for cup adjustment prevents binding, Nylon Leno power net fabric, semi-low back and light side boning complete quality features. White. **$5 00**
Sizes 32 to 36A, 32 to 38B or 32 to 40C cup.

#3052 SWORD POINT
Perfect sweater bra points up bosom glory. Youthful support and comfort assured by fine quality satin Lastex. Colorful daisies on sheer Nylon marquisette upper bust. Peek-a-boo straps between busts. Low back. White only. **$3 95**
Sizes 32 to 36A, 32 to 38B, 32 to 40C cup.

#3232 MOLD 'N POINT
Stop drooping and dragging, slumping and sagging—these cling-ing cups lift you up a full 2 inches! Upper cup is of sheer, see-through Nylon with pretty, embroidered flowers. Rest of this curvaceous pointer is of breathing Dacron leno elastic. Satin shoulder straps and center straps lend luxurious touch. White. Sizes 32 to 38B, **$3 95**
32 to 40C cup.

#3090 KEY HOLE
Light weight Dacron elastic bra has embroidered Nylon net "key-holes" to reveal a glamourous you. Light side boning combined with unique design molds bust to high point firmness. Accentuates small bosom, and remodels large ones. White. 34 to 40, B or C cup. **$5 00**

#3124 NATURE GAL
If nature blessed you with a full bosom, this new model bra is for you! It offers the complete comfortable control you need — plus the shapely high pointed look you want. In fine quality Dacron Elastic that extends from cup base through supporting bandeau. Side boning coaxes your bosom into the cup and keeps it there. Upper bust is exquisitely embroidered Nylon Sheer. Faggoting accentuates point. Wonderful separation and support. Controls! 3-hook closing. Elastic back. White. Sizes 34 to 40 B C Cup. **$4 50**
Sizes 34 to 44 D cup, $5.00

#3263 LADY "K"
Count on Frederick's to be "fustest with the bestest"! Fabulous new Fiber "K" makes this lovely new bra lighter, stronger, non-allergic—and even machine-washable! Fashioned for give-and-take freedom! Light side boning, nylon lace over net upper cup. White. Sizes 32 to 36A, 32 to 38B or 34 to 40C Cup. **2 for $5 95**

You asked for it!

New!

New!

PADDED HIPS AND SEAT!

#3277 TWO-TIMER
Another Frederick's "first!" The answer to hundreds of requests. Miracle under-an-ounce foam rubber pads fit into miraculously shaped pockets on hip and derriere. Feels real. Knitted Rayon Acetate Powerflex. White. Sizes S, M & L. **$15**

Paris Points

FRENCH FANTASY
A FREDERICK'S first!
The Frenchiest little glamour bra you've ever seen is no more than a half-bra! What **isn't** there reveals the **most**! What **is** there supports and lifts with the swing of youth! Beautifully scalloped edging trims this beauty in exquisite Rayon Satin Stitched half cup. Wear as a halter, wide-set, or strapless.
Black, White.
Sizes 32 to 36A, 32 to 36B Cup. **$5.95**

FRENCH CAPER
Nylon lace lined with nylon net. Wear it for new bosom beauty, perfect comfort! French-designed bra has cut-out cups that are light as a feather! Gives a young, natural look. A Hollywood favorite! White Ice or Black Frost.
Sizes 32 to 38, B-cup only. Just **$4.50**

Imported from France

BETTER HALF →
Only the French would think of it — the bra that isn't a bra at all! Only the under bust is covered, but gives small busted women complete uplift with gleaming satin under-cups, lightly boned. Wide shoulder straps for perfection with plunge necklines and decollete styles.
White or Black. Sizes 32 to 36. Will fit A or B cups **$5.00**

YOUNG MISCHIEF
A marvel for youthful molding, support and pointed uplift! Four-section stitched cotton cup has encircling curve-mold of rayon satin, and cushioned, wired undercup for support plus separation. No cut wide shoulder straps. Lined with nylon net.
White only. Sizes 34 to 38, B; 34 to 40, C and D- cup **$5.00**

The Way...
in French Follies Bras

FROM FRANCE!

BOU-BOU
Imported from France
From Paris — Frederick brings you one of the finest strapless bras ever made! Fabulous patented design absolutely prevents it from shifting or slipping. Thin over-wiring plays "Frenchy" tricks — separating and lifting busts. Deepest front plunge you ever saw! In extremely fine quality nylon fabric. White, Black.
Sizes 32 to 38, B cup; 34 to 38, C cup. **$750**

Dare To Be Different

frederick

frederick's —
AS TALKED ABOUT BY

Abendzeitung

Von Frederick aus Hollywood

Walter Winchell In New York and Hollywood

Innaresting Jobs Section: Frederick of Hollywood (he designs those scandalous scanties for the Hollywood-be-stars) does the "measuring" himself . . .

Earl Wilson

. . . . Frederick of Hollywood the underwear designer, returned from Europe and announced, "The under-all picture there is good."

Don't Be Half Dressed

To make the most of your glamorous new costumes be just as glamorous underneath! Among these bras, you'll find the secret to daring high curves that will capture men's hearts.

AS SEEN IN

LOOK · Esquire · CHARM · GLAMOUR · VOGUE · Mademoiselle

is a genius at figures!

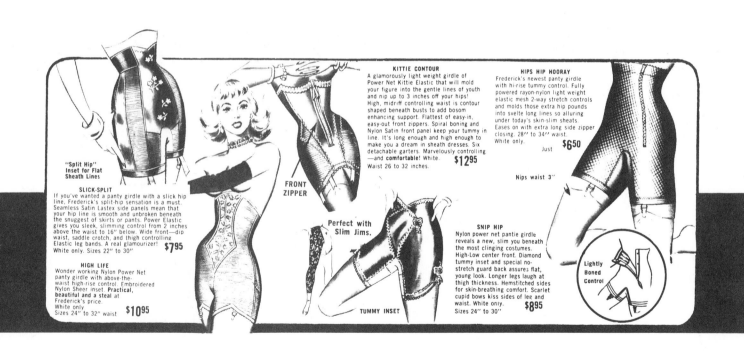

**"Split Hip"
Inset for Flat
Sheath Lines**

SLICK-SPLIT
If you've wanted a panty girdle with a slick hip line, Frederick's split-hip sensation is a must. Seamless Satin Lastex side panels mean that your hip line is smooth and unbroken beneath the snuggest of skirts or pants. Power Elastic gives you sleek, slimming control from 2 inches above the waist to 16" below. Wide front—dip waist, saddle crotch, and thigh controlling Elastic leg bands. A real glamourizer! White only. Sizes 22" to 30" **$7.95**

HIGH LIFE
Wonder working Nylon Power Net panty girdle with above-the-waist high-rise control. Embroidered Nylon Sheer inset. **Practical, beautiful and a steal at** Frederick's price. White only Sizes 24" to 32" waist **$10.95**

FRONT ZIPPER

KITTIE CONTOUR
A glamorously light weight girdle of Power Net Kittie Elastic that will mold your figure into the gentle lines of youth and nip up to 3 inches off your hips! High, midriff controlling waist is contour shaped beneath busts to add bosom enhancing support. Flattest of easy-in, easy-out front zippers. Spiral boning and Nylon Satin front panel keep your tummy in line. It's long enough and high enough to make you a dream in sheath dresses. Six detachable garters. Marvelously controlling —and **comfortable!** White. **$12.95**
Waist 26 to 32 inches.

Perfect with Slim Jims.

TUMMY INSET

SNIP HIP
Nylon power net pantie girdle reveals a new, slim you beneath the most clinging costumes. High-Low center front. Diamond tummy inset and special no-stretch guard back assures flat, young look. Longer legs laugh at thigh thickness. Hemstitched sides for skin-breathing comfort. Scarlet cupid bows kiss sides of leg and waist. White only. Sizes 24" to 30" **$8.95**

HIPS HIP HOORAY
Frederick's newest panty girdle with hi-rise tummy control. Fully powered rayon-nylon light weight elastic mesh 2-way stretch controls and molds those extra hip pounds into svelte long lines so alluring under today's skin-slim sheats. Eases on with extra long side zipper closing. 28" to 34" waist. White only. Just **$6.50**

Nips waist 3"

Lightly Boned Control

DON'T LET A BUDGET FIGURE SPOIL *your figure* !

Just say "CHARGE IT" at — Frederick's of Hollywood!

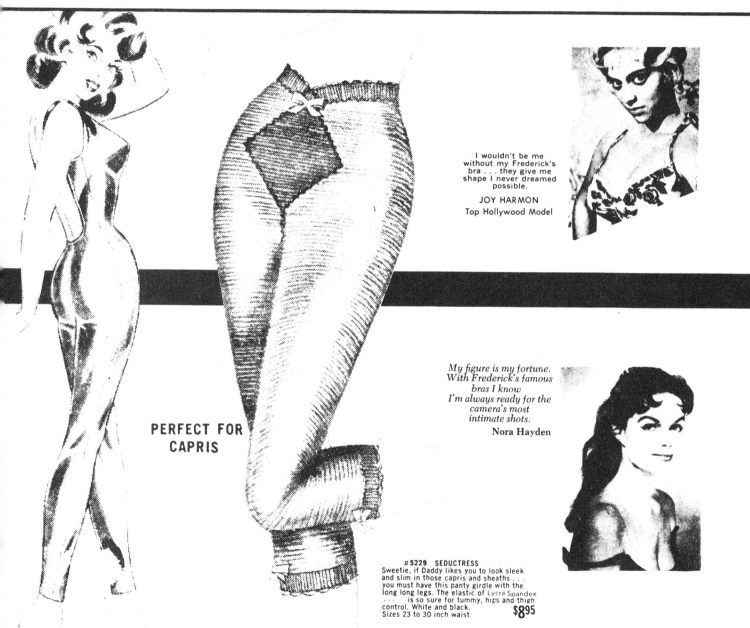

PERFECT FOR CAPRIS

I wouldn't be me without my Frederick's bra . . . they give me shape I never dreamed possible.

JOY HARMON
Top Hollywood Model

My figure is my fortune. With Frederick's famous bras I know I'm always ready for the camera's most intimate shots.

Nora Hayden

#5229   SEDUCTRESS
Sweetie, if Daddy likes you to look sleek and slim in those capris and sheaths . . . you must have this panty girdle with the long long legs. The elastic of Lycra Spandex . . . is so sure for tummy, hips and thigh control. White and black. Sizes 23 to 30 inch waist. **$8⁹⁵**

I've learned the secret of magic-cleavage, through my introduction to those fabulous Frederick's bras!

CHERIE FOSTER
Top Fashion Model

I wouldn't be me without my Frederick's bra . . . they give me shape I never dreamed possible.

CHARLOTTE FLETCHER
Well Known Filmland Star

I want to tell you how happy I am with Frederick's bras & girdles . . . they're fabulous!

MARILYN TURNER
Fashion Model

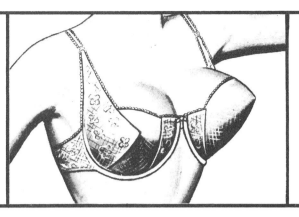

#5321 MAM'SELLE
You're irresistable, you're shaped like never before, and you're oh-so-comfortable . . . intricately made in sheerest of Marquisettes, delicate Nylon Lace, Lovely Lingerie straps. French White. Sizes 32 to 36 B, C. **$5**

ONLY FOR THOSE WITH SOFT BOSOMS!

#5430 DARLING DECEIVER
Frederick's designed an entirely new push-up pad, called "THE SHELF." This scientific design is contoured and shaped to completely lift and raise the breast, and put it "on the shelf!" This new bra is especially created for gals wanting that PLUS look. Polyester, Acetate and Nylon Satin. Black, White, Sizes 32 to 36 A or B cup. **$6⁹⁹**

PUSHES UP   PUSHES IN

#5292 TEMPTRESS
Paris inspired this new demi-bra . . . shows just enough of you to entice! Self adjusting Acetate Satin-demi cup. . . . gently wired for hi rising deep cleavage. Acetate, rubber and polyester. contrasting top ribbon trim. Black, White. Sizes 32 to 38 A, B, C. **$6⁹⁹**

BLOW UP TO STREAMLINED "A" CUP BEAUTIFUL "B" CUP. # BLOW • UPS! *YOUR FIGURE CAN BE MADE TO ORDER!*

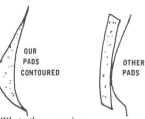

OUR PADS CONTOURED   OTHER PADS

What others promise . . .
Frederick delivers!
Frederick's pads are like no others! Each pad is **hand-sculptured** by an artist who works from life, following the natural, delicious curves of a woman's body.
Then the pads are cast . . . molded in softest, bounce-back poly-foam. They're curved . . . natural . . . delightfully feminine! Very femme fatale!
The pads slip in wherever they're needed. **Only you will know they're not all you!**

AIR-LITE INFLATABLE

#5439 LIGHT 'N' LOVELY
Pick your size . . . and BLOW UP! A funtabulous blow-up bra, complete with straw . . . to add inches without weight! Light airy design, with delicate edging of fine lace. Elastic criss-crosses under bust for support! Nylon, Acetate, Spandex. White or Black. Sizes 32 to 36 A or B. **$5**

Just wouldn't be me without my Frederick's shape-up bra! I've got that model bosom now! **CAROL HOLLAND** new Leading Model

intimately Yours!

. . . your public appearance begins in private . . . . **you owe it to yourself** to measure up! These magical foundations are the hidden powers of persuasion that give you the perfect figure — Mr. **Frederick**

GARTER PANTY

CROTCHLESS

#5752 BIKINI BELT
Too kicky to keep under cover! Mr. Frederick has attached Nylon Lace bikini panties at an elastic garter belt. An all-in-1 piece of below-the-waist beauty! Panties are crotchless. Garters detach, if you wish. White or Black. In sizes **22 to 30 inch waist** $5.99

COPY OF AN IMPORT!

COPY OF A PARISIENNE IMPORT!

#4473 FANCY PANTS
This heart-shaped Bikini's a little bare nothing! You'll sigh for its thigh-free cut-up legs . . . love the lace trim and front button bow. Just a wisp of a panty . . . but it's very big in Europe! Choose in White, Black or Pink Nylon. Waist sizes 23 to 30 inches. **2 FOR $5.75**

#4475 MIGHTY MITE
This brief, brief panty has no crotch at all! Nothing but lovely-lovely lace! High-cut legs leave little to the imagination. Elastic waist . . . lace, and more lace trim. Wouldn't you know it's a copy of a bizarre Continental import? In White, Black or Red Nylon. Waist sizes 23 to 30 inches. **$3.99**

#4474 FIG LEAF
Scanty, but oh my! Frederick's copy of a Bikini Pantie imported from Paris has legs *cut way-up-to-there,* a Nylon net crotch. Flower trim is appliqued at strategic spot. Tiny satin bow and dropped lace waist. In White, Black or Blue Nylon. Waist sizes 23 to 30 inches. **2 FOR $5.75**

MARIBOU POUF

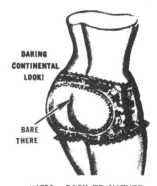

DARING CONTINENTAL LOOK!

BARE THERE

#4662 POUF PANTY
Fluffy Maribou poof gives a flirtatious French look to this sheer nylon panty with high cut legs. Black or Red. Sizes Small, Medium or Large. **$2.00**

#4706 BACK TO NATURE
All nylon sheer lace brief pantie has daring derriere cutout edged in lace. Matching ruffled lace trims the legs. Black in sizes Small, Medium and Large. **$2.99**

#4—5928 PARIS INSPIRATION
So French, so fancy, so pretty, so practical! Lightly boned waist cincher with appliqued rose on center panel gives you a "handspan" middle. Attached nylon tricot lace skirted panties make it *the complete undergarment.* 4 attached garters. Black or White. Sizes Small, Med. or Large **$16.50**

"Frederick's changed me to a celebrity — over night. It's these sensational Frederick foundations that did it. They make a girl a woman, and a woman all the more so."

Gro Dinger
Miss Hollywood 1962

"Modelling is fun . . . Frederick's made me a cover girl once . . . twice . . . three times . . . courtesy of those fabulous Frederick foundations that caress a girl's curves to model proportions."

Carol Holland
TV Star

before · after

Why a Frederick's Panty Girdle?
Nothing else can make your rear so admirable! Frederick's is noted for Hollywood panty girdles that trim the thighs . . . raise the fanny up and out . . . delineate natural cleavage . . . mold hips, waist and tummy . . . redistribute flesh for fabulous balance! Try one! It'll fib years off your figure!

I can't be without my Frederick's girdles — they make all my clothes look great for personal appearances

Linda Edds

Hollywood Model

urges
bust
upward

cinch
waist

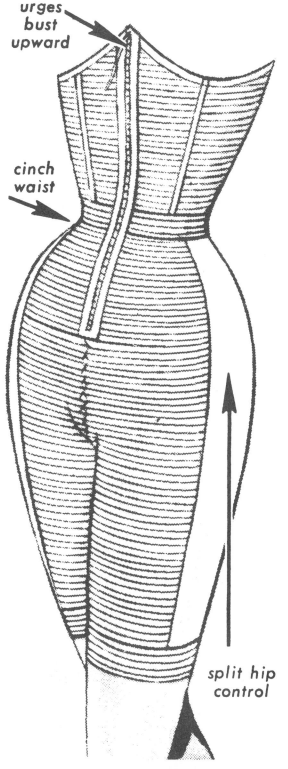

split hip
control

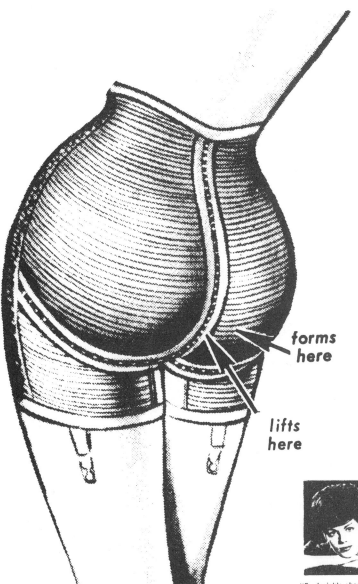

forms
here

lifts
here

"Frederick's changed me to a celebrity — over night. It's these sensational Frederick foundations that did it. They make a girl a woman, and a woman all the more so."

Marilyn Manning
Hollywood Actress

#4–5779 SECRET HELPER
This French styled panti-girdle gives you that perfect uplift for unrivaled curves. Center separation for that natural look. Finely knit nylon, acetate; cotton rubber lastex. Trim elastic band below derriere. Garters detach. White. Sizes 22, 24, 26, 28, 30. **$7⁹⁹**

#4–3362 SECRECY
Want to keep a figure secret?
No one needs to know that shape is only partly yours! Amazing girdle starts just below the bust . . . zips to tummy! Built-in waist cincher. Side panels take in inches at the thighs. Convenient snap crotch. White. Waist sizes 26, 28, 30, 32, 34 inches. **$16⁵⁰**

43

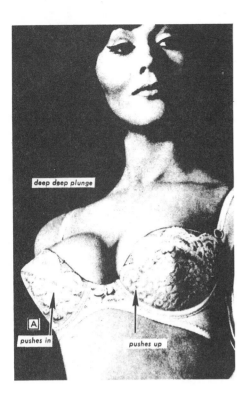

HOLLYWOOD SAYS:

PAD IT!

A #5596 **SEE-SHELLS**
* bare plunged cleavage
* fine lace
You'll surge to new heights on these sexy scalloped See-Shells! They're the most for new nude fashions! Bosoms are cradled on IN-UP PUSH-UP pads that provide an eye-catching uplift. In sheer Nylon Lace, with Lycra sides and back. White, Black
  Sizes 32 through 36;
△ B and C cups. **$6.99**

PAD!

PAD!

Mr. Frederick says:

"YOU'LL NEVER SUE ME FOR NON-SUPPORT!"

THE SECRET CIRCLE

pushes in
pushes up

before   after

The instant, magic of Frederick's "Secret Circle" lifts you up as it pushes you in! It's all done according to a scientific formula . . . and only Mr. Frederick knows the secret! Like magic, an exciting cleavage is created to make "A" and "B" busts bloom to new dimensions! "C" and "D" bosoms are higher . . . firmer . . .

C cotton
D nylon

pushes up
pushes in

Bobby Jordan

My Frederick's bra wardrobe is as important to me as my make-up . . . no matter what fashion I'm called upon to model — plunge neckline, bare shoulders, low back . . . I know I have the perfect Frederick's bra.

You wouldn't dream of going out with just lipstick to beautify your face! Every facial feature needs an aid, and there's a cosmetic designed for every *inch* of you, pretty one. From the neck down, you may need even more help. That's why Frederick's bras and girdles are the *most important* fashion investment you can make.

new "shelf" padding raises the soft bosom completely for plus cleavage!

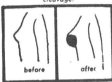

before   after

My Frederick's bra wardrobe is as important to me as my make-up . . . no matter what fashion I'm called upon to model — plunge neckline, bare shoulders, low back . . . I know I have the perfect Frederick's bra.

Carolyn Nelson

HOLLYWOOD MODEL

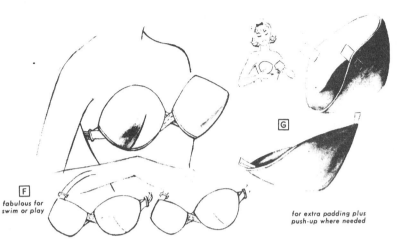

F — fabulous for swim or play

for extra padding plus push-up where needed

F #5487 WATER LILY
New undercover aid, exclusive with Frederick's . . . a Push-Up pad swim bra that repels water. Pin in your swimsuits, or dresses if you wish, or use the elastic backstrap and hook to side tabs. Nylon Tricot covering. White. A or B cups. **$3.99**

G #1320 PUSH UP
Add inches in seconds and become more alluring! New improved water-proofed plastic foam 5/8 pad, with magic tabs to pin in or out of your favorite swimsuit, dress or bra. Fits all cup sizes. Two sets $4.65 **$2.50**

to be perfect!

C #3073 RIDIN' HIGH
• Peekaboo Cotton Eyelet!
Here's your favorite *cleavage-plus* bra! (Like fabulous #3155 above), except it's made of Cotton Acetate Eyelet, specially laminated to a light foam rubber shell for support. White only. Sizes 32 to 36. A, B, C cups. **$6.99**

D #3155 HOLLYWOOD PROFILE
Magic "In-UP" angle foam rubber pads for that youthful look. New inner circle shell pad can never lose its shape. Fine Acetate Rubber, Polyester Leno-elastic and underwired for support. Slipper Satin Acetate Nylon lower-bust, exquisitely stitched Acetate Nylon above. Petal White or Midnight Black. Sizes 32 to 36A, 32 to 36B, 32 to 38C. 2 for $13.50 32 to 38D $7.99. **$6.99**

HOLLYWOOD APPROVED SCREEN STYLE

Mr. Frederick says...

You already have your figure. Make the most of it! The right bra spells the difference between *sag* and *surge*. A well-fitted strapless bra shows off a bare-topped sheath. Stretch capris need panty girdles to *lift* up the seat, *smooth* the tummy. Every Frederick's foundation is designed to make the most of your hidden assets. So shop this catalog . . . put your figure in balance for the greatest Holiday season ever!

BODY...

. . BY FREDERICK'S

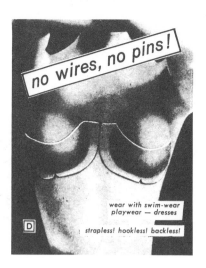

no wires, no pins!

wear with swim-wear
playwear — dresses

strapless! hookless! backless!

D #4—3260 SULTRY
The new self-supporting half-bra for
natural curves. Adjustable, no straps,
no hidden wires or bones. Has a
magic patented shape-controlling
feature that holds you, molds you to
the perfect young bustline. Soft,
pliable, long wearing. Order sizes,
A, B, C. **2 PAIR $3⁹⁹**
3-months' supply.

#4523   SLEEP GLAMOUR
Dainty s-t-r-e-t-c-h Nylon Helanca bra
gives you dreamy bedtime comfort . . .
provides gentle all-over support so you
sleep or relax at ease. Wear it under
your nightie, or with sleep shorts. Slips
on or off simply, with front snap fast-
ener. White or Black. Comes in **$1⁷⁵**
A & B cup or C & D cup.

Dotti Synder

*I can't be without my
Frederick's bras — they
make all my clothes look
great for personal
appearances*

Hollywood Model
and Screen Star

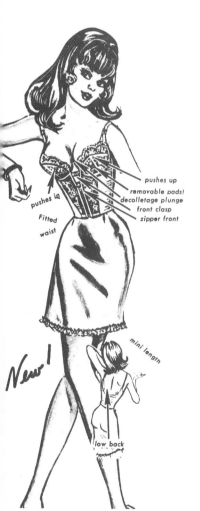

pushes up
removable pads!
decolletage plunge
front clasp
zipper front

pushes in

Fitted
waist

New!

mini length

low back

**#4—5986   WAISTS
AWAY!**
For you who need a little taking in
at the waist and a push-up in your
bra, Frederick's has done it again.
Stretch straps, 100% nylon lace
cups with removable push-up pads,
zip front, nylon spandex waist.
In White or Nude.
Sizes: 32, 34, 36, 38 B Cup;   **$15**
32, 34, 36, 38 C Cup.

make him look

TWiCE

(ONCE IS NEVER ENUFF)

*I wouldn't be me
without my Frederick's
bra . . . they give me
shape I never dreamed
possible.*

Georgi La Peer

Top Hollywood Model

Pad Wardrobe

**FABULOUS WARDROBE
SET OF ALL SIZE BRA PADS**

#9476   THREE IN ONE
Three ways to elevate yourself to new
heights! Frederick's wardrobe of pads
is designed for bosom appeal! Set contains angled push-up pads,   **$5⁹⁹**
sweater pads and beauty tips.

IDEAL
FOR ONE
SHOULDER
DRESSES

J #4722   UNBELIEVABLE
Only at Frederick's would you expect
to find this one-derful one-cup bra.
Sheer all nylon lace cup has satin
shoulder strap with ribbon tie under
the bust. Great gift idea! Black or
Red.   **$2⁰⁰**
Sizes 32 to 38.

G-R-E-A-T
frenchy look

E

D

import

D #4-3304 OOH, LA, LA!
bosom lacking young uplift?
Frederick's copies a fabulous French
import to bring you that youthful
look. Circular stitched cup urges your
bosom forward and "OUT." Fabulous
under sweaters or silks. Acetate
Satin. White or Black.
Sizes 32, 34, 36, 38 B cup;   **$6**
    32, 34, 36, 38 C cup.

E #4-3244 "FRENCH" LIFT
Are you woman enough for this
sensational French lift that bares
your bosom becomingly? Plush edge
Nylon Taffeta acts as a sling for
each bust, leaving you free but
supported. Perlon Nylon Jersey back
insures neat line. Black, White.
Sizes 32, 34, 36, 38 B cup;   **$6**
    32, 34, 36, 38 C cup.

Eunice Dee, fashion model,
says "I depend on my
Frederick's bra wardrobe! No
matter what fashion I'm called
on to model...plunge neckline
...low back...bare shoulders
...I know I'll have the perfect
bra to fill the perfect dress."

The Sensuous Woman
Wears Frederick's Originals!

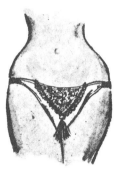

spider web fringe bikinis

#3-4298 HAVE A HEART
Give him the key to your heart! Wee bikini panty comes equipped with heart and chain. Share the secret, and you're his love slave for sure! In Black, Red or Sand-colored Nylon, lace trimmed. Sizes 5-6-7. **3 FOR $4.50**

#3-4144 COBWEBS
The winning way to weave a web! With spider web bikini panties, bound to you with the narrowest of elastic straps! To cover you almost decently, three tiers of shimmy fringe are hung on a sheer lace backing. In Black or Red.
One size fits all. **3 FOR $8.50**

#3-4295 TASSY
Tassy the Tassle-Twirler adores these bikinis! Made of 'wet' look nylon with elastic sides, they're hung with black tassles and trimmed with black lace. In Hot Pink, Black or Lime, all with black trim. Sizes Small (5), Medium (6) and Large (7). **2 FOR $6.95**

THE NEWEST!!

A B C

#3-4299 STAR GAZER
Whether you dig astrology or not, the high sign is yours in our new zodiac panty. Box of 3 (100% nylon, 15 denier). Order by the month sign and date for inscription. Set colors are Black, Red, Pink. Sizes: Small, Medium, Large. **the set $9**

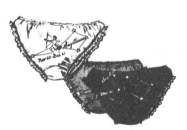

I believe you MUST look truly feminine to enjoy life. Our aids to nature assure that look INSTANTLY! Order yours now.
Mr. Frederick

BIRD CAGES
Turn into a peacock and strut your stuff! Excite him . . . delight him in bra and bikini built like bird cages of bands of nylon lace. (How he'll long to set you free!) Red or Black.

A **#4-5087 FANTASY BRA**
Sizes 3 4-36-38.
No cups sizes needed. **$12**

B **#4-5089 FANTASY PANTY**
Small (22-24''), Medium (25-27''), Large (28-30''). **$6.50**

C **#4-5789 BEWITCHIN'!**
Want to look pretty from the skin out? Hitch your hose to a star! Headlining in lingerie glamour, is this Lace-and-Ribbon Garter Belt—too provocative to pass by! White, Black or Red. Elasticized, so one size fits all. **$3**
2 For $5.50

#3-4266 PANT 'O MINES!
Suit the mood and say it with sass. Your set of three flirtatious and delectable panties is a real gone come-on. It's "Yes," "No," or "Maybe" In Black, White and Peach. 100% nylon, washable. Sizes: 5, 6, 7 **the set $5**

48

#3—4442 HOT SEATS
Underpinnings, cut to cling under Hot Pants! Sheer little Nylon bikinis slash up high on the thighs. Provide minimum coverage! Buy by the half-dozen, in a NEW color assortment of Lilac, Pink, Blue, White, Black. Sizes 5,6,7.

6 for $9

#3—4396 BARE ESSENTIAL
This tantalizing bikini panty has high-cut one-inch elastic sides. Made of 40 denier Nylon, comes in Black, White or Pink—buy all 3 colors! Small (5), Medium (6), or Large (7).

3 for $8 50
$3 ea.

#3—4475 MIGHTY MITE
This brief, brief panty has no crotch at all! Nothing but lovely, lovely lace! High-cut legs leave little to the imagination. Elastic waist . . . lace and more lace trim, wouldn't you know it's a copy of a Continental import! Nylon White, Black or Red. Sizes: Small (5), Medium (6), Large (7).

3 for $8 50
$3 ea.

SCANTY LACE
Four delightful strips go from crotch to side of bikini panty. Lace trim. In beautiful assortment of colors. 100% Nylon. Small, Medium and Large

#3—4912 $3

PANTS TO PLEASE
Find out how it pays to advertise! Wear our "Try It! You'll Like It!" panty! Chances are. . . . he will! Choose your Acetate bikini briefs in set of 3 colors Lilac, Coral or Yellow, each with contrast trim and "Try It!" stitching. In Sizes 5, 6, 7

#3—4908   3 for $4.50

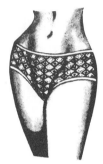

#3—4471 STRETCHIES
Go beautiful from the pants up! S-t-r-e-t-c-h lace bikinis fit and feel like nothing at all! Woven in a harlequin pattern in a rainbow assortment of lingerie colors, you'll want to own a drawerful! In easy-wash quick-drying Nylon. One size fits 5,6,7.

3 for $6 99

SEX IT UP . . . WITH FREDERICK'S SIZZLERS

FUNDERWEAR!

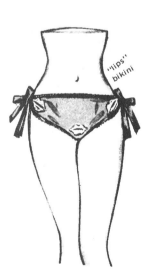

#3—4558 KISSIN' SWEET
Scanty bikini panty is embroidered with LIPS at the nicest spot! Gives a guy ideas! In sheerest Nylon, to tie with bows at both high-cut sides. In Black, White, Purple. Small (5), Medium (6), Large (7).

2 for $8
$4 50 ea.

BEASTLY BIKINIS
Primitive pelts for the best undressed woman! Wear our animal print pants . . .in pure Acetate Jersey with elasticized waist and leg bands. Go really WILD with a set of 4. Small, Medium and Large.

#3—4967   set of 4 $5

49

A **#4—5062 "SLING" DING**
Better than no bra at all! Suspension-type bra defies the laws of gravity . . . lifts you and molds you as nature intended. Bares you up for the most daring exposure under new, cling-close fashions. In soft nylon tricot with adjustable elastic straps. In Nude only.
Sizes: 32 to 36,
A, B and C cups. **$6**

#4—5060   NICELY NUDE!
You're more alluring wearing this transparent "skin" bra. Thin Underwiring gives all the support that's necessary — gentle spandex wings give smooth "under-sheers" appearance. Nude-skin color chiffon with dainty bow between breasts. Sizes: 32 to 36 B and C cups. **$6**

#4—5072 THEY MOVE!
Yes the cups slide away at each side to give bare dramatic separation and deep plunge. Soft crepeset cups add to the illusion of naturally you. Narrow lycra spandex wings and back eliminates gapping at the underarm sections. Sizes 32 to 36, B and C cup. White and Nude. **$5⁵⁰**

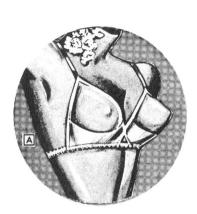

It's New!

adjustable cups

FREDERICK'S
25 Years of SHAPING America

#4—5082   TENDER TIPS
For the gal who can't make it on her own...but would like to! Soft rubber nipple pads fill you out all the way, just like nature intended! Most natural look and feel in the world, even under see-through tops. White. One size fits all.
THE PAIR **$3**
2 for **$5⁵⁰**

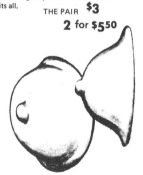

#4—5093   SHEER UPRISING
NUDER THAN NO BRA. . .yet gives individual shaping every day in every way! Tricot sheer bra is so ultra see—through it looks like another layer of sensuous skin. Peasant shirring at the top gives and takes with the fullness of your bust. All—but invisible underwiring for exciting elevation. In nothing—at—all Nude or Black Sizes 32 to 38, ~~WAS $7⁵⁰~~
B and C cups. **NOW $6⁷⁵**

New!
New!
New!

B,C,D,DD
SIZE YOU UP
FOR EVERY FASHION LOOK!

Great for Halters!

Wild Wild Cleavage!

Push-up Pads

imported underwired half cups

NATURAL LOOK under knits and Banlons

Mr. Frederick knows where it's at . . . I've never looked so good in those bare-back fashions since he got me into Frederick's low-back bras!

Mary

NATURAL NIPPLES
lets everything show naturally under Banlons and Knits! Underwired Nylon lace half-cups lift the breasts, leave the nipples uncovered to press forward provocatively. Ribbon trim on adjustable straps. White with Blue trim.

32 to 38, B cups;
34 to 38, C cups

#4—5150 $7

OUT OF SIGHT
This backless beauty has a back strap of non-skid rubber that always clings waist-deep. Wide-apart frontage gives better-than-no-bra cleavage. Cups have sewn-in push-up pads, are of Tricot-lined Kodel Polyester
                    White only.
Order in C or D cup sizes.

#4—5186 $7

Mr. Frederick says...

We know you expect a lot from your Frederick's fashions! But remember, please, an attractive woman NEVER lets her figure down! ALWAYS wear the right bra for the right fashion . . . to be SURE.

Great for Halters

3-way convertible straps

BARE WEAR
Sensational shaping for the bare-fashioned look. Bandeau converts from shoulder-strapped to strapless to halter. Hooks in front. . . so you cup your breats IN, arrange them UP, and SNAP! They're pillowed in place on removable push-up and in pads. Delicately pleated Nylon lace shells, lightly contoured, are wide-apart spaced for extreme plunge. Black or White.
#4—3190
32 to 36 A, 32 to 38 B cups.

WAS $9.50
NOW $8.77

32 to 38 C,
32 to 36 D cups

WILL BE $10.50
NOW $9.50

When my figure needs to be at top advantage, Frederick's is where I shop.

Odessa

Darlings for Daylight...

Magic for Moonlight

DARINGLY DIFFERENT!· NEW! DRAMATIC!

"Mad Moment"

only $14.98

"Breathless Beauty"

only $17.98

Jewel Clip FREE!

"Movie Queen"

only $14.98

"Million Dollar Look"

only $14.98

Exotic! Does things for figures! Romantic style with "peek-a-boo" slits on shoulders and neckline. Softly draped bust and hips; LACE midriff. Rayon "Paradise Crepe". Sizes: 10 to 20. Angel White, Lime Green, Sea Aqua, Black. (All with Matching Lace.)
Style No. 3110

Divinely flattering! Filmy "French" lace yoke, sleeves and inset are SO alluring! Slit neck, draped shirred skirt. Rippling peplum in back. "Symphony" rayon crepe. Sizes: 10 to 20. Blush Rose, Black, Turquoise Blue. (All with Matching Lace.)
Style No. 306

You'll look stunning . . . have the time of your life in this "movie queen" style! He'll love the daring neckline, shirred molded lines, and insets of filmy rayon sheer— back and front! Sizes: 10 to 20. Superb rayon crepe in Black with Black Sheer; Sea Aqua or Shy Pink with Nude.
Style No. 314

Exact copy of a thrilling Paris creation! Here's a dress to catch a dream man—with its portrait collar, draped lines, darling swishy "fish-tail" peplum. Thrilling value! Finer rayon Crepe Divine. Sizes: 10 to 18. Glamour Grey, Daring Red, Sea Aqua, Black.
Style No. 319—

ORIGINAL *HOLLYWOOD* CREATIONS!

"Silver Sequins"

For that New, Naughty NUDE LOOK!

only $14.98

Wear it if you dare! Enticing, eye-catching, heart-stealing! Slim lines with gorgeous drapery to mold a beautiful bust and hips. New slit halter neck, sparkling "silver" sequin trim. **ONLY AT FREDERICK'S!!** Rich rayon crepe. Sizes: 10 to 18. Black, White, Lime Glow, Aqua.
Style No. 315—

"Temptress"

only $15.98

Be first to wear the rage of Paris . . . the dress with one bare shoulder! Look like a Hollywood star in this gorgeous draped fashion with rippling skirt and fluffy flower to accent the bustline. Rayon "Paradise Crepe".
Sizes: 10 to 18. Lime Green, Naughty Black, Angel White.
Style No. 313—

"Social Butterfly"

only $15.98

Has matching bolero jacket— wear it in the daytime, too! Darling butterfly bow back gives bustle effect. Boned, shirred bodice gives gorgeous bustline—stays firmly in place. Rayon Taffeta.
Sizes: 9 to 17; 10 to 18. Happy Red, Tender Green, White, Black.
Style No. 307—

"Show-off"

Worth Every Cent of $20.00

SALE PRICE— *only* $10.98

Daring, head-turning yoke of black sheer rayon . . . frilly cap sleeves of black REAL LACE! Fitted bustline, draped skirt. Fine "Exotic" rayon crepe. Sizes: 10 to 20. Daring Red, Black, Sky Aqua (with BLACK Sheer & Lace).
Style No. 317—

You'll **Stand out** *in a Crowd!*

Frederick's Fashion Guarantee . . .

"Stand Out" FASHIONS... Dramatic Full Sleeves!

"Moon Mist"

SPECIAL PRICE

only $10.98

(But looks like $35!)

Imagine the allure of flowing sheer sleeves, plunging neck veiled with daring filmy lace, draped skirt! A dreamy dress every woman can afford—no woman can do without! Fine rayon crepe with Black rayon sheer sleeves and yoke. Sizes: 10 to 20 Shocking Red, Black, Foam Aqua. Style No. 318

56

$14.98

"SEQUIN SPARKLE" Dress

For that "Hollywood" look! Rich rayon crepe with full sleeves and "peek-a-boo" yoke of sheer BLACK net, sprinkled with gay sequins. Slim skirt, smart back interest. Midnight Black, Foam Aqua, Glamour Grey (All with BLACK Net). Sizes: 10 to 20

STYLE NO. 24

NOW! DATE-GOING GLAMOUR *in* GLEAMING RAYON *Satin*

HOLLYWOOD GLAMOUR at a
New Low Price!

NOW! Genuine *Hollywood* ORIGINALS

High Style at Low Prices!

DATE TIME DRESSES
ONLY $12⁹⁸ EACH
SPECIAL PRICE

"GALA EVENING"
Flatters figures! Dreamy draped lines to mold bust and hips glamorously. Brand new . . . priced for value. Shimmering rayon SATIN.
Sizes: 10 to 18—Mist Blue, Black, Sun Bronze
STYLE NO. 108
"GALA EVENING" IN RAYON CANTON CREPE!
Romance Red, Black, French Grey
STYLE NO. 109 $12⁹⁸

"NIGHT CLUB"
GOLD SEQUINS glitter on deep midriff insert. Gorgeous date dress of silky smooth rayon crepe with "choker" neck, graceful fishtail peplum, slit skirt. Thrilling value!
Sizes: 10 to 20
Peacock Blue, French Grey, Romance Red, Black
STYLE NO. 110 $12⁹⁸

YOU ALWAYS GET A FREE GIFT
If you send payment with order! Enclose check or money order and we will send you a lovely gift FREE.

THRILLING LOVELINESS in CREPE or SATIN
at a
SENSATIONAL LOW PRICE
ONLY $11⁹⁸ EACH

"DATE GETTER"
Lovable lines — back and front! Smoothly draped bust and hips, head-turning little "bustle" back falls in soft folds. Rich rayon SATIN at the lowest price ever!
Sizes: 10 to 18 — Black, Mist Blue, Copper Glow
STYLE NO. 99

Designed By . *Frederick* Sold Only By . . . FREDERICK'S

"ALLURING HOUR"
Exciting "nude" look of real BLACK LACE daringly draped from shoulder to waist and forming one entire sleeve. (Darling built-in "camisole") Canton crepe Stunning skirt.
Sizes: 10 to 20—Blush Rose, Turquoise Blue, Siren Black (All with Black Lace)
STYLE NO. 100

57

"Wardrobe Magic"

only $14.98 each

You'll want **BOTH . . .**

"HEAVENLY BODY"

You'll look glamorous in this stunning, easy-to-wear dress with its draped wrap-around skirt. The low, square neckline is shirred and draped across the bust. Sash tie is adjustable for perfect fit.

"Sunset" rayon crepe
SIZES: 10 to 20
DAWN GREY,
58 NEW NAVY, RICH RED,
MIDNIGHT BLACK
STYLE NO. 56

"TEMPTRESS"

Your waist never looked so small! Bust and hips have soft lines for eye-catching curves. Matching FRENCH LACE forms a fitted midriff band . . . trimmed with glittering simulated jewels.

SIZES: 10 to 20
SURF AQUA
LIPSTICK RED
DAWN GREY
MYSTERY BLACK
(All with Matching Lace)

STYLE NO. 49

"PARISIAN PRINT"

Gorgeous draped hipline, smart front fullness, molded bustline daring low-cut "V" neck. You'll wear this colorful print dress everywhere–! Creamy pattern on vibrant backgrounds is dramatic!

"Sunset" rayon crepe
SIZES: 10 to 18
RICH RED, DAWN GREY
MIDNIGHT BLACK
STYLE NO. 57

"ENTICING"

Hollywood favorite! Exotic low-cut neckline held snugly with hidden ties and shirred bustline; stunning draped skirt falls in graceful folds. So different—you be first to wear it!

SIZES: 10 to 18.
GARDENIA WHITE,
GLAMOUR GREY
MIDNIGHT BLACK
STYLE NO. 46

"ENCHANTMENT"

Adorable TWO-PIECE charmer! Flared peplum ends in fish-tail back. Striking neckline has inset of nude sheer, trimmed with beautiful lace. Skirt is slim . . . waist is tiny .

SIZES: 10 to 20
TURQUOISE BLUE,
GLAMOUR GREY
MIDNIGHT BLACK
GARDENIA WHITE
STYLE NO. 47

The Dress with MALE APPEAL

Paris loves its adorable shirred "hour-glass" look . . . you will, too! "Glitter" trim on choker neck, new flowing draped panel in front is graceful. Silky rayon "Princess" crepe in Heavenly Aqua, French Grey, Siren Black.
Style No. 134

"LOVE AFFAIR"

Smart double peplum of rayon taffeta sweeps to one side; sweetheart neck is taffeta-trimmed. Molded bust; tiny waist.

STYLE NO. 82

- TURQUOISE BLUE
- FRENCH GREY
- GARDENIA WHITE
- SIREN BLACK

"Midnight Mood"

Stunning original design that makes you the belle of the ball! Lovely rayon sheer is draped over rich rayon crepe in exciting "Harem" effect. Molds bust and hips!

Black, White, Lime Green, Turquoise Blue.
Style No. 301—

"NIGHT LIFE" DRESS

It's NEW . . . EXCITING . . . Daringly DIFFERENT!
The most breathtaking style Hollywood has seen! Designed for figure magic, it drapes your bust with gentle folds, hugs your waist, glamorizes your hips with stunning drapery! Rayon sheer yoke gives the new "naked" look . . . rich LACE forms ruffled cap sleeves. And the back is gorgeous, too, with its sheer yoke, graceful drapery and zipper for a dreamy fit! Priced for every pocketbook—

SIZES: 10 to 20
Smart "LUXURA" Rayon Crepe in
- MYSTERY BLACK with BLACK sheer yoke; black lace
- ROMANCE ROSE } with NUDE SHEER
- TURQUOISE BLUE } and
- GLAMOUR GREY } MATCHING LACE

STYLE NO. 55

"BEST BEAU" Dress

Stunning molded lines flatter your figure! Two saucy bows on shoulders, rich jeweled embroidery trim. Looks far more expensive! Smooth "Angel-Skin" rayon crepe. Turquoise Blue, Dawn Grey, Black, Lipstick Red.
Sizes: 10 to 18

STYLE NO. 22

Yes! FREDERICK'S Hollywood Originals Give You GLAMOUR and ALLURE . . Really "Do Things" for You!

It's No Secret!

California's Favorite

"'ROUND THE TOWN"
Darling, colorful, flattering! You'll wear it EVERYWHERE. Gaily printed fine one-denier rayon "Four Season" fabric. For shopping, street, school, or office wear. 2-way collar, full skirt, self-belt. Rainbow Print on dark grounds.
Sizes: 10 to 18
STYLE NO. 103

$7.79

only **$9.98** EACH

At last you can buy the gorgeous, flattering filmland fashions you've admired at prices you can afford! Lovely new shades, smart fabrics!

"EYE-CATCHER"

Crisp, crease-resistant rayon GABARDINE that buttons all the way down; contrasting saddle-stitching, 2-way collar, action back.

SIZES: 10 to 20

SUN GOLD
SURF AQUA
DAWN GREY
BLACK

STYLE NO. 61

... *Yes, It's No Secret That* **FREDERICK'S of HOLLYWOOD** Is First In ✓NEW FASHIONS ✓QUALITY ✓SERVICE ✓VALUE

Glamorous Hollywood 'Dress Up' Styles Trimmed with Imported French Lace

Casuals

PHOTOGRAPHED IN HOLLYWOOD!

"FUN EVERYWHERE"
2-tone glamour! Figure-flattering dress with gay "gold" glitter chain forming necklace and belt trim. Smooth rayon GABARDINE.
Sizes: 10 to 18 — Lime Top & Brown Skirt; Aqua Top & Black Skirt; Red Top & Black Skirt
STYLE NO. 105 $**10**⁹⁸

"FOUR STAR" JERSEY
Soft 100% PURE WOOL JERSEY! You'll love the turtle neck, perky pockets, "dog-leash" belt. Skirt has soft fullness.
Sizes 10 to 18 — Gold Top & Brown Skirt; Grey Top & Red Skirt; Green Top & Black Skirt
STYLE NO. 106 $**11**⁹⁸

ONLY $**8**⁹⁸
($15.00 VALUE)

Style No. 312

"Queen of Hearts"
Win hearts, win compliments in this princess style dress with flattering fullness in bust and skirt . . . tiny waist, plunge neck! Fine rayon crepe.
Sizes: 10 to 18. French Aqua, Dawn Grey, Black—All with WHITE trim.

"HAPPY DAYS" — Sun Dress & Matching Stole. Dress has boned bodice and back zipper for alluring bustline & beautiful fit! Cape-stole covers bare shoulders and back . . . has cute pockets, too!
SIZES: 10 to 18
Multi-Color Cotton Print
STYLE NO. 85 $**9**⁹⁸

These are the *Dream Dresses* Chosen by the HOLLYWOOD STARS!

HOLLYWOOD ORIGINALS

Heavenly Glow

"Forbidden Fruit"

"Romantic Mood"

only $15.98

DETACHABLE HOOD Forms DRAPED COLLAR!

Style No. 347
$14.98

Style No. 334
$12.98

IT'S NEW!

This is the dress that has Hollywood agog! Models and Hollywood stars paid much more for this gorgeous creation!

Man-catching flared tunic of "Shadow Sheer" over silky Rayon Crepe. Sleeves and cuffed yoke of luscious sheer, too! Sizes: 10 to 20. Black or Seafoam Blue with Black Sheer; White with White Sheer.
Style No. 334

Deep-slashed neckline held by 2 slim straps, softly draped bustline, backswept peplum, and VELVET BOW! "Paradise Crepe" in Silver Cloud Grey, Black, Seafoam Blue.
Style No. 347 Sizes: 10 to 18.

It has EVERYTHING! Molded bust, daring neckline, draped collar, flattering skirt, back zipper —and a HOOD that buttons on or off for real glamour. Smooth Rayon "Exotic Crepe". Sizes: 10 to 18. Black, Royal Blue, Grey, Kelly Green.
Style No. 344

with that "COME HITHER" look!

"High Life"

"Night of Love"

"Perfect Evening"

Style No. 343
$14.98

Wear-if-you-dare! He'll kiss you when he sees this form-fitting style of smooth, fine "Paradise Crepe". Cowl neck with deep plunge; gorgeous draped skirt. Sizes: 10 to 18. Aqua, Black, Lime Green, Passion Purple.
Style 343

Romance can be yours—in this dress! It has everything—shirred bustline for pretty curves . . . draped skirt . . . "peep-show" shoulders . . . sparkling trim of Sequins! Then there's a darling MATCHING JACKET for daytime wear. Gorgeous Rayon "Paradise Crepe." Sizes: 10 to 18. Black, Emerald Green, White, Lime-Gold.
Style No. 326
$17.98

Dreamy draped lines give you a perfect figure! Rich, gleaming Slipper SATIN* with shirred, boned top that really stays up. You'll adore it for special dates, and add the cute bolero jacket for daytime wear.
A FREDERICK'S FIRST at a new low price! Sizes: 10 to 18. Black, Lime Green, Cherry Wine.
Style No. 325
$12.98
*rayon

FREDERICK'S NEW FABRIC STORY—

Now we can bring you the fabrics you've seen at MUCH HIGHER PRICES at Frederick's low price! You'll love the shimmering new rayon crepes . . . the gleaming rayon satins . . . the fine cottons . . . and crisp rayon gabardines.

MEN AGREE - THESE ARE TOPS FOR DATES!

"EXOTIC EVENING"
He'll want to hold you close in this romantic dress of sweetly shirred "Crepe Supreme" with Paris-inspired "peep-show" shoulders, tiny waist, draped bust, rich FRENCH LACE trim. This is YOUR dress—so buy it! Lime Green, Peacock Blue, Black. Sizes 10 to 18.
Style No. 372-only $15.98

"LOVER'S DREAM"
Rustling TAFFETA!* Profile collar, sideswept skirt, perky bow. He'll love it! Emerald Green, White, Ruby Red, Black. Sizes: 10 to 18.
Style No. 322—only $17.98

Sale! $10.98

"DREAM MATE"
Stunning choker neck, portrait collar, draped skirt! MARVELOUS VALUE! "Exotic Crepe"* in Black, Shocking Red, Seafoam Blue. Sizes: 10 to 20.
Style No. 331—SPEC. PRICE—$10.98

You **Must** *Take a* **Peek**

"Screenland Sparkle"

Wonderful, wearable . . . flatters every figure! Fine, crease-resistant sheen GABARDINE (rayon) with gorgeous lines, deep dolman sleeves and glittering trim of "gold" nailheads. Sizes: 10 to 20. Lime Green, Honey Beige, Black, Foam Aqua.
Style No. 294

SPECIAL PRICE—

only **$12⁹⁸**

"Party Polka"

only **$16⁹⁸**

Silver-dollar size velvet-y polka dots to catch his eye! They're embroidered on filmy sheer rayon that plays peek-a-boo with bosom and shoulders. Shirred bust, draped skirt, big bustle-bow in back. Fine TAFFETA in Naughty Black. Sizes: 10 to 18.
Style No. 337

Best Buys in Glamour

STYLE
271

STYLE
279

ELASTIC
WAIST-CINCHER
BELT

STYLE
286

STYLE 271—"CURVACEOUS"— 100% WOOL JERSEY, with daring low-cut, fitted bodice and peg-top skirt. Smart fashion details include jewelled buttons, waist-whittler belt, 2 pockets. Smart, 1-piece style. Black, Emerald Green, Lipstick Red. Sizes 10 to 18 *$15⁹⁸*

STYLE 279—"SWEET SURPRISE"— 6-PLY BENGALINE*. Biggest surprise ever is the tiny price! Looks pert and fresh all day, and thru the wee hours . . . thanks to the gorgeous fabric. Pert collar, fine fit, ELASTIC WAIST-CINCHER BELT. Blonde-Beige, Date Red, Bewitching Black. Sizes 10 to 18 *$9⁹⁸*

STYLE 286—"DANCING DUET" DRESS AND MATCHING BOLERO Adorable yarn-dyed taffeta** date-dress will make your date rating zoom! Unusual bra-fit bodice is boned, has pretty petal effect neckline. Full circle skirt. Jewel and silver trim from top to hem . . . glitters as you dance. Black, Green, Cherry-Wine. Sizes 10 to 18 *$18⁹⁸*

*Rayon-and-Cotton   FOR BOTH
**Rayon-and-Acetate

FREE GIFTS FOR YOU WITH ALL ORDERS . . . .

except C.O.D.'s. We surprise you with jewelry, hankies, lots of pretty little gadgets for your pocket-book. ALL FREE!

SMART, FASHION-WISE WOMEN ORDER CLOTHES BY MAIL FROM FREDERICKS OF HOLLYWOOD BECAUSE:

"SWISS MISS"
Tyrolean Suspender-Skirt
Wear it with or without suspender-straps! Finest faille* with multi-color wool embroidery and huge patch pockets. Sizes: 10 to 18. Black, Emerald Green, Royal Blue.
Style No. 398—only $7.98

"Sheer Dear" Blouse
"Oo-La-La Georgette* in White, Lilac, Lime. Sizes: 32 to 38.
Style No. 64—$6.98

I See SAVINGS for YOU!

FILM FAVORITES YOU'LL LOVE . .
ARE EASY ON YOUR BUDGET!

Stop . . Look . . and Whistle

STYLE 312—"IN THE SWING"
Brilliant flash of red ruffle at hem and glimpse of red lining on the snug Black bodice will hold his interest! Looks like separates but it's a new 1-piece dress of TAFFETA*. Skirt is checked; wide cummerbund belt in red. Darling for dates. Holiday parties, etc! Sizes 10 to 18
$15⁹⁸

STYLE 309—"TAKE A TWIRL"
and show the bright red lining of your full-circle skirt! Dream of a dress with plunge neck, big platter buttons and passionate red rose. New "CHROMSPUN" color-locked, no-fade TAFFETA* stays fresh and glowing for life of the dress. Black or Navy— each with RED skirt-lining. Sizes 12 to 18
$10⁷⁹ SPECIAL

MONEY BACK GUARANTEE

STYLE 310—"PARTY NEWS"
COPIED FROM A PARIS IMPORT!
Newest shape for a date dress! Crisp lining makes skirt whirl gaily . . . soft pleats bell out to form full-circle skirt. Cuffed bust line has bra-look inset of Black Alencon Lace, lined in nude crepe. CHROMSPUN TAFFETA* in Black, Red, Royal. Sizes 10 to 18.
$16⁹⁸

*Rayon-and-Acetate

• Our own copies of fabulous French imports that "he" will love.

STYLE 312

STYLE 309

STYLE 310

SKIRT LINED IN RED

---

1. **FASHION FIRSTS**—We're way ahead with the latest styles!

2. **HOLLYWOOD ORIGINALS**—Unusual designs, made in Hollywood!

3. **MONEY BACK GUARANTEE**—If you are not entirely satisfied, we will gladly refund ALL your money and postage, too!

4. **MORE FOR YOUR FASHION DOLLAR**—FREDERICK'S offers new, different styles, well made of fine fabrics.

AND REMEMBER, A FREE GIFT WITH ALL PREPAID ORDERS!

#309—"TAKE A TWIRL"
The most amazing "buy" we have ever offered! The full circle skirt is lined in bright red to catch his eye! Big platter buttons, plunge-neck, red rose at hip. No-fade, color-locked Rayon-and-Acetate CHROMSPUN Taffeta. Black, Navy, both with Red lining. Sizes 12 to 18
$10⁷⁹

He'll Love These Hollywood

#412 "PICTURE OF PARIS"
Satin Date Dress and Coat.
You can't tell it from the original French creation that cost $200! Coat alone is worth the price of the outfit! Dress has boned bra-top, draped and jewel-studded; hip-hugging skirt. The dressy date coat in matching satin is fully lined. Wear over all your dressy clothes! Both of new "Angel Skin" Satin* backed with glowing Taffeta for a duller luster. Black or Champagne Beige. Sizes 10 to 20.
$3998
FOR BOTH

#437 "DESIRE ME"
For gals who want to live dangerously! Hear him whisper "Darling, you're beautiful!" Yarn-dyed Taffeta* dream dress with hundreds of shimmering sequins on the boned-bra inset. Daring cuffed bodice and draped halter that may be tied in back, too. Flirty bustle bow-back with flowing fullness in skirt. Glamorous matching bolero. Black or Mink Brown. **$1998** Sizes 9 to 17.

Hits!

#298—"FASHION SHOW" Glamour-Gown and Bolero. Both with Lavish Jewelled Trim. Strapless, boned dress has rhinestone trim on bust and arched pockets of slinky skirt. For dressy dates, parties, dinner-dances. Matching Bolero. Rich, silky Bengaline** in Black or Teal Blue. Sizes 10 to 18. **$18.98**

#298A—IN IMPORTED VELVET:* lined bolero. Black, Red. **$28.98**

#361—"DANGER AHEAD" Copied from Hollywood's top Glamour Queen! Revealing Honeymoon Crepe* cocktail dress with daring bare midriff. Bust and hips have magic shirring for gorgeous curves. Be first to wear this sensational daring style!! Brought to you only by Frederick's at an amazingly low price. Black, Glamour Gold, Heavenly Aqua. Sizes 10 to 18. **$14.98**

#380 "TEMPTATION" Make him all yours in this smart curve-cuddling date dress! Two-tone combinations in glowing "Hollywood Crepe"*. Bosom-hugging drape points up your alluring torso; ditto for the draped hipline. Jet Black with White; Navy with Sky Blue; Emerald Green & Gold; **$15.98** Sizes 10 to 20.

#381 $15.98

#381—"MISS MISCHIEF" Two colors are smarter than one—and this wickedly becoming, new, naughty creation proves it! SO easy to wear—cut to flatter all figures! Halter-neck; Grecian bust-draped, softly flowing skirt. "Hollywood Crepe"*. Black with White; Navy & Powder; Black with Silver Grey. **$15.98** Sizes 10 to 18.

CURVE-Y CREPE CREATIONS

Slinky CREPE SHEATHS

#330

#340

#341

#336
$15.98

FREE BIRTHDAY GIFT*
JEWELLED CLIPS
*with purchase of dress shown

Birthday Bonus Special

#330 "HEAVENLY DRAPE"
A charmer—if there ever was one! Shirred panels hug torso closely from bust to thigh; zipper back. Sweetheart neck has a glamorous look with FREE jewelled clips that are Frederick's birthday gift to you. California crepe.* Sizes 10 to 20. Black, Red, Turquoise Blue— **$16⁹⁸**

#336 "MIDNIGHT SUPPER"
Dressy two-tone crepe ablaze with dozens of rhinestones. Revealing neckline; draped sheath skirt. Waist-hugging two-tone belt. For movie-dates, dining, dancing in your favorite spots. Specially priced. Rich Rayon and acetate crepe. Sizes 10 to 20. Black & White; Royal Blue with Grey. **$15⁹⁸**

#340 "LOVE AFFAIR"
Frederick's Original Design
Simply sensational! Silky "Siren Crepe"*. Scalloped off-shoulder has Portrait neckline; skirt has smart sunburst drape. Glittering rhinestone trim accents bust; daring halter-effect back. Deep Purple, Royal Blue, Black. Sizes 10 to 18— **$16⁹⁸**

#341 "DOUBLE CROSS"
"Angel Crepe"* siren-sheath clings tenderly to curves. Draped halter criss-crosses to let lots of skin show! Hipline is deftly draped in a peplum effect. Sure to be voted "Dream Dress of The Year". Low-priced! Black, Red, Turquoise Blue. Sizes 10 to 18— **$14⁹⁸**

*Rayon and acetate

DATE CRAZY DRAMA

DARING
DEVILISH
DARLING

#338 "FALLING IN LOVE"
Taffeta Dress and Tiny Bolero
Right from the wardrobe of a top
Hollywood screen star! It has the
new sideswept peplum that gives
graceful lines to the body, with
an accent of glittering sequins.
Boned bra-top for a pretty bust.
Very dressy! Add the brief jacket
for cocktail dates. Colorfast rich
Chromspun Acetate Taffeta in Red,
Black or Peacock Blue. **$24.98**
Sizes 10 to 18—

#366 "FRENCH FRINGE"
Fabulous fabric, delicious drape
make this perfect for dates! Satin finished Chromspun Acetate Taffeta is fringed with rows and rows
of silky "eyelashes" to wink at
men who look your way! Scoop-neck;
low-cut back; sliver-slim sheath
skirt. White, Mist-Grey,
Jewel Blue. Sizes 10 to 20. **$24.98**

#328 "POLKA PARTNER"
Has everything from the man's
point of view! Velvet ribbon dips
from shoulder to encircle bust, and
it's caught with a romantic rose.
Draped, boned bustline; swirling
skirt has attached petticoat in
brilliant red with double net
flounces. Acetate Taffeta. Black
with White Dots.
Sizes 10 to 18 **$22.98**

Taffeta GOES DANCING

#338
TWO-PIECE

#366

#328

STRAPLESS SORCERY

HOLLYWOOD ORIGINALS
. . . Mean MORE for your fashion dollar,
because they're new and different . . . beautifully made of fine fabrics . . . designed
in glamorous HOLLYWOOD!

Kissin' Cocktail Cottons

#592 POUFF PET
Be his pet in this exotic cotton satin halter neck sheath! Lap-over surplice neck with pointed bust line is fabulously flattering and *fits!* Double self-pouff riots from hip to hem, and from side to bottom in back to give you added excitement and glamour. Lilac or Aqua, on White background.
Sizes 10 to 18. **$25⁹⁸**

Frederick and glamorous
Italian model stroll
in Roman Forum.

South of The Border Siren!
#243 "SPANISH SERENADE"
You'd swear it was imported! As colorful as fabulous hand-painted styles, but it's a glowing border print. One-piece cotton in Fiesta Red, Black Magic, or Golden Glow.
Sizes 10 to 18. SALE— **$11.88**

COMING SOON!!
FREDERICK'S NEW
"LUCKY MOMENT"
CONTEST

Frederick EXPORTS styles to France!

Frederick poses an attractive French model in his original Style #291 (shown on Page 10) in front of Jacques Fath's. She adores this American creation!

Frederick found the French loved the lace allure of his style #250 (shown on Page 3). The background is the famous Arc de Triomphe, in Paris.

CAREFREE COTTONS

IMPORTED
← from →
HAWAII

BUY NOW
...while our
stock of
new styles
is complete.
Don't wait!

MONEY-BACK GUARANTEE ON
ALL OF OUR MERCHANDISE!

#239 "ISLAND MAGIC" Cotton
Imported Print—New Long Torso! Frederick brings you a tropical creation at a price so LOW you won't believe it! Draped bust, bow-tied shoulders, shirred skirt. Sizes 10 to 18. Sun-Gold, Red, Sea Green. JUST— **$9.98**

#233 "HAWAIIAN HEAVEN"
Exotic Bamboo Print Cotton Duo Sarong-drape dress gives you the lush curves of native charmers! Built-in boned bra. Wear strapless or with halter. Tiny bolero. Sizes 10 to 18. Aloha Rose, Palm Green, Tropical Blue. **$14.98**

#237 "INDIAN PRINCESS"
2-piece Playtone Squaw-Dress Colorful cotton needs no ironing! Blouse and full, tiered skirt have rows of ric-rac and gay embroidered braid. Low-priced! Sizes 10 to 18. Melon-Red with Black; Gold with Jade-Green. **$12.98**

Last Chance

to buy these sensational favorites!

#263

#461

#462
JACKET

#594
GENUINE
COWHIDE
BELT

frederick
OF HOLLYWOOD

#263 CAIRO CURVES
He'll adore you in this exotic-sheath Frederick-styled with accents from far-away Egypt. Square neck and pockets trimmed in notched self-petals with tantalizing white tassels. Alluring princess fitted waistline. In cruise rayon linen. Turquoise, Navy or Lime with White. Sizes 10 to 20. **$16⁹⁸**

#594 SWEET AND SASSY
A rayon linen cutie, sassy as sin with its high turtle neck. Darts under the arms from the waistline emphasize the alluring curves of bust section. Hide his heart in the two little secret hip pockets. Frederick's' *Free* belt with a huge metal buckle is made of genuine cowhide. Natural, Navy, Petal Pink. Sizes 10 to 18. **$12⁹⁸**

#461 TEMPTRESS
Long, lean, lovely rayon acetate taffeta sheath with pencil-slimming satin stripes flowing with every curve; intriguing shoestring straps; snugged to you with back zipper. Black Multi-Stripe. Sizes 10 to 18. **$10⁹⁸**

#462 MATCHING JACKET
Rayon faille . . . Black with multi-stripe trim flared shortie with huge satin-striped roll-up cuffs. This mate to the dress #461 is a real purse-mate, too! Sizes 10 to 18. Only **$10⁹⁸**

#450
CURVACEOUS

#227

#429
SATIN

#450 SHAPELY DRAPE
Wear this when you want to look glamorous! Stunning sheath in rich rayon and acetate crepe features low-cut surplice neck, draped bust and cummerbund waist. Skin-slim skirt; back zipper. Turquoise, Red, Black. Sizes 10 to 20. ONLY **$12⁹⁸**

#227 V VIXEN
A vampy little sheath with deepest V from here to there! Shimmering acetate taffeta makes it a demon of a date dress! Black Check, or Solid Black. Sizes 10 to 18. **$8⁹⁸**

#429 MIDNIGHT MADNESS
Paris-inspired sheath of rayon and acetate slipper satin molds torso from choker neck to gored skirt. Back zipper; shirred bust. Black, Twilight Rose, Turquoise. Sizes 10 to 18. SALE **$12⁹⁸**

SAMPLE

FREE DIVIDEND CHECK FOR YOU!

74

#247

#266

#203

#601

#247 ADAM'S RIB
He'll love you in this carefree shirtmaker tickled with little brass buttons from throat to waist; wide belt with brass buckle cinches in waist. Full circle skirt flares in riot of unpressed pleats. Attached petticoat. Drip dry striped cotton. In Buttercup Yellow, Petal Pink, Toffee Tan stripes. **$18⁹⁸**
Sizes 5 to 13.

#266 TORCH SONG
Your wardrobe's not complete without this glamorous date sheath! Tightest torso, flatteringly shirred at back and sides, has smooth down-the-front panel, parting to form hip-flattering cuff at torso line. He'll adore scoop neck! Polished cotton. Flame Red, Sultry Black, Oyster White. **$19⁹⁸**
Sizes 5 to 13.

#203 LOVE CAPTIVE
Oriental mystery enfolds you in this exotic creation of Oriental taffeta. Reed-slim sheath is alight with fabulous Oriental pattern; revealing side-slits in skirt. Different—alluring. Rayon acetate. Panther Black, Turquoise, Shell Pink. **$19⁹⁸**
Sizes 10 to 16.

#601 DRAGON FLAME
Exotic lace over skin-slim acetate taffeta sheath! The taffeta contrast-piped slit neck and side skirt slits add exotic Oriental Lure. Tiny cap sleeves. Zipper back closing. White Lace over Blue or Toast. **$19⁹⁸**
Sizes 10 to 18.

Junior Jeze

...and wear a SHEATH

#351
SALE—
$14.98

#365
SPECIAL—
$12.98

#291
FAILLE

#365 "PARIS BEAUTY"
Loads of Paris tricks in a tiny-priced Chromspun acetate taffeta treat! Alluring portrait collar dips so low! Slim skirt has "Frou Frou" drape to flatter hips. Red rose accents fitted bust. Wine, Date Black, Teal Blue. **$12⁹⁸**

#351 "NEW YOU" Sheath
Slinky rayon and acetate SATIN caresses every curve! Halter neck has deep V-plunge; draped bust. Buttons accent the snug fit, but a back zipper fastens it. Daring slit sheath skirt; low-cut back. Black, Lilac, Slate Blue. **$14⁹⁸**

#291 "KISS ME AGAIN"
Lace-trimmed Twosome
Shapely strapless sheath and tiny matching bolero with rich Venise lace applique, studded with daz-zling rhinestones! Faille* with thrilling boned bra-top and hip-hugging sideswept drape. Black, Beige or Petal Pink. **$19⁹⁸**

#201 "SLINKY SIREN" Crepe
Flattery goes to your figure! New glamorous Crepe* sheath with rows of luxurious fringe. Daring neck-line, back and front; slim strap displays a pretty shoulder. Self-belt has jewelled trim. Sun-Gold, Riot Red, Black. **$18⁹⁸**

*rayon and acetate

Please the MAN in your life!
Wear Frederick's creations!

#201
FRINGED
CREPE

FREE GIFTS...
with all orders of $15 or more, and get your thrilling, beautiful surprise gift FREE!

bels

11-13-15

#2172

#2171

Sleeve Story

#2233

Lace Elegance

#2189

#2172 DEVIL DARLING
You're darling and devilish in this rayon and acetate tissue faille crepe strapless cocktail dress! Swooping long stole is reversible and can be worn as halter or hood. Contrast facing at boned bust section peeks out alluringly for that oh-so-daring effect. Black, Red, White. **$29⁹⁸**

#2171 PARIS WILD
Copy of a $150.00 Paris Original!
Wildly bouffant sleeves accentuate the broad, bare sweetheart neck of this gorgeous French-inspired creation! Softest shirring at bust enhances bosom beauty and creates the slimmest of midriffs. Equally slimming darts mold skirt to your figure. Huge rhinestone ornaments at sleeves. In exquisite tissue faille crepe (rayon and acetate) with taffeta top. Black only. **$39⁹⁸**

#2233 HIP BEAU
For the cocktail sheath that will be the envy of everyone you know, choose this exciting new black and white creation in gorgeous matte satin (rayon & acetate). Sensational styling has satin pleated into bust, with matching pleated hip cuff that ends in huge bow at left hip. Startling color combination, plus figure-hugging lines and off-shoulder look make it a beau catcher you can't do without! Gold with Brown, Black with White. **$27⁹⁸**

#2189 CHAMPAGNE
Like bubbles in champagne you'll go right to his head (and Heart) in this Frederick creation of nylon lace over nylon tulle sheath. Lined in champagne colored limelight rayon and acetate taffeta. Unusual scallop edge, stand-up collar and sheer yoke back.
A unique combination of rich fabrics and luxury design! Black or White. **$44⁹⁸**

#2176

#2219

Fringe Flirt

Voluptuous Velvet

Sequin top   **#2169**

Iced Sequins

Buy NOW—pay later with Frederick's NEW, FREE TIME PAYMENT PLAN!

#2176 PERSIAN FRINGE
High fall fashion in an all-wool sheer sheath, alive with glamour! Gorgeous imported fabric is tweed-flecked, forming horizontal stripes that feather into alluring fringe that's woven right in. Wrap-around skirt has tricky button back. Richly lined in taffeta. This imported "fringe-fabric" will be the envy of everyone you know!
Black and Spice Brown. Black and Powder Blue. **$39⁹⁸**

#2219 VELVET BEAU
Your beau will adore you in this exquisite imported rayon velvet sheath copied from a $200.00 Italian original! Triangular bodice plunging to point at waist, is gorgeous nylon lace over nude satin, and is pinned with huge velvet bow at bosom. Wide velvet shoulder straps, low back with zipper close. Crush resistant. Black or Red. **$39⁹⁸**

#2169 LIVE AND LOVE
You can live, love and dance all night in this most luxurious, cloud-like creation! The skirt is actually **three** skirts, with whirling yards and yards of nylon tulle drifting over underskirt in shimmering taffeta. You're all aglow with thousands of sequins which completely cover the top. Halter neckline — low, low back! Bronze, Black, Silver. **$49⁹⁸**

Smash Hits from Hollywood!

LOOK

#2230

FABULOUS FALL
...AND WINTER
Knit Fits

#2126

#2127

KNIT
50% orlon
50% vicara

#2125

Angora Trim
100% Wool

#2230 MAGIC TOUCH
Copy of a star's favorite!
Slip into this slinky sheath, and
enjoy the magic touch of figure
flattering allure! Fabulous 2-tone
styling creates utterly exciting
slimness with light front panel
enclosed by dark sides and back
that literally eat up the inches!
Yet, your bust takes on new,
beautiful proportions. Graceful
Italian cowl neck and deep V back.
Exquisite rayon and acetate crepe
make this the perfect costume for
the dressiest occasions! Brown and
gold. Black and white. **$15⁹⁸**
Sizes 10 to 18.

#2126 FAIR FLATTERER
Designed to flatter! Two-piece
all wool zephyr suit dress. Tricky
button front with jeweled rhinestone trimmed buttons. Metallic
thread angora trim forms two
stripes over the bust and out to
shoulders. Same angora trim is
featured on tiny-stand-up collar.
Mist Grey, Tahiti Red, Turquoise.
Sizes 10 to 18. **$19⁹⁸**

#2127 CURVACEOUS CUTIE
Watch his heart melt when you
wear this plaid one-piece sacque
dress made of washable 50% orlon
and 50% vicara. Adjusts to hug
curvaceous lines. Cannot shrink.
Cannot stretch out of your
delightful shape. Wide patent
leather belt. Sunset Red,
Heather Green, Midnight Black
plaid. **$16⁹⁸**
Sizes 10 to 18.

#2125 KISSIN' COUSIN
Naturally you'll be kissed when he
sees you in this 100% wool knitted
two-piece suit dress. Ribbed skirt
so figure flattering! S-o-o soft
angora trim on short sleeves and
plunge neckline. A terrific value
at this price! Navy, Monaco Red,
Turquoise. **$13⁹⁸**
Sizes 10 to 18.

78

at these flatterers

READ FOR YOURSELF...

What these movie people and thousands of other women say about Frederick's clothes!

"I want to thank you for your feminine creations and styles, and I wish you also had a store in New York City."

LINDA LOMBARD

"I'm just wild about your clothes and nobody believes me when I tell them how little I paid. They've helped me to success—but definitely!"

JUNE SVEDIN

"I'm on my way to starring roles in two big pictures — and I know it was my Frederick's dress that helped me get my first role."

ALLISON HAYES

"I was wearing a Frederick's creation while I auditioned for a singing job and was happy to have gotten it. My Frederick's dress **really helped!**

Angela Perry
Chicago, Illinois

"I was wearing a Frederick's of Hollywood creation when I met my future husband. That stunning date dress **caught his eye** (and his love."

Mrs. Kathleen Morgan
Clear Fork,
West Virginia

"When I dressed for our 12th anniversary in my Frederick's creation, **I felt like a million dollars.** The love and admiration in my husband's eyes is something I will always treasure."

Mrs. Harry Barbish
Cincinnati, Ohio

"Was doing the mambo in my Frederick's fringe creation when a professional dancer spotted me. He said my hips were pips and asked me to be his partner. Am now on the way to a dancing career, **thanks to Frederick's.**"

Ruth Seppala
Jamaica, New York

KAREN SCOTT
International star of London, Paris and Hollywood: "In Paris it's Dior; here it is definitely Frederick's"

✣*Robin Stanley:*
"...glamourous Frederick's clothes are the "secret weapon" of my career..."

*Lovely young starlet of Movie, TV and the night-club circuit.

MRS. ROD CAMERON
"Among the movie set . . . Frederick's is a favorite both on and off the screen"

"Being the mother of 7 children and 38 years old, people think I am still a teen age girl, thanks to Frederick's of Hollywood Fashions which have that **glamorous** and **stay-young magic.**"

Mrs. Irene Apodaca
Las Vegas, New Mexico

79

Fredericks
OF HOLLYWOOD

1438 NORTH CAHUENGA BOULEVARD • HOLLYWOOD 28, CALIFORNIA

BE HIS CHRISTMAS STAR!

Ahead -- for the most wonderful customers anyone ever had -- 40 pages of Christmas Glamour in an all-new catalog simply packed with hundreds of star-styled Hollywood fashions that will make you his Christmas Star!

Be tops on his list with an exciting new holiday wardrobe of the _fashions that are right_ -- and the height of _fashion_. NOW, the fabled Frederick's label ushers in the season's most sparkling creations -- to make you a sparkling Christmas Eve.

Don't miss the alluring glamour of bare backs -- and new back interest creations that will keep him coming back long after the holidays! Look forward to a dazzling evening in a new gold or silver metallic lurex cocktail dress. Do yourself over in a new curve-clinging sheath that makes your figure as exciting as the kiss under the mistletoe!

There's nothing like these new fashions in regular stores. You won't meet yourself coming and going at the biggest (or smallest) party of the season. But you will meet plenty of Tom and Jerrys who'll want to meet _you_ -- if you're wearing a Frederick's.

And remember! Whether the gifts you choose are from you to you -- or from you to your friends -- they're the gifts that will be long remembered and cherished.

Don't wait! These Christmas arrivals won't last forever. So, if you're caught short, rush your order NOW -- with Frederick's fabulous Credit Plan. Send no money for a full 30 days! What's more, you _must_ be satisfied, or every single penny will be cheerfully refunded.

My staff and I wish you the merriest Christmas ever and a joyous New Year.

Frederick

DATE FASHIONS SELECTED

#2310   HOLLYWOOD COQUETTE
For a glamour eyeful of coquettery choose this exotic trumpet sheath! Tantalizing empire lines accentuate your curves from bust to flaring mermaid flounce. Bows right where they belong—between busts and at skirt. The bare shoulder look is emphasized by tiniest shoestring straps. It's the eye-catcher of the season. Black Rose, Lime. Sizes 10 to 20 Acetate taffeta **$12⁹⁸**

#2267   JEWELED GYPSY
Jeweled drama is yours in this shockingly slim sheath in gorgeous Mystere* that highlights every curve! Deceptive simplicity is daringly accented by hundreds and hundreds of blazing rhinestones in three-tiered trim that streaks from shoulder to deep V-front and back. An exotic holiday party-goer that your friends will envy! *Acetate and rayon. Red, Black or Sapphire Blue. Sizes 10 to 20. **$24⁹⁸**

Romantic Crepe!

Metallic Lurex!

#2554   MANDARIN MAGIC
The mysterious lure of the Orient beckons from every stitch of this shapely sheath with long narrow sleeves bewitchingly tapered at the wrist. Fitted like a coat of lacquer to emphasize every graceful charm of your figure. Fabulous gold tone scroll print on solid color Rayon and Acetate Satin is so exotic it's almost sinful! Jade Green, Fire Blue, Dragon Red. Sizes 10 to 18. **$16⁹⁸**

#2320   TEMPTRESS
Long, lean, lovely rayon Tissue Faille (Rayon and Acetate) Crepe sheath with pencil-slimming lines flowing with every curve; intriguing shoestring straps; snugged to you with zipper back closing. Black, White or Coral. Sizes 10 to 20. **$14⁹⁸**

#2243   SHOCK SHEATH
Whether you choose this glamorous new sheath in genuine Lyon velvet, or in gold or silver metallic lurex, it has a curve-hugging fit that looks like it was born on you! Tiny shoestring straps are for laughs only, because this sensation keeps itself up with what you've got! And when you've got this sheath — you've got plenty! Silver or gold lurex, Black Velvet. Sizes 10 to 18. **$19⁹⁸**

BY OUR MALE JURY

#2252 DAGGER DANGER
They'll envy you in this stunning sheath in curve-catching Moire *Taffeta! Bare shoulders are accentuated by rhinestone dusted halter neck plunging to dagger point in front, and streaking down the low, low back in vampy straps! Peek-a-boo lattice work at both sides of hem add to the look they'll envy! *Acetate taffeta. Midnight Black, Star White, Champagne. **$24⁹⁸**
Sizes 10 to 16

#2300 CLEOPATRA
You're all seductive temptress in this exotic Egyptian drape rayon and acetate crepe sheath. The secret is in the soft shirring that flows and clings along every curve, front and back, moulding the hip-line into an Egyptian drape. Moulded, boned bustline with pleated folds accentuates a curving bosom. Self-material bow dramatizes the sinuous back line. Back zipper closing. Vivid Red, Wicked Black or White. **$24⁹⁸**
Sizes 10 to 20

FREDERICK SAYS, "Famous Movie Stars wouldn't be without Glamour fashions. Why should you?"

"Snare Him with Back Interest"

≠2531 HI-LO BELLE
Exotic sheath features face-framing collar in imported Velvet, with back excitement that plunges to the waist! Wool Jersey snuggles to your curves with outspoken flattery. Taffeta lined skirt guarantees your shapeliness. A dreamy cocktail-dater . . . worth so much more! Bewitching Black .
Sizes 10 to 20.
$24⁹⁸

≠2503 SWAGGER
Glamorous 2-piece Crystalline* cocktail costume copied from expensive French original gives you that sleek-hipped look with a sheath skirt (lined), and bold swagger in a Blouson top that cinches down to a whisper at your waist (even in the back). It's a true lap-over, so wear it as plunged as you dare! Broad self belt and buckle Black, Rose, Turquoise.
Sizes 10 to 20.
*Acetate.
$24⁹⁸

≠2100 TORRID PLAYMATE
Watch his temperature rise when you wear this play suit and skirt ensemble. Gold tone cotton in oriental print with mandarin style top. Plunging neckline faced with solid color cotton. Little-boy shorts, faced in same solid color, can be turned up or down. Slip-into skirt, faced with solid color all around saucy slits for added adventure. Black-Gold Tone, Red-Gold Tone.
Sizes 10 to 20
$12⁹⁸

1-Piece Playsuit with Matching Skirt
≠2100

"Dear Frederick:
It was a Frederick's dress that helped get me my very first role in the movies — so I know you'll believe me when I say I'm a Frederick's girl from now on . . . and forever!"
Allison Hayes

FREDERICK SAYS, "Don't DREAM of glamour — BE glamorous in Star-styled Fashions!"

Bouclé

#2294 HEART'S DELIGHT
Cuddly, curvaceous two-piece knitted bouclé 100% wool dress. One of the loveliest and finest quality knit dresses we've ever carried. Beautiful cuff motif forms heart shape alluringly outlining bosom, continues on shoulders and stand-up collar plunge neckline. Sleeve cuffs and dress bottom have hand knit look. Slimming panel knit effect skirt has elasticized waistline. Black, Crimson Red, Pheasant Brown.
Sizes 10 to 18
$29⁹⁸

Allison Hayes

#662 **SAINTLY SINNER**
Saintly little cotton checked sheath has positively sinful allure from bare-shoulder top to can-can skirt with five flirty flounces. Fits so it's held up by your curves alone— making tiny shoe string straps needless, but tantalizing.
Jet Black, Iced Pink, Green.
Sizes 10 to 18. **$16⁹⁸**

#2146 Same stunning lines as #662. Perfectly detailed in rayon acetate taffeta. Choose from Jet Black, Emerald Green or Violet.
Sizes 10 to 18. **$16⁹⁸**

"Dear Frederick:
It was a Frederick's dress that helped get me my very first role in the movies — so I know you'll believe me when I say I'm a Frederick's girl from now on . . . and forever!"

Allison Hayes
popular young TV and Film Star

Allison Hayes
loves Frederick's "Dazzling Dots"

#566 **DAZZLING DOT**
Luscious styling and intriguing shoestring straps make this rayon linen sheath a date-time wonder in dancing dots! Curve-hugging snug fit is assured by back zipper.
Navy Dot on White,
White Dot on Black.
Sizes 7 to 15
10 to 18. **$10⁹⁸**

Don't miss the Filmland shoes that do the most for you!

#2131 **CLINGING VINE**
Copy of an original created for Hollywood's most glamorous star, this stunning sheath in curve-clinging wool jersey is skin tight from top to hem. Daringly reveals every contour of the body. Long, long back zipper closing and rollover collar styling. Order Black, Red or Goldtone.
Sizes 10 to 18. Only **$19⁹⁸**

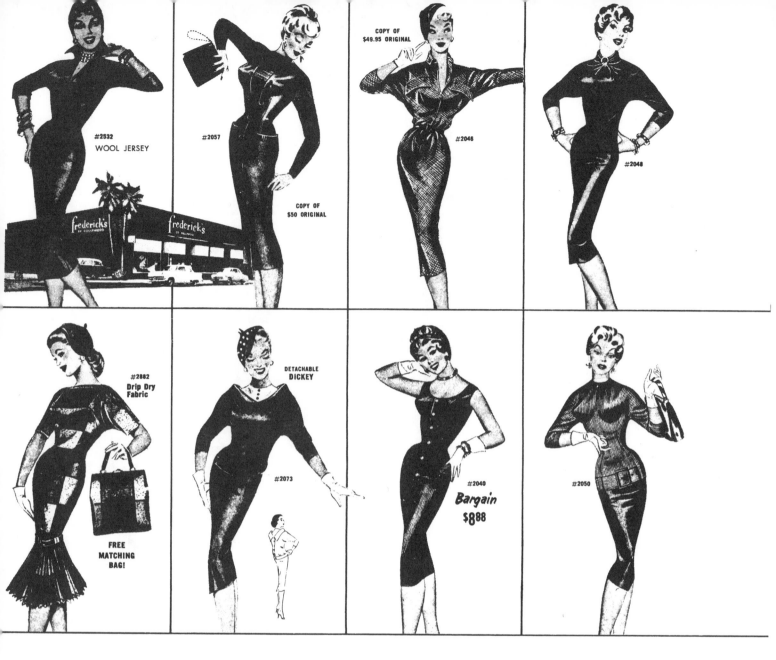

Darlings for the Daylight.......

#2532 SHAPE SORCERY
It's witchcraft . . . what this 100%
Wool Jersey sheath does for you! Fitting
like a second skin; it glorifies every
curve with daring flattery. Fabulous
wing collar takes off for a plunge into
decollete excitement! Rump lining
disciplines your shapeliness. Midnight
Black, Romance Red, Azure Blue.
Sizes 10 to 18.   **$19⁹⁸**

#2882 KNEE NAUGHTY
Wash 'n' wear dark tone box print
cotton chemise clings casually to above
knee, flounces flirtatiously below.
Patent leather belt beautifies your walk.
Same fabric and patent bag is 11 x 12
big . . . and FREE! Plum, Copper. **$22⁹⁸**
Sizes 8 to 16.

#2057 PARIS FALL
Clinging all Wool Jersey buttons up the
front for a French-style sheath fit.
Ribbed Wool Knit. V shaped inset
plunges to waist. Copy of $50. Black,
Parsley Green, Ketchup Red or Persian
Blue. Sizes 10 to 20.   **$19⁹⁸**

**EVERY PENNY REFUNDED
IF NOT 100% SATISFIED**

#2073 LOVE MATCH
Pretty pair of coordinates for that
cute, curvaceous look! Sheath skirt is
new, narrow look, blous-on fullness
makes it delightfully feminine. Wear
dicky in daytime, remove for daring,
date-time appeal. Wool Jersey.
Black, Radiant Red or Cobalt   **$17⁹⁸**
Blue. Sizes 8 to 16.

#2046 TWIN TRIUMPH
You chance at $49.95 styling at
Frederick's fabulous price! This
couturier twin is cut on bias for
sensational sheath fit, trimmed with
pockets to enhance bosom. In Rayon
and Acetate, with free patent belt.
Royal and Red, or Black and
White Check.   **$17⁹⁸**
Sizes 8 to 18.

#2040 JOY JUMPER
Here's a morn-to-midnight wonder at a
wonderful price! Sleek cotton corduroy
scoop necked jumper combines with
blouse for beautiful daytime look,
cunningly solo's it at night! Smart
back has bloused shirring, self
half-belt. Washable.
Lilac, Red, Blue or Green.   **$8⁸⁸**
Sizes 8 to 16.

#2048 LOVERS LOOP
Wear this anywhere and see what
happens! Cloud-soft Wool Jersey is
draped into sensational sheath with
new eased waistline. Bust building
gathers through looped "gold" color
pin. You'll love the look! Winterberry
Red, Black or Royal Blue.
Sizes 8 to 16.   **$24⁹⁸**

#2050 MOVIE QUEEN MAGIC
Works like magic on your figure. Soft,
soft Rayon and Acetate men's wear
flannel weave wondrously hugs your
every curve with the newsy new torso
line, accented by slimming
pin-stripes right down to dramatic
hip belt. Solid skirt. White with Black,
or Black with White.
Sizes 8 to 16.   **$22⁹⁸**

84

Magic for the Moonlight!

#2069 SHEER DELIGHT
You'll feel like you're floating on a soft cloud when you wear this filmy Rayon and Nylon chiffon. Shirring at bust and hip and skin tight bodice make this feminine plus! Siren Black. Flame Red, Midnight Green. Sizes 8 to 16. **$22.98**

#2070 PROMISE
Flatter your femininity with ounces of flounces in a striking trumpet effect, and rows on rows of softly draped shirring from shoulders to hips. In Rayon chiffon over Rayon taffeta lining. Jet Black, Aqua, Sea Coral or Pearl White. Sizes 8 to 20. **$35.00**

#2049 VICTORY SHEATH
Supreme figure flattery for your most gala affairs! Plunged V neckline gives you a luscious lowdown look. Softly feminine draping caresses your curves. Matte jersey. Seat lined. Black, White, Turquoise or Pink. Sizes 10 to 20. **$19.98**

#2491 GLOVE FITTED
No glove has ever fit so well as this rayon-acetate linen look sheath. From the crisscross halter, across bosom and over hips to slit hem, your curves are captured and faithfully repeated. For daytime or datetime, you're glamorous. White, Black or Lilac. Sizes 10 to 20. **$14.98**

#2892 DRAPED DRAMA
Peek-a-boo slit above bust emphasizes seductive interest of dramatically draped cowl neck, spectacular shirred bosom and front. Slits at knee are neatly naughty . . . dolman sleeves add drama. In curvaceous all wool jersey. Oriental Gold, Black or Flame Red. Sizes 8 to 20. **$19.98**

#2829 VAMPIRE WEB
Plunge neck unearths eye-catching cleavage enhanced by fully-boned, bosom-building bust. Shimmering rayon and acetate faille snuggles your skin in seductive sheath style, slits in front to reveal barely enough leg. Back lunges to lovely low depths too, with dramatic web of grosgrain weaving Black, Red or Turquoise. Sizes 10 to 18. **$19.98**

#2056 TENDER TRAP
Bare minimum sheath in luxurious Rayon and Acetate crepe has soft shirring from bosom to hip for gently enhanced roundness. Slip it on and see your curve blossom! Black, Turquoise or Gold. Sizes 8 to 18. **$14.98**

#2064 SKIN O' GOLD
Glamour, glamour in every stitch, and priced within your reach! Gleaming Rayon Lurex sheath cups bust in soft shirring, accents waist with midriff binding on hip and beneath waist. Dips down in back for added drama. Gold or Silver. Sizes 8 to 18. **$19.98**

Dramatic Stars!

in the new look

WOMENS AND MISSES SIZE CHART							
Sizes	8	10	12	14	16	18	20
BUST	33	34	35½	37	38½	40	41½
			26½	28	29½	31	32½
WAIST	24	25				40½	42
HIPS	34	34½	36	37½	39½		

#2055
★ TRAPEZE

#2086
★ BUBBLE

EMPIRE BUST!

#2095
★ DRAPED BACK

#2051
★ DRAPED BACK

Frederick says:

What you wear in underwear makes all the difference

Dressy

#2055 PAGE ONE
Absolutely the latest fashion, a must for every style-conscious woman! Soft Rayon and Acetate crepe is cut in smartest Trapeze lines, with scoop neck and black nylon lace over daring nude taffeta bodice. Skirt has sheath front, femininely full back. Black only. Sizes 10 to 18. **$24.98**

#2086 DOUBLE BUBBLE
The look that all Paris is talking about! Divine adaptation of the new bubble skirt with shirred pick-up front. Semi-nude shoulder. Pelon lined skirt. Rayon and lurex. Precious Silver or Gold. Sizes 8 to 16. **$29.98**

#2095 WATERFALL
Sensationally draped matte jersey gives you that powerhouse appeal! Waterfall of softly shirred draping feminizes your derriere, fulfils your bust beautifully. In acetate and nylon. Lined seat. White, Black or Turquoise. Sizes 8 to 18. **$19.98**

#2051 NIGHT LIFE
Long for a beautiful bustline? This dress gives it to you plus a "young" look! Rayon and Acetate crepe sheaths you sheerly, with enhancing Empire bustline accented by high-waisted satin cuff. Back has softly pleated overlay of Rayon Chiffon for extra-feminine effect. Siren Black only. Sizes 10 to 18. **$24.98**

#2083 BUTTERFLY
Drape yourself in the crepe shape that shows the smartest side of you— Frederick's new "fluttering" original. Snug sheath skirt, latest butterfly bodice. Free rhinestone clip, too! Rayon and Acetate. Black, Beige or Royal Blue. Junior Sizes 7 to 17 or Misses Sizes 8 to 18. **$17.98**

#2083
★ BLOUS-ON

Daring

JAYNE
MANSFIELD
glamorous motion
picture star

#2081
★ BLOUS-ON

#2081 COCKTAIL QUEEN
Fall fashion says "blous-on" and
Frederick's brings it to you with that
typically Hollywood touch! Cuddlesome
crepe is softly draped round bosom,
snugly sheathed round waist and hips.
Tricky bow detailing points up a pretty
figure. Rayon and Acetate crepe. Red,
Green or Black. Junior Sizes 7 $17.98
17 or Misses Sizes 8 to 18.

STARS SAY

"My Frederick's
clothes get the stares!
I'm a Frederick's fan
. . . and you can quote
me. Thanks for the
speedy service."
TINA LOUISE

"I don't think there
is a thing I welcome
like my Frederick's
catalog . . . What
would we do without
you?"
JAYNE MANSFIELD

"I want to thank you for
your feminine creations
and styles, and I wish you
also had a store in New
York City."
LINDA LOMBARD

"I'm just wild about your
clothes and nobody be-
lieves me when I tell them
how little I paid. They've
helped me to success—but
definitely!"
JUNE SVEDIN

DAZZLING

LUREX $17⁹⁹

BROCADE

#2418 NITE LIGHT
Sparkling and twinkling, you're the delite of his eyes, the life of the party . . . star-studded in our glistening full length Lurex Sheath. Cued-in to every curve, with your favorite spaghetti-strap styling gives added glamour to gorgeous shoulders. Back slit. Rayon, Metallic. Black, Gold or Silver. Sizes 8 to 18. $17⁹⁹

#2416 EVENING ESCAPADE
Be the smashing hit of the party! Slip into our Oriental Brocade number with exotic full length styling that is the newest, sassiest fashion for hostessing and dress-up evenings. Tantalizing high mandarin collar, three frog diagonal closing, leg-revealing side slits for high jinks! Acetate and Cotton; Black, White or Chinese Blue. Sizes 8 to 20. $19⁹⁹

#2751 HEART THROB
Give him plenty to think about . . . let him see you delectable and delicious in this heady sheath of cotton lace . . . sleeveless, nylon sheer covering your back and shoulders. Black, White, Beige. Sizes 8 to 20. $17⁹⁹

COPY OF $100.00
ORIGINAL

#2952 MILLION $ BABY
Imagine . . . Ravishing Rayon Metallic Lurex that gives noticeable curves, new interest with two slashed straps, one-shoulder extravaganza. Gold, Black or Silver. Sizes 8 to 18. $15⁹⁹

#2235 DAZZLING DUPLICATE
A rare steal just for you! Slimmifying
sheath with a high neckline and long
sleeves. that suddenly provide the surprise
of his life with the long descent of
squared-off plunge back. Arnel
Triacetate Jersey. Black, Coral
or Aqua. Sizes 8 to 18.

$12⁹⁹

LOOK!

It's the way you look...coming and going...that draws all eyes ...makes women envious and strong men whimper. What's UNDERNEATH makes all the difference!

Let Mr. Frederick show you how to play up your good points... improve what's less than perfect. Only he can create these miraculous figure-shapers. The stars depend on them...so will YOU!

#2152 FLAMENCO
Be sheathed bust-to-toe in shimmering, crackling Acetate Taffeta! Dramatic Spanish swirl breaks knee-high. Straps, one-inch thin, anchor torso and daring bare back. Entire gown is covered with dotted net, edged with elegant lace. Black over Red, as shown, or All Black. Sizes 8 to 16.
$35

be Seductive in a
SHEATH!

#2658 TORCHLIGHT PARADE
Ooh la la...this is it! The dress of the year and a direct copy of one of the most famous styles now in a Paris collection. Cotton Lace sheath with enchanting top and sleeves. The bust ...a flame that fans into a deep 'V'. Black, White or Beige.
Sizes 8 to 18.
$17⁹⁹

COPY OF AN EXPENSIVE PARIS ORIGINAL!

COPY OF A $200.00 ORIGINAL

#2950 EYE-CATCHER
You have a date with fashion—tingling, *exciting shoulder baring fashion!* A slim streak of linen-weave rayon, delightfully dressed up with a big bow of dainty cotton eyelet that moves across the bustline and nestles on the shoulder. This is a copy of a $200.00 original. In Black with Black Eyelet, or Pink with White Eyelet. Sizes 8 to 16.
$17⁹⁹

#2933 **RARE GEM**
A dress like this one is as elusive and hard to find as the most precious of jewels and you'll sparkle like a diamond in it. This *fabulous Orlon acrylic knit* has so many wonderful features. The sweater is glamorously trimmed with jets and rhinestones and has a jewel neckline and a back zipper. The slim skirt will fit like a dream because of the superb styling and the elasticized waist. Eggshell White. Sizes 8 to 18. **$22⁹⁹**

2-PIECE KNIT JEWEL TRIM

#2297 **SMOOTH LINE**
The "line up" with the spotlight on YOU...Mitred stripes that swerve with every curve! V-shaped at the bust exposing your best parts! Expensive looking Cotton. Jet Black or Candy Pink with White. Sizes 8 to 18. **$8⁹⁹**

ONE PIECE LOOKS LIKE TWO

#2212 **AVANT GARDE**
Here's a swinger of a dress for bistro hopping and much dancing! Rayon and acetate crepe scoop neck sheath, graceful with all around fringe from neckline to hipline. Self belt. Black, white or bright orange. Junior sizes 7 to 15. **$17⁹⁹**

#2924 **HOE-DOWN**
A city slicker with rustic charms! This tomboy sheath buttons straight up the front. The bib's an optical illusion ...it's all one piece! Skirt and suspenders are solid blue, the jaunty shirt is checked red and white. Push-up sleeves. All Rayon. Sizes 8 to 16. **$8⁹⁹**

Frederick's is the store, where I get all my film-star fashions!

JEANNE BRETT, HOLLYWOOD STARLET

Jeanne Brett

You bet I'm a Frederick's of Hollywood fan . . . because I know I can order clothes that do so much to brighten every occasion.

Donna Kane

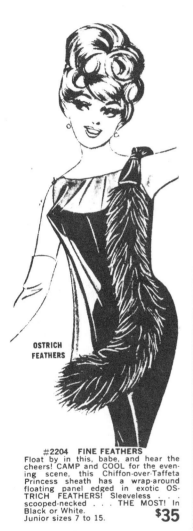

OSTRICH FEATHERS

#2204   FINE FEATHERS
Float by in this, babe, and hear the cheers! CAMP and COOL for the evening scene, this Chiffon-over-Taffeta Princess sheath has a wrap-around floating panel edged in exotic OSTRICH FEATHERS! Sleeveless . . . scooped-necked . . . THE MOST! In Black or White.
Junior sizes 7 to 15.   **$35**

G
ARNEL

H
**2-Pc.
JERSEY**

G   **#2954   FUN-DAMENTAL**
What a lovely look for summer! Carefree Arnel Triacetate fashions a sleeveless shift-sheath that shirtmaker-buttons three-quarters down its shapely front. So comfortably step-in! Wear self-material belt high, low, or not at all. Pink, Blue or Maize.
Sizes 10 to 18.   **$7.99**

H   **#7005   JERSEY JOY**
No excuse to look LESS THAN TERRIFIC when this 2-pc. Jersey print costs so little! V-necked top has a notched man's collar, ¾ sleeves. Elastic waistband on the pullon skirt molds to every figure. Acetate Jersey, abstract printed in Pink, Aqua or Gold. Sizes 12 to 20.   **$8.99**

Frederick's is the store, where I get all my film-star fashions!

Bobby Jordan

get that "marry-a-millionaire" *look!*

Money couldn't buy the compliments I get on my Frederick's of Hollywood styles . . . I love them!

Marylen Fee

Most girls I know in my business are ardent Frederick's of Hollywood fans . . . because we know how important it is to dress in exquisite fashions.

Desda Morris

DESDA MORRIS
Filmland Model

#2320 PARTY GIRL
Sparkle in the party spirit! Fitted Crepe sheath drapes to the side, leaving one shoulder completely bare. Sheer shirred Chiffon inset over one exposed bust glitters with jewel trim. All completely lined, with a long back zipper. In White or Pink. Sizes 8 to 16. **$19.99**

new mini skirt

B **#2387   FLY-A-WAY MINI**
Get out of your cocoon and swing in
this butterfly sleeved A-Line mini-skirt
dress. Have the newest look in this
checked Polyester and Cotton. Pink with
White only.
Junior sizes 5 to 13. **$16**

HOLLYWOOD APPROVED SCREEN STYLE

C **#2500   MAGIC NECKLINE**
Nope . . . it isn't done with mirrors!
Magic is wrought with hidden elastic
inside the bustline! Enhances a
small bosom . . . entrances those
larger! Fully lined
and Cotton is sheathed in solid color.
Flat midriff . . . low back. Black,
Bermuda Lime, or
Golden Yellow. **$17**
Sizes 6 to 18.

trench coat-dress

E **#1—2656   TRENCH,
TRENCH,
TRENCH!**
The boys will come marching right
up to you when you're wearing this
kodel and cotton trench coat-dress
(can be worn as either). Button down
front, flap cuffs, belt. Beige **$21**
only. Junior Sizes 5 to 15.

94

more of you
SHOWS NOW!

*bonded lurex
low, low back*

HOLLYWOOD
APPROVED
SCREEN STYLE

E #1—2680 FREDERICK'S
SPECIAL
Here's the way to look more
glamourous than you ever dreamed
possible! Our special body-clinging,
spaghetti strapped bonded rayon
lurex. Choose Blue, Gold $15⁹⁹
or Silver. Sizes 6 to 16.

wrap

YUMMY

...crepes suzettes

arnel jersey

#1—2897   RANSOM
A king's ransom couldn't buy a greater creation than our V neck wrap dress with tie that pulls through the side seam attached to this fabulous dress. Tie loops at side and falls to hemline shirring the bodice diagonally for the most in dramatic fashion glamour. Long sleeves are trimmed in banded cuff. Dress is unlined rayon acetate crepe. Light Blue or Bright Red. Misses sizes 8 to 18.   **$22⁸⁸**

#1—2870   SASSY SWIRL
Swirl around in this ultra-feminine Jersey dress that shows soft pleats at shoulders which drape down into a surplus bodice for comfort and allure. Gathered skirt is topped by a 2½" Black Patent belt to show off your tiny waist. Bonded Arnel Triacetate Jersey with long belled sleeves. Tones of Brown, Black and Gold in Animal Print only. Sizes 10 to 18.   **$23**

rajah coat-dress

#1—2492   RAJA GLITTER
Exotic India inspires this glamorous Rajah coat-dress. Paisley pattern of golden Lurex glitters on a rich Black background. BONDED BODY fits and flairs . . . holds ITS shape . . . shows off YOURS! Split, gold-buttoned front has a high standup collar, long belled sleeves. In Black with Gold. 85% Rayon, 15% Metallic. Junior sizes 7 to 15.   **$18**

#1—2524   LOVE GODDESS
Classic sheath! With low scooped neckline drapes into a Grecian cowl . . . makes much of a beautiful bosom! Slim and supple in Acetate-Rayon Crepe. Zips in back. Pink or Black. Sizes 6 to 18.   **$23⁹⁹**

96

"I WEAR FREDERICK'S OR NOTHING AT ALL!"

Money Back Guarantee
Purchase Price
Refundable if
not 100% satisfied

#1—2978   PLEATED PLUNGE
Catch his eye . . . wearing a swirl of permanently pressed pleats with a wide, plunging decolleté to the empire waistline! Built-in bra cups hold you in . . . and show you off. Soft narrow belt cinches the high waist. Sleeveless dress has back zipper and is made of soft arnel triacetate jersey. White or shocking pink. Misses sizes 8 to 16. **$23**

#1—2711   UP-STANDING
If you're proud of your bust . . . SHOW IT OFF! Scooped-neck Empire charmer accents the bosom up high and handsome over a drawstring tie. Bonded Rayon and acetate crepe holds its shape and flatters yours. Long sleeves; back zipper. Pink, Black or White. In sizes 8 to 18. **$18**

#1—2698   KABUKI DREAM
You'll have that subtle Oriental charm for him in this lovely nylon Enkalure empire with Kabuki sleeves. Squared off neckline front and back. Elastic around front and back of neckline and under bust holds the Empire look and fit without buttons or zipper. Comes in Black or Yellow. Sizes 6 to 16. **$17⁸⁸**

SIZZLE THAT SLINKS IN THE NIGHT

chavacete

HOLLYWOOD APPROVED SCREEN STYLE

#1—2301 SWEET BEAT
Come on strong, girl! Catch the beat
with these batwing sleeves . . .
sheer and see-through . . . absolutely
angelic! Cuffs and stand-away collar
sparkle with rhinestones. Dress of
rayon chiffon is body-lined in taffeta.
Pink or Black.   **$28**
Misses Sizes 8 to 16.

#1—2297 TWO TIMER
If it's attention you're needing, in this
it's attention you're getting, in this
conrast-panelled two-toned swinger.
Sleeves and skirt are fit to flare . . .
neck's a cut-out "U." Zips in back.
Black-and-Grey textured chavacete.
Junior Sizes 9 to 13;   **$26**
Junior Petite Sizes 5 to 7.

DEME SAYS: *frederick's OF HOLLYWOOD*
Where but
could you find such a
great selection of fabulous
date dresses . . . my dates
really go for the gal with
the Frederick's Look!

With the new
styles emphasizing
shape, I find
I am shapeliest
in Frederick's
Fashions.
Metihi

98

marabou trim

WICKEDLY Glamorous

...IN FABRICS THAT SLINK

#1—2291   FLUFF STUFF
Tickle his fancy with fluffs of marabou, hung in puffs around the deep scoop neck, cuffing the wide bell sleeves. A-line shift is the sheerest of polka-dotted acetate nylon net, body-lined in taffeta. Marabou-tiful in Black or in White. **$30**
Misses Sizes 8 to 16.

When I want to look glamourous, I always go to Frederick's. It's wonderful!

Gloria
Model-Actress

When your
appearance counts,
Mr. Frederick is
one of your
best friends.

Stephanie

Model/Actress

27

B
washable
fake
leather

B #2—7569   LEATHER BIT
When it comes to catching male
eyes . . . a little bit of leather goes
a long way! Terrific trim for our
wonderful, washable turtle neck
shift, in sharp Black and White.
Great for travel, in polyester
leather and acrylic knit.
Junior sizes 5 to 13.   **$23**

IT'S WHAT'S
DOWN FRONT
THAT COUNTS!

I really dig the new Frederick's
BARE look. It's sexy. It
shows me off. It's a whole new
way of dressing.

Marie

D

lavishly
hand beaded
fine double knit

I have to show off
my figure to the
best advantage all
the time so I always
shop the Frederick's
catalog.

Lucy
Model

D #1—2238   SOUL MUSIC
You're beautiful, baby, so show off
the REAL YOU! Double knit imported
wool mini is gold-beaded to the
wide-plunged waist, jewel-braceleted
around the cuffs. Slit thigh-high at
the sides, Exciting in Lime or White.
Misses Sizes 8 to 1o.
Junior sizes 7 to 15.   **$45**

wear neckline
open or closed

DO SOMETHING SEXY!
{show your stuff}

" In my career, I have to look glamourous all the time,... And Frederick's Fashions do it for me!!"

Debbie

I love your clothing + what is more important so does my husband too
Patricia Y. Cotter
Radley Park, Pa.

My dress was simply a knockout—It made me feel great but most of all my husband was so terribly proud of me. Thanks again for making a wonderful evening.
Vicki Kelley
Addison, Ill.

assorted prints

I have to show off my figure to the best advantage all the time so I always shop the Frederick's catalog.

Mary L.
MODEL

D #1—2590 DYNAMITE
Start with "wet look" nylon cire. Hang a brief skirt from an elasticized waistband. Up an Empire waistline. Add a top that's V'd to the waist . . . back-fastens with two skinny straps. Wear this, gal, and you're dynamite! Black or Red.
Junior Sizes 5 to 15. **$26**

M #1—2659 SCANT PANT
A blue denim mini-romper that bares your back, loves your legs and encourages your cleavage! That's a lot of sex-appeal in a "casual" sport fashion! Halter-styled V-neckline buttons at back of neck, shapely seam points upward under bust and all make for a great take-off on hot pants! In Cotton and Nylon stretch denim.
Junior Sizes 5 to 15.
Misses Sizes 6 to 16. **$15**

L #1—2663 SHIRRED BEAUTY
Saturate his senses with the all-female impact of a maxi-frock that's nipped-in with solid shirring from bust to waist. And what a gorgeous bustline when the elasticized scoop-neck seems to cling undecidedly over shoulders and bosom! Add to all this appeal the sweep of a maxi skirt over a ruffled flounce. 100% cotton and irresistible!
Junior Sizes: Small (5 to 7), Medium (9 to 11), and Large (13). **$15**

MR. FREDERICK SAYS

MAKE
YOUR
MAN-HOURS
COUNT!

sheer
top

opaque
skirt

low
bare
back

bare up-show off

TOP ATTRACTION

If your guy's a BUST guy he'll LOVE
this gown! The bodice is utterly sheer
and see-through. Doesn't conceal a
thing! The back is bare and very low . .
elasticized for SNAP! Opaque long skirt
for contrast. Sexy Black Nylon ,
Bust sizes 32 to 38.

#3—4741 $12

BARE
SHOULDER!

SOFT SHOULDER!

Dangerous curves ahead! This bare-
shouldered maxi forgets all the STOP
signs! Slithers down to maxi length.
Slits high on the side. All GO-GO in
pure Arnel Triacetate Jersey. Blue,
Wine or Black print (give 2nd. color
choice).
Misses sizes 6 to 14,
Junior sizes 5 to 13   **WAS $25.00**

#1—2291   **NOW $14**⁸⁸

"Poured-In"
Perfection!

Dress up and live! Take a tip
from the master designer of
fabulous filmland fashions. For
clothes to suit **you** Frederick's
has the answer.

Mr. Frederick

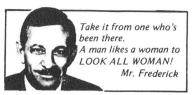

*Take it from one who's been there.
A man likes a woman to LOOK ALL WOMAN!*
Mr. Frederick

Mr. Frederick says

Keep the love in your life — the life in your love! Look your most appealing — Like a Frederick's woman always does!

LIVING TOGETHER
A sleeveless dress and matching ribbed jacket to make your season sensational! Both in packable, go-able Acrylic double knit. White or Powder Blue. Misses sizes 8 to 16.
C #1–2424 **JUST $17⁸⁸**
A $35.00 VALUE

2-piecer

#1–2916 PARTY PEEKER
A peek-a-boo knit that's great when you wear very little beneath! Open neck gathers into circle with a drawstring for a full and flattering fit. Manipulate it as you like! Flare skirt. Back zipper. Acetate and Nylon Lace Knit, in Blue or Pink.
Junior Sizes: 3 to 11 . **$15**

peek-a-boo
lace knit

LIGHT BRIGHT THING
to swing with! Check-patterned mini ties at the back or bows up under the bust. Low V-neck, A-line skirt. Red or Brown Acetate and Nylon Jersey. Junior sizes 5 to 13.
D #1–2423 ONLY $14.88

2 pc. set!
Glittery
Flashlight

SHOW GLOW!
Strike sparks! Signal come-on sex signs in glittery Flashlight Jersey! Deep-V'd to below the bust. Buttons behind the neck. Silver Black or Light Blue Acetate and Nylon Mini with matching bikini. In Misses sizes 6 to 14. Junior sizes 5 to 13.
#1–2450 $22

Blouse Beauties

ALL STYLES
SIZES 32-38

"RIVIERA RAGE" Two way sanforized cotton broadcloth shirt. Wear buttoned up or open & tied. **White, Aqua, Pink, Gold** (fast color). STYLE NO. 76 $3.98

"MOVIE DATE" Exotic cowl-drape and deep plunge form a stunning neckline. Dressy enough for dates! "Cal-ura" rayon crepe. White, Black, Rio Red. Style No. 141 only $3.98

"SWEET and LOW." New low neck and "capelet" sleeves with eyelet-embroidered organdy trim. "Angel Skin" rayon crepe in WHITE. STYLE NO. 75 $4.98

"BEGUILING" — Rows and rows of lace trim this cap-sleeved charmer. Back buttons, tiny collar. Rayon crepe. **WHITE or BLACK.** STYLE NO. 73 $3.98

"MY BELOVED" Wear on or off shoulders! "Naughty" yoke and cuffs of lace. Superb rayon crepe. **Red, Aqua, or Black with Black Lace; White with White Lace.** STYLE NO. 74 $5.98

Flattering, feminine BLOUSES for ROUND · THE · CLOCK wear

"HOLLYWOOD POLKA"
with **FREE** Scarf

Yes, it's true! Darling "Cavalier" collar, polka dot rayon crepe blouse AND harmonizing sheer rayon two-tone scarf. Wear scarf in hair, as sash, too . . . blouse is smart by itself. White, Navy-Blue, Red Backgrounds with Contrasting Dots & Scarf. **Style No. 414 — ONLY** $4.98

"EYELET APPEAL" Flattering blouse of rich WHITE rayon crepe with wide ruffles of fine eyelet embroidery. STYLE NO. 34 $5.98

BACK IN FRONT!

PLUNGE NECK!

"HOUR GLASS" — Fine WHITE cotton batiste with black ribbon drawstrings and eyelet embroidered trim. It's adorable! **STYLE NO. 77** $3.98

"TANTALIZER" Wear It Three Different Ways!

Wear it off-the-shoulders, with deep plunge neck, or backwards! He'll adore you in this "quick-change" style of fine "Ambrosia" rayon crepe. Radiant Red, Glamour Gold, Black, Lily White. **Style No. 413 — ONLY** $4.98

Beautiful BLOUSES Feature DARING Necklines!

ALL STYLES SIZES 32-38

"BARE BEAUTY" Rich rayon SATIN with embroidery and gay "jewel" trim. Choker collar is removable. Red, Black, Blue, White. Style No. 153 $5.98

"LOOK AGAIN" He can't resist this "bat wing" blouse with new deep sleeves, draped bust, slit neck. Rich rayon. White, Kelly Green, Rio Red. Style No. 140 $4.98

"DANGEROUS" He'll adore that daring, draped neckline! Full, bow-tied sleeves. What VALUE! Smooth rayon crepe. Gold, White, Red, Green. Style No. 152 $3.98

"ONE AND ONLY"— REAL LACE ruffled collar and sleeves, peek-a-boo neck. Rich rayon crepe in Black or White. Style No. 155 $5.98

★ **HOLLYWOOD ORIGINALS!**

More for your fashion dollar — because they're NEW . . . different, beautifully made. Be first to wear them!

FEMININE AND FLATTERING!

MIX OR MATCH THESE BLOUSE and SKIRT 'SEPARATES'

FREE GIFT
WITH ALL
PREPAID
ORDERS!

"LACE LOVE" BLOUSE
Alluring REAL LACE
with draped bust, shirred
sweetheart neck, back
buttons. Wear in or out!
Black or White
Sizes: 32 to 40 **$5.98**
STYLE NO. 123

"HOUR GLASS" Skirt
Full and graceful as can be! Rich rayon
faille with gold tabs and buckles. Gives
you a tiny waist! BLACK only.
Sizes: 10 to 18

STYLE NO. 40

$6.49

"SWEETHEART SET"

Silky WHITE rayon crepe
blouse with cut-out eyelet
yoke for glamour, PLUS a
"go-together" BLACK faille
skirt with perky pockets,
button trim, back zipper,

Blouse only;
Sizes: 32 to 38 $4.98
STYLE NO. 65-A

Skirt only;
Sizes: 10 to 18
$5.98
STYLE NO. 65-B

only **$10.49**
FOR BOTH
STYLE NO. 65

← SATIN
"EVENING-OUT" SKIRT
Gleaming BLACK
SATIN . . . beautifully
draped; sash tie is looped
through bright metal
buckle. Back zipper.
Sizes: 10 to 18
STYLE NO. 124

$6.49

**WESTERN QUEEN
SHIRT and SLACKS**

$17.98
FOR BOTH
SHIRT
ONLY
$9.98

BOTH
SIZES
10-18

RICH
"ALL-YEAR"
RAYON
FABRIC

"DRAPED DARLING" Skirt
WEAR IT THREE WAYS: Draping and
button trim may be worn in front, back, or
at side! Fine rayon faille. BLACK only.
Sizes: 10 to 18

STYLE NO. 38

$6.49

"DRAGON LADY"
Exciting! Multi-color drag-
ons with dazzling "gold"
embroidery. Choker neck.
"Luxury" rayon crepe in
Gold, Rio Red, Black, White.
Style No. 194 —
only **$5.98**

BLOUSE STYLE NO. 43
FOR BOTH STYLE NO. 44

• Dashing Western
outfit from Hollywood!
Shirt has color contrast,
bright embroidered trim.
Hi-Rise **Slacks** fit smoothly!
• White or Grey SHIRT
with Black SLACKS;
• Beige SHIRT with Brown SLACKS

ORDER A COMPLETE BO   DROP
SEND PAYMENT AND   G

"FOLLOW ME"

only $9⁹⁸ FOR BOTH

WHITE rayon blouse has puff sleeves and trim of dainty lace; BLACK rayon faille skirt has lace "peek-a-boo" insert. A "Buy"!

SIZES: 10 to 16   **STYLE NO. 63**

FILMLAND'S LATEST FANCY   **WEAR IT 2 WAYS**
"QUICK CHANGE" Weskit-and-Skirt

$9⁹⁸ FOR BOTH

NEW! A darling, fitted cap-sleeved vest to wear on the print or plain side! Beautiful pearl studs help it hug your figure. Full, full skirt is trimmed with matching print. "Year-Round" linen-weave fabric.

SIZES: 10 to 18

SILVER GREY
ROMANCE ROSE
MYSTERY BLACK
(with Harmonizing PRINT Trim)

STYLE NO. 50

Be a Pal...
HELP YOUR FRIENDS...
Get $1⁰⁰ Friendship Certificate
ABSOLUTELY FREE!!!

Help your friends look smart! Send us TEN names and addresses of friends who have NEVER BOUGHT FROM FREDERICK'S. We will send them our folders—and we send you a Friendship Certificate worth $1⁰⁰* ABSOLUTELY FREE.
*on merchandise

"BRIGHT LIGHTS"—New and daring in SATIN—be first to wear this BARE MIDRIFF two-piece style! Draped skirt has front fullness; the top has "peek-a-boo" neckline, molded bustline.

SIZES 10 to 16 ONLY.
BLACK, GLAMOUR GREY.
STYLE NO. 69

ONLY $14⁹⁸

SATIN

HOLLYWOOD ORIGINALS!
We are again proud to bring you Hollywood Original Creations — designed and made in the Glamour Capital of the world!

BE FASHION-RIGHT!
Wear clothes chosen for you by FREDERICK, famous Hollywood stylist. Be first to wear all the new styles!

"COME HITHER"
Peasant Twosome

Darling blouse and skirt . . . made for each other! Blouse is finest gingham in gay **red-and-white** checks . . . trimmed with lots of eyelet ruffles. Black fine cotton gabardine skirt has flirty petticoat flounce and daring inset of eyelet-edged gingham.

Sizes: 10 to 18   Only $10⁹⁸

STYLE NO. 10
(Give Bust & Waist Size)

Crisp Rayon TAFFETA *Skirts*
FOR DAY OR DATES!

"PARTY PRETTY"

DRESSY! BLACK with White accents in lining of big pouch pocket and lacing.
Sizes: 10 to 18.
Style No. 402 $6⁹⁸

"PROUD PEACOCK"

Hand-Painted Multi-color peacock on rich Black rayon taffeta.
Sizes: 10 to 18.
Style No. 197

$6⁹⁸

Hand Painted

109

Special Sale OF THRILLING NEW BLOUSES $3⁸⁸ EACH

Sizes: 32 to 38

"Sun Dater"

Demure—but daring! Fine sheer WHITE cotton with colorful trim of ribbon and embroidery. Puff sleeves, drawstring neck. Style No. 418 $3⁸⁸

"Eyelet Honey"

His eyes will gleam when you wear this lacy cotton eyelet style with eye-catching sleeves and shirred bust! Black or White. Style No. 419 $3⁸⁸

FREE GIFTS! With all prepaid orders.

"Male Magic"

Smart draping and shirring does things for figures. Rayon "Exotic Crepe" in Shy Pink, Gold, Black, White. Style No. 420 $3⁸⁸

"Summer Romance"

Adorable boned "camisole" top for skirts, slacks, shorts; zipper back. Silky cotton in Red, Lime, Black, White. Style No. 421 $3⁸⁸

$3⁹⁸

"LOVE LETTERS"

Crisp broadcloth with cute eyelet bib and ruffled cuffs. **White, Pink, Yellow, Blue. Sizes: 32-38** (All with white eyelet)

STYLE NO. 35

$5⁹⁸

"EYELET ANGEL"

WHITE rayon crepe with collar, "Angel Wing" ruffles, cuffs, and insert of eyelet embroidery. Perfect for suits or skirts! Sizes: 32 to 38

STYLE NO. 36

$4⁹⁸

"CIRCUS SHEER"

Colorful! Soft, white rayon sheer, printed with a rainbow of big polka dots in gay shades. Lace edges, collar and cuffs. Sizes: 32 to 38

STYLE NO. 19 Only $4⁹⁸

$5⁹⁸

"PRETTY PIRATE"

HAND-PAINTED pirate scene in gay colors on creamy white rayon crepe. Pearl buttons, ¾ "push-up" sleeves. Sizes: 32 to 38

STYLE NO. 17 Only $5⁹⁸

$3⁹⁸

"SAMBA" Midriff-Blouse

Smooth WHITE cotton with elastic neck . . . lacy eyelet ruffled shoulders. Perky! Sizes: 32 to 38

STYLE NO. 18 Only $3⁹⁸

YOUNG, COLORFUL CALIFORNIA CASUALS!

TWO-PIECE
only $14.98

HOLLYWOOD LOVES JUMPER-DRESSES! Smart with or without blouses . . . Be first in your crowd with one!

BLOUSE
$5.98

JUMPER
$10.98

$11.98 FOR BOTH

"BEAU-PEEP" Pinafore

Full-skirted, tiny-waisted pinafore of rich BLACK rayon faille has gold clasps on bodice, wide band of WHITE eyelet embroidery at hem. Matching blouse is fine white eyelet embroidered cotton with puff sleeves, black bows. Pinafore may be worn as a dress, too! Sizes: 10 to 18

STYLE NO. 28

"GOLDEN GLAMOUR" Jumper-Dress

Picture yourself in this darling cap-sleeved style with rich, jeweled GOLD BRAID trim! Peg-top pockets, fly-front skirt, deep square neck. BLACK rayon faille. For dress-up, wear without a blouse! Sizes: 10 to 20

STYLE NO. 29
"Glitter Blouse"—Trimmed with jeweled braid, too! Rayon crepe in Kelly Green, White, Red. Sizes: 32-38

STYLE NO. 30

"DANCING DOLL" Blouse and Skirt
STYLE NO. 37

Dreamy, dress-up twosome! Blouse is smooth WHITE crepe . . . ruffled, gold-buttoned, frosted with lace. Skirt is ever so full, in rich BLACK faille-taffeta, trimmed with gleaming gold braid. Buy both and save! Sizes: 10-18

Blouse—$5.98; Style No. 37-A
Skirt—$6.49; Style No. 37-B

"COCKTAILS for TWO"
Cocktail glasses, jive music
are HAND-PAINTED on
gorgeous twosome! Gay,
colorful, NEW! Sizes: 10-18.

Blouse—Rainbow colors on
WHITE Rayon Crepe.
Style No. 160—$5.98

Skirt—Rustling BLACK
Rayon Taffeta.
Style No. 161—$6.98

Lucky Stars

Traffic Stopper

"LUCKY STARS" Blouse
Be lucky FOREVER—when you wear this "Good Luck" blouse—HAND-PAINTED with signs of zodiac, lucky dice, lucky stars, gay rainbow on gleaming WHITE Rayon Crepe. Sizes: 32-38.
Style No. 158—$5.98

"TRAFFIC STOPPER" Skirt
Be first to wear one—watch his eyes pop! Bright Red and Green "Signal" pockets are HAND-PAINTED with the words "Stop" and "Go"! Fine quality BLACK Rayon Taffeta. Sizes: 10 to 18.
Style No. 198—$6.98

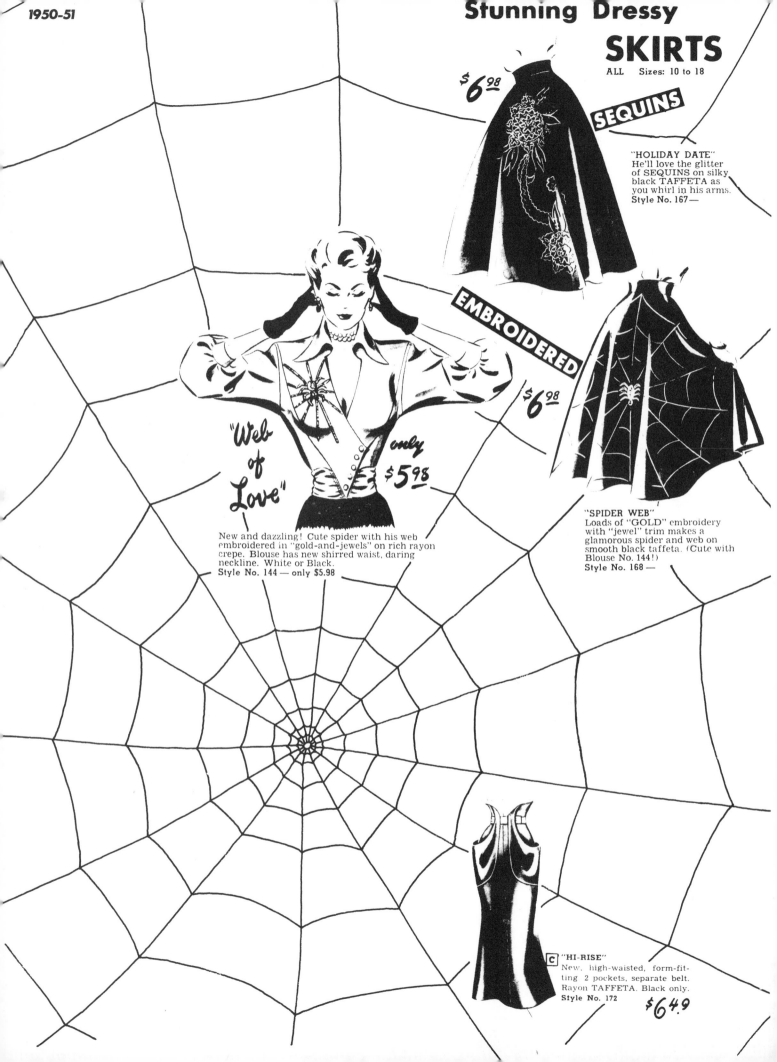

Stunning Dressy
SKIRTS

ALL   Sizes: 10 to 18

$6.98

SEQUINS

"HOLIDAY DATE"
He'll love the glitter
of SEQUINS on silky
black TAFFETA as
you whirl in his arms.
Style No. 167 —

EMBROIDERED

$6.98

"Web of Love"

only $5.98

New and dazzling! Cute spider with his web
embroidered in "gold-and-jewels" on rich rayon
crepe. Blouse has new shirred waist, daring
neckline. White or Black.
Style No. 144 — only $5.98

"SPIDER WEB"
Loads of "GOLD" embroidery
with "jewel" trim makes a
glamorous spider and web on
smooth black taffeta. (Cute with
Blouse No. 144!)
Style No. 168 —

C "HI-RISE"
New, high-waisted, form-fit-
ting 2 pockets, separate belt.
Rayon TAFFETA. Black only.
Style No. 172

$6.49

"SAILOR GIRL" "GLAMOUR GADABOUTS"

PEEK-A-BOO NECKLINE
ONLY
$5.98

"CHINA BELLE"
Glamorous DRAGONS on each sleeve, embroidered in rainbow colors, threaded with gold.
"Luxury Crepe" in Rio Red, Black, White, Glamour Gold.
Style 143

GOLDEN GLEAM

$6.79

"GOLDEN GLEAM" Skirt
Metallic threads make it look SO expensive; gorgeous draped lines; rich rayon fabric. Black, Purple, Emerald Green.
Style No. 169—
SPECIAL PRICE—$6.79

"TRIM 'n' SLIM"
Fine quality, braid-trimmed skirt of rich rayon GABARDINE with hourglass lines, 2 pockets. Grey, Black, Brown, Plum.
Style No. 170—$5.98

SIZES 10 to 18

$5.98

Slacks and Shirt; Style No. 59 only $9.98

THE SET— Style No. 634 only $13.49

SLACKS *for the* HOLLYWOOD LOOK

"SAILOR GIRL" Slacks-and-Shirt

Slacks—Firm rayon GABARDINE; 6-button closing, 2 pockets. Sizes; 10 to 18 Black, Grey, Navy. Style No. 58—$6.98

Shirt—Striped sweater-knit cotton. Red, White or Navy. Sizes: 10 to 18. (NOT SOLD SEPARATELY)
ORDER BOTH and SAVE !
Slacks and Shirt; Style No. 59 only $9.98

"GLAMOUR GADABOUTS"
For Street, TV, etc.

Blouse—Sheer rayon GEORGETTE, plunge neck, lantern sleeves, "jewel" buttons. White, Lilac, Lime. Sizes: 32 to 38.
Style No. 64—$6.98

Slacks—Rayon SATIN with hi-rise waist, zipper, trim lines. Sizes: 10 to 18. Black, Royal Blue, Red.
Style No. 63—$6.98
Slacks and Shirt; Style No. 634—only $13.49

115

$5.98
STYLE NO. 69

$6.98
STYLE NO. 60—"SATIN SIREN"

$5.98
STYLE NO. 50

$5.98
STYLE NO. 67

"SHOCKING"
He'll adore the eye-catching neckline—but beware! Rayon crepe with corded trim on collar and cuffs. Lime Green, Lilac, Black, White.
Style No. 69—$5.98—SALE PRICE

STYLE NO. 60—"SATIN SIREN"
Exotic rayon SATIN; portrait neck; French Lace trim. Black or White.
$6.98

STYLE NO. 50—"MY DESIRE"
Deep scoop neck with criss-cross of BLACK LACE. Black, Aqua, Red, or White Rayon Crepe.
$5.98

"HALF ANGEL" Tulip-Collar Blouse
Romantic—yet so daring with deep round neck and bust-molding drape; perky petal collar, full flattering sleeves. Rayon crepe. Royal Blue, Green, Purple, White.
Style No. 67—WHILE THEY LAST—ONLY $5.98

EMBROIDERY!

STYLE
533

"STAGLINE"
Dashing cut-out neck with cute choker collar
and metallic embroidery trim. Full sleeves.
"Crepe Ideal"* in Black, Red, White, Lime-Green.
Style No. 911—$6.98

*RAYON

2-Way
blouse

$6⁹⁸

$6⁶⁹

"PARIS PORTRAIT" Over-Blouse
New tunic-look to spice your wardrobe! Flared
TAFFETA* with plunge neck, pretty posy trim,
stand-up collar, shirred yoke, patent-leather belt.
NEVER AGAIN AT THIS PRICE!
Date Red, Black, Royal Blue.
Style No. 907

STYLE
519

**STYLE 533—"DATE GLEAM"
JEWELLED JERSEY BLOUSE**
It has everything—daring
scoop neck, draped bust, peaked
lapels, "silver-and-jewels" trim
—and a LOW price!
Sizes 32 to 38.
White, Black, Kelly, Royal Blue
$6⁹⁸

**STYLE 519—"EMBRACEABLE
YOU"—100% WOOL JERSEY
TORSO Blouse.** New PARIS-
INSPIRED style in a fitted,
long-line blouse to wear over
skirts or slacks. Shirred and
molded to hug every curve.
Daring! Sizes 10 to 18.
Black, Winter White, Lime-Glow
$6⁹⁸

117

HOLLYWOOD'S NEWEST "PLAY-GIRL" STYLES

Style No. 10—"SECOND SKIN"–Curve-cuddling TWO-PIECE play-suit of fine striped cotton jersey. Shorts are cotton-lined, zip in back. Navy & White; Red & White.
Sizes: 10 to 16 . . . .$7.98 for BOTH

Style No. 14—"HI, BEAUTIFUL" Shirt–Printed heavy TERRY-CLOTH pullover; zipper-front; white ribbed trim $7.85
Style No. 15—Matching shorts; back-zipper, cuffs. . . . $6.50
BOTH– Sizes: 10 to 16. White with Red or White with Navy.

Style No. 14
Shirt $785 →
Style No. 15
Shorts $650

Style No. 263—"LITTLE LOAFER"–Rugged, zippered denim 1-piece coverall. Elasticized waist; print trim on collar; print hanky in pocket. Sea-Spray Blue Denim.
Sizes: 10 to 18 . . . .$6.98

Style No. 952—"DUDE RANCH"
Bolero & Pedal-Pushers of
Sea-Spray Blue Denim,
fringe-trimmed! Fitted &
flattering.
Sizes: 10 to 18. . . **$7.49 for BOTH**

"GET TOGETHERS"—Shirt—Cool "Cal-Aire"*
fabric, striped trim, ribbed waist.
Red, Navy, or White.
Sizes: 32 to 38. **Style No. 956**. . . **$4.49**

Culottes—Fitted, full-cut Faille*.
Red, Navy, or Black.
Sizes: 10 to 18. **Style No. 957**. . . **$6.49**

**MONEY-BACK GUARANTEE
PROTECTS YOU! FREE GIFT**
with all prepaid orders! Yes,
and **FREE POSTAGE,** too – so
send payment with your orders–save real money, and receive a gorgeous gift.

Style No. 468—"VACATION DAYS"
Bra-top is boned, fully-lined; culottes
are full-cut, pleated. Looks like a
one-piece dress! Crisp Faille* in Red,
Navy, or White. Sizes: 10 to 18. **$11.98**

Frederick's OF HOLLYWOOD
SMART SEPARATES

22

Work or Play

WHILE THEY LAST!

#537
Blouse
$6.98

#538
Skirt
$6.98

STYLE
528

STYLE
767

STYLE
188

"TULIP TOP" High-Rise Skirt
Thrillingly lovely – does wonders for your figure! Boned petal top hugs waist, arches bust into high, firm curves...gives him ideas! Zipper back.
BLACK TAFFETA*.
Sizes: 10 to 18.
Style No. 181— **$7⁹⁸**

"BACHELOR BAIT" Skirt
Graceful sunburst pleats twinkle as you move; wide belt.
Silky TAFFETA*.
Green. Black. Royal.
Style No. 173— **$7⁹⁸**

"QUILTING PARTY" Skirt
New – the rage in Hollywood! QUILTED TAFFETA* beauty at the lowest price ever – but hurry! Extra full and swishy – perfect for dancing!
Kelly Green. Red. Black.
Style No. 184— **$7⁹⁸**

#537–"PERFECT PACKAGE"
New Wool Jersey Envelope Blouse. Opens and closes like an envelope. Wear it backwards or front! Buttons form a stunning yoke.
White, Pink, Blue.
Sizes 32-38. **$6⁹⁸**

#538–"SLIM LINES" Skirt
2 peaked points accent hi-rise waist. Button trim on fly front. Form-fit, 2 perky pockets.
New! Navy or Grey.
Sizes 10 to 18. **$6⁹⁸**

STYLE 767—"TAKE IT EASY"
Work-or-Play Cover-All
New! Trimly tailored one-piece zipper Cover-All with elastic waist-cincher belt. Non-crush Rayon GABARDINE.
Navy, Grey, Red.
Sizes 10 to 18. **$13⁹⁸**

STYLE 528—"ZIP-TEASE"
CORDUROY JACKET
Ribbed at collar, cuffs and waist. Cute over slacks or skirts. Zipper closing.
Red. Green, Gold.
Sizes 10 to 18 **$6⁴⁹**

STYLE 188—
"CUMMERBUND"
Hi-Rise Slacks with a trim pleated waistband, back zipper for smooth fit. 2 pockets.
Menswear fabric*.
Black, Grey, Navy.
Sizes 10 to 18. **$6⁹⁸**

*Rayon-and-Acetate

#22–"FARMER'S DAUGHTER"
Shorts and halter of crisp denim. Shaped, lined halter-bra with white pique trim on lapels and shirred drawstring bust. "Baby Boy" shorts have 2 pockets and pique trim on cuffs. Back zipper.
Blue or Grey.
Sizes 10 to 18. **$5⁹⁸**

#589–"PARTY MOOD"
Exciting "Parisienne Crepe*" blouse is so sexy! Sweetheart neckline and shirred bodice gives you an illusion of bareness . . . bring out pretty bosom curves. Huge bell sleeves. Perfect blouse for that special date! White or Black. SPECIAL— Sizes 32 to 38.
$788

#541–"I'M IN THE MOOD"
HAND-PAINTED design of words and musical notes on date blouse of White "Calura Crepe".* Sizes 32 to 38.
$698

#506–"I'M YOURS"–100% Wool
Initialed Sweater-Blouse. Two gold-color snap-on initials come with this smart style. (Print ones you want on Order Blank**). White, Red, Sea Aqua. Sizes 34 to 40
$598

#582–"MY THRILL"
The daisies on this darling blouse will tell that he loves you! Dazzling NYLON sheer looks so expensive! Permanently tucked yoke . . . exciting low-cut back. Perky embroidered lace daisy trim. White only. Sizes 32 to 38.
$698

#592–"STRIPED SIREN"
Right from the men's department . . . but flatters feminine curves! Shimmering striped taffeta* vest is tucked and tapered in just the right places. FULLY LINED! Divine for anything from cocktails to casual wear! Black with White; Red with White. Sizes 32 to 38.
$698

*Rayon-and-Acetate
**No V or Y

BEST BLOUSE BUYS

#589 CREPE! $7.88

#541 $6.98

THRILLING LINGERIE ON PAGES 16 thru 19

I'm in the mood

FH

#506 $5.98

#582 NYLON $6.98

#592 FULLY LINED! $6.98

122

JUST FOR FUN!

#578
$4.98

#583
SALE!
$3.98

(SHOWN ALSO ON PAGE 27)

HAND-
PAINTED

#581
$8.49

#152
JEWELLED
$3.95

#585
$4.98

#578–"GYPSY SWEETHEART"
Gay, colorful peasant blouse.
Shirred yoke. Multi-color rick-
rack trim on short puffed
sleeves. Elasticized neckline,
to wear on or off the shoulders.
Pearl buttons. White only. Soft,
flower-fresh broadcloth.
Sizes 32 to 38. *$4.98*

#583–"ANGEL WINGS"
Frilly, flirty and strictly
feminine! Cotton broadcloth
peasant blouse has elasticized
neckline for enticing off-the-
shoulder line. Two "Angel Wing"
ruffles with eye-catching
eyelet embroidery trim this
daytime darling. A bargain!
White only.
Sizes 32 to 38. *$3.98*

#581–"YOURS ALONE"
Fascinating Flamingos hand-
painted in vivid tropical tones,
play on a smooth-fitting linen*-
weave glamour skirt. Pouch pocket
accents this original design . . .
created just for you!
Gold, Aqua or Pink.
Sizes 10 to 18. *$8.49*

#152–"PLAY-BRA"
New and different! Snow-white
waffle pique with sparkling trim
of rhinestones. Fully lined; new
"camisole" back. For sun, sports,
or beach. Sizes 32 to 38.
B-Cup only. *$3.95*

#585–"COOL PLUNGE"
A new low in necklines! This
eye-catching polished cotton
blouse is open all the way
down to your waist! (Or wear
it demurely wrapped and tied.)
Pert cuffs and face-framing
collar. White, Navy,
Jade Green.
Sizes 32 to 38. *$4.98*

*Rayon and Acetate

the HOLLYWOOD look

#566–"LADY LOVE"
For a terrific torso! Long-line over-blouse that sends men's glances your way! Mandarin neck, clever tucks on bust and sleeves; cuff-effect at bottom. White, Black, Sky-Aqua, Tissue Faille.*
Sizes 32 to 38 **$6⁹⁸**

#545–"DELICIOUS DREAM"
Dressy date-blouse of lovely new NYLON and acetate crepe. Full sleeves, frilly lace insets and soft pleated ruffles. White, Black.
Sizes 32 to 38 **$6⁹⁸**

#565–"ONE AND ONLY"
Perfect suit blouse in NYLON LACE! Sweetly sexy, too, worn with skirts or dressy slacks... Stunning turtle neck with deep V-plunge; back buttons. Black, White, Aqua.
Sizes 32 to 38 **$5⁹⁸**

#557–"TRAFFIC STOPPER"
Deep-plunge neck on an adorable fine White cotton broadcloth style, with rainbow ric-rac trim, dolman sleeves, winged lapels. Looks demure but it's daring!
Sizes 32 to 38. **$6⁹⁸**

*Rayon-and-Acetate
**No V or Y

#566
$6.98

#565
NYLON LACE
$5.98

#545
$6.98

#557
$6.98

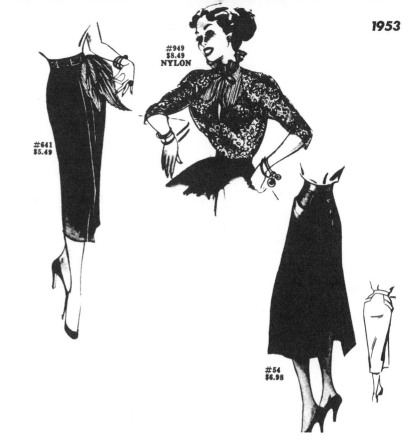

#641 "GABARDINE GLORY"
Slim-lined gabardine* skirt has
fly-front, self-belt and a bright
color permanently pleated scarf
for that "extra-special" appeal.
Wrinkle-resistant; spot-repellant
. . . this fabric wears and wears!
Black or Navy.
Sizes 10 to 16. **$5.49**

#949 "BIG MOMENT" Blouse
100% NYLON LACE
Exact copy of a $40 original!
Sheerest Nylon Lace with Nylon
net yoke and smart velvet trim.
Pink with Black; All-White;
All-Black.
Sizes 32 to 38. **$8.49**

#54 "BACK TALK" Skirt
Wrap-around style buttons in
the back . . . legs peep out as
you walk. Rich gabardine
fabric*. Autumn Wine, Black,
Also in Grey Rayon Menswear
Flannel.
Sizes 10 to 20. **$6.98**

#635 "MOVIE DATE"
Figure-glorifying 100% wool
jersey blouse designed for male
admiration! Sleeveless ribbed
charmer clings to every curve.
Demure turtle neck; back zipper.
Red, Dawn White or Black.
Sizes 32 to 38. **$5.98**

#639 "MAD WHIRL"
100% Wool Jersey blouse is trimmed in gorgeous whirling loops of
metallic embroidery and glowing
pearls. Scoop neck dips into a V
just to be different! Dressy
enough for dates. Black, White
or Shocking Pink.
Sizes 32 to 38. **$6.98**

#949
$8.49
NYLON

#641
$5.49

#54
$6.98

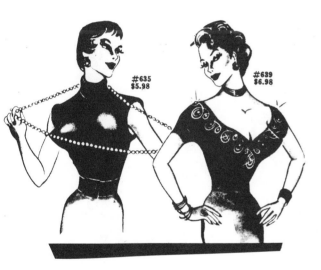

#635
$5.98

#639
$6.98

#644
$6.98 ➡

**GENUINE
MINK!**

#644 "MINK MAGIC"
Genuine MINK edges sweetheart
neck of this silky Taffeta* date-
blouse. (Your guy will think you
have millions!) Tiny buttons accent molded bustline . . . Greatest
value in Frederick's history!
White, Pink or Black.
Sizes 32 to 38.
Birthday Sale Priced! **$6.98**

SKIRT STARS

#580 "LET'S GO" Quilted!
Chromspun Taffeta** full-circle skirt for dance dates. Hi-rise waist; double-stitched design. Black, Red, Kelly Green, Navy. Sizes 10 to 18— **$7⁸⁸**

#522 "BACK INTEREST" Two-Faced Skirt
Silky, slinky Taffeta* with hip-balanced pockets. Back zipper for extra cling; triple-button trim on pockets and double slits at back of hem. Red, Black, Grey. Sizes 10 to 20. **$5⁹⁸**

#585 "SIDE SWIRL" Draped!
Molded sheath lines swish out at side and rippling hemline. New! Colorfast Chromspun Taffeta** Black, Red, Green. Sizes 10 to 20. **$6⁹⁸**

#533 "MERMAID MAGIC"
Form-fitting, hip-molding sheath of Taffeta* has flirty "Mermaid" flounce that ripples as you move. Date Red, Black, Lilac. Sizes 10 to 20. **$7⁹⁸**

#547 "NIGHT CLUB"
Rows and rows of eye-fluttering French Fringe on a hip-hugging slim sheath skirt. Glamour Crepe* Black, Red, Royal Blue. Sizes 10 to 18. **$12⁹⁸**

#488 "TWO FOR THE MONEY"
2 skirts for one tiny price! Rich yarn-dyed iridescent Taffeta* Wear with overskirt looped up to show the ruffled petticoat, or wear as a full skirt with a hidden petticoat. Black with Red Petticoat. Sizes 10 to 18. **$7⁹⁸**

*Rayon and Acetate   **Acetate

#580
QUILTED
$7.88

#522
$5.98

#585
$6.98

#533
$7.98

#488
$7.98

FRINGE

#547
$12.98

DATE DARLINGS

#546
$5.98

FRINGE

#603
$14.98

#582
$6.98

CREPE

Embroidered
LACE

**WEAR IT
TWO WAYS**

#614
$9.98

LUREX

#597
$8.98

#581
$5.98

VELVET

TAFFETA

#546 "PARTY MAGIC"
Bra-fit blouse with deep plunged neck. Yoke has eye-catching row of fringe across bust! Glamour-Crepe*. Black, White, Red. Sizes 32 to 38. SALE— **$598**

#603 "LACE ANGEL" Exotic Embroidered Lace Sensation—has daring cut-outs and exquisite trim of velvet, pearls, and rhinestones. Form-fitting; truly glamorous! White or Jet Black. Sizes 34 to 40— **$1498**

#582 "WEB OF LOVE"
Spider-web metallic Nylon bib is detachable; wear this dazzling style as bare scoop-neck blouse, too! White, Black or Gold-glow "Crepe Allure*" Sizes 32 to 38. **$698**

#614 "SPECIAL SPARKLE"
Metallic Lurex* makes your curves gleam in the moonlight! Portrait collar, Empire bust; jewel buttons. White, Aqua, Black. Sizes 32 to 38. Smart! **$998**

#597 "DATE MOOD" Dressy Rayon Velvet Blouse. Soft draped fullness, back and front. Puff sleeves; glitter buttons. Black Magic. Sizes 32 to 38— **$898**

#581 "BEAU-BLOUSE"
If you wondered how a blouse could be sexy and demure all at once, here is how! Bow-tied, bold-striped Acetate Chromspun Taffeta. Black or Red with White. Sizes 32 to 38— **$598**

*Rayon & Acetate

FREDERICK'S ORIGINALS

#653 "SAILOR GIRL"
Brand-new long-torso middy blouse
of crisp cotton hugs your hips!
Braid trim sailor collar, cuffs
and dickey (which tucks in for a
lower neckline.) White
with Navy. Sizes 32 to 38. **$3⁹⁸**

#470 "ANGEL STRIPES"
Gorgeous striped Taffeta* blouse
with low scoop neck; cuffed dol-
man sleeves, jewelled buttons.
Red and White; Black and White.
Sizes 32 to 38. **$3⁸⁸**

#602 "LEOPARD LOVE"
FREE SILK GLAMOUR SCARF *
All the exotic lure of the jungle —
deep V-neck, back and front. Zipper
closing. Sizes 32 to 38.
Cotton Leopard print— **$3⁹⁸**

#553 "JERSEY JEWEL" Nylon
Clinging draped NYLON jersey
blouse for days or dates. Full
flowing sleeves. Deep plunging
V-neck. Gleaming jewel tones:
Jet Black, Pearl White,
Lapis-Blue, Rose-Quartz.
Sizes 32 to 38. **$5⁹⁸**

#608 "GLITTER SHIRT"
Diamond-tucked and jewel-trimmed!
Acetate Chromspun Taffeta spark-
ling with rhinestones and jewelled
FREE* adjustable Velvet tie.
Black or White.
Sizes 32 to 38. **$4⁸⁸**

#612 "SEE-THRU" Date Sweater
100% Orlon that wears and washes
so beautifully. Slashed neck and
brief sleeves. Dressy for dates!
Black or Snow White.
Sizes 34 to 40. **$6⁹⁸**

#615 "DATED UP" Taffeta
with Daring Corselet Lacing
Rich Acetate Taffeta with petal
collar. White, Fireman Red,
Gleaming Black.
Sizes 32 to 38. Sale— **$5⁸⁸**

*with purchase of blouses shown

#470
$3.88

#653

#612
$6.98

NYLON

#608
SALE
$4.88

#553
$5.98

FREE
JEWELLED VELVET TIE

100% ORLON

#602
SALE
$3.98

#615
SALE
$5.88

FREE
SILK GLAMOUR SCARF

#667 "POODLE PARADE"
Perky poodles with their bright leashes are printed on a whirling back-zippered skirt. New no-iron cotton fabric has a pleated look that's smart! Red, Navy, Black. Sizes 10 to 18. **$5.98**

#665 "POCKETS A-PLENTY"
TEN corded pockets on an unusual full, gored skirt of brocaded silky cotton Chromspun with an iridescent glow. Back zipper. Sizes 10 to 18. Navy Blue, Paradise Green. JUST— **$7.49**

#519 "WHIRL ME 'ROUND"
Brilliant Aztec Indian print skirt will make you his favorite squaw! Dazzling cotton flares into dozens of unpressed pleats — stays flower fresh; needs no ironing! Blue or Grey prints. Terrific! Sizes 10 to 18. What a value! **$5.49**

#521 "TOREADOR"
HAND-PAINTED Skirt! All the excitement of a trip to Mexico! Thrilling rainbow skirt shows a brave bullfighter. Your date will be fascinated! Finest cotton; adjustable waist ties snugly. Full swirling flare. Fiesta colors. Sizes 10 to 18. **$8.49**

#495 "TROPICAL TREAT"
Longing for an exotic vacation on some enchanted isle? This swirling, border-print cotton broadcloth skirt shows colorful scenes of native high-life. New in Red, Tropic Gold, or Blue prints. Sizes 10 to 18 SALE— **$4.98**

#525 'LACE ILLUSION"
Tiny Waist . . . Tiny Price! Be the first to wear this thrillingly full whirl-skirt. Hi-rise to girdle your waist like your most passionate beau! Wonderfully washable, crisp embossed printed cotton. Looks exactly like expensive French lace! Navy Blue. Black or Red (all with White). Sizes 10 to 18. **$6.98**

Fashion Sensations at Special Savings! Look for our amazing values on every page.

#519
$5.49

IMPORTED!

#521
$8.49

HAND-PAINTED BACK AND FRONT

#495
$4.98

#525
$6.98

LACE LOOK

"FARMER'S DAUGHTER"
Suspender-slacks plus adorable
peasant blouse. Order both!

#492 Blouse. Cotton cutie with
contrast ric-rac trim. (See it
on P. 11, too.) Red, Black,
White. Sizes 32 to 38. **$3⁸⁸**

#1617 LOVE BUG
A love of a little blouse! Cotton
wrap-around with different
detailing at yoke top. Flattering
folds over bust. Side ties with
cummerbund effect in back.
Excitingly new! Luscious Lilac,
Turquoise, Cruise White,
Deep Black. Sizes 32 to 38.
$4⁸⁸

Riotous Romancers

the REAL YOU! revealed in Clinging *Jersey!*

#1635 TARZAN'S MATE
Curve-cuddling elasticized cotton topper with ravishing stripes to help matters! He'll adore it and so will you. Turtle neck. Red with White Stripe, Black with White Stripe. Sizes 32 to 38. **$2.88**

#1638 SEE CHASE
The chase is on when he sees you in this bare shoulder ribbed cotton pullover. Very low sun back and elasticized top fits skin tight. Versatile! Wear as a beach blouse or with dressy or casual skirts. Sea Froth White, Vampire Red, Bewitching Black. Sizes 32 to 38. **$2.88**

#1636 GAY TIME
Fun! Frolic! Flirt! All three for you in this curve clinging sweater type knit cotton pullover. In multi-color Blazer Stripes, it's sleeveless. Wear inside or out. Rose and Turquoise, Maize and Royal. Sizes 32 to 38. **$4.98**

#1605 HOODWINKED!
He'll adore this striped Jaguar cotton jersey pullover just for the way you look under it! Wear hood on or off! Vibrant stripes, in Butterscotch with Lime or Turquoise with Coral. Sizes 32 to 38. **$4.98**

#664 MAGIC FIT
Shirred, elasticized cotton knit top is perfect with shorts, slacks or skirts. Red or Black with White Stripes. Sizes 32 to 38. Buy several at this tiny price! **$2.88**

"PIXIE POINTS"
New and different corduroy duet! Both top and pixie pants come in Black, Purple, or Ivory-Glow. Order both in sizes 10 to 16.

#538 Top—Pullover style with notched trim on sleeves and bottom. Italian-look! **$7.98**

#539 Pants—Slim-cut; notched trim; zip-back. **$6.98**

#1577 PARIS BISTRO
Sleeveless French pullover of clinging cotton jersey looks like two garments! Solid color bodice is alluring contrast to gay striped yoke with apache side-tie and deep V-front and back. Arm edged to match. Wear with anything! Jet Black with White. Sizes 32 to 38. **$4.98**

#1635

#1605

#1638 RIBBED COTTON

#1636

#538 Top

#539 Pixie Pants

#1577

#664

carefree knits

NEXT TO *YOU...*
HE'LL LOVE THESE

#708 DANGER
Danger is in every line of this exotic 2-piece Toreador suit that fits like a second skin! Brief bolero has flirting frog and tassel at throat of standup collar and slit back. Taffeta-lined, bull-fighter pants have hi-rise boned, waist-minimizing, bust-emphasizing glamour and fit like a glove! A terrific hostess or play costume! Fine cotton corduroy.
Matador Red, Turquoise, Black. **$16⁹⁸**
Sizes 8 to 16

#707 TORREADOR TEMPTRESS
You can more than just tempt him in this fine quality cotton broadcloth blouse. Torreador styled with lace ruffled bib effect front and interesting yoked shoulders. Velveteen shoe string ties and jewel buttons add sparkle!
White only. **$6⁹⁸**
Sizes 32 to 38

film
star
loungers

SO nice to come home to! Three glama-jamas and a cute "baby doll" set are perfect for glamorous lounging.

MONEY-BACK GUARANTEE ON EVERY PURCHASE!

#919

#714

#920

#921

#3500 TURTLE DOVE
For fun days wear this cotton jersey, turtle neck pullover. Gay, exciting collar and cuffs are ribbed. Wear this with #3501 and fill his arms with glamour! Black only. Sizes 32 to 38 **$3.88**

#3501 FOOTPRINTS TO HEAVEN!
Heavenly cotton corduroy Capri pants. So unusual multi-color footprints, rhinestone trimmed, race right up the left ankle to the right hip. Slit sides. Excitingly different! Black, Turquoise. Sizes 10 to 16 **$8.98**

Jigger Sweater

#3503 TRAFFIC STOPPER
Spend exciting nights in this evening sweater with that heavenly cashmere feel (60% lambswool, 30% fur fibre, 10% nylon). Waist length shawl collar of O'llegro (man made fur) that you would be sure to think real fur fastens with lovely rhinestone buckle at waist. Colors Black, White, Blue. Sizes 34 to 40 **$29.98**

#1663 CROSS CUT
Daring darling of a cocktail sweater for those who want the most glamorous new styling. Orlon tube knit fits like a second skin up to alluring arm bands that emphasize "bare" look. Bust cuff and arm bands of ribbon knit dusted with glistening rhinestones. Black, White, Pink, Blue. Sizes 32 to 38 **$7.98**

#919 "EASY LIVING"
Tunic-top TV pyjamas with slim, tapered pants. Striped-with-solid silky 80-square cotton broadcloth. Terrific value! Red & White with Red pants; Blue & White with Blue. Sizes 32 to 38. **$4.98**

#714 "TWO'S COMPANY"
Two-Piece Satin Cocktail-jamas
Shirred, slinky siren style in shimmering rayon Satin. Strapless top is fully lined and boned. Back-zipped pants have lined stay-up waist. Black, Red. Sizes 10 to 16. **$18.98**

#9Z1 "PRETTY BABY"
Cute companion to Style #920! Same stunning tunic tops a pair of baby-brief bloomers. 40 denier Nylon jersey. White, Red. Sizes 32 to 38. **$10.98**

#920 "PYJAMA GAME"
Two-piece creation for lounging, at-home entertaining or watching TV. Flared tunic-top is frosted with insets of Nylon lace. The slim, tapered pants fit like a glove! Shimmering 40 denier rich Nylon jersey. Black, Red. Sizes 32 to 38. **$17.98**

WHO WILL WIN THE TRIP TO LUCKY LAS VEGAS?

133

"CHOOSE YOUR

*Mightier than the Sword

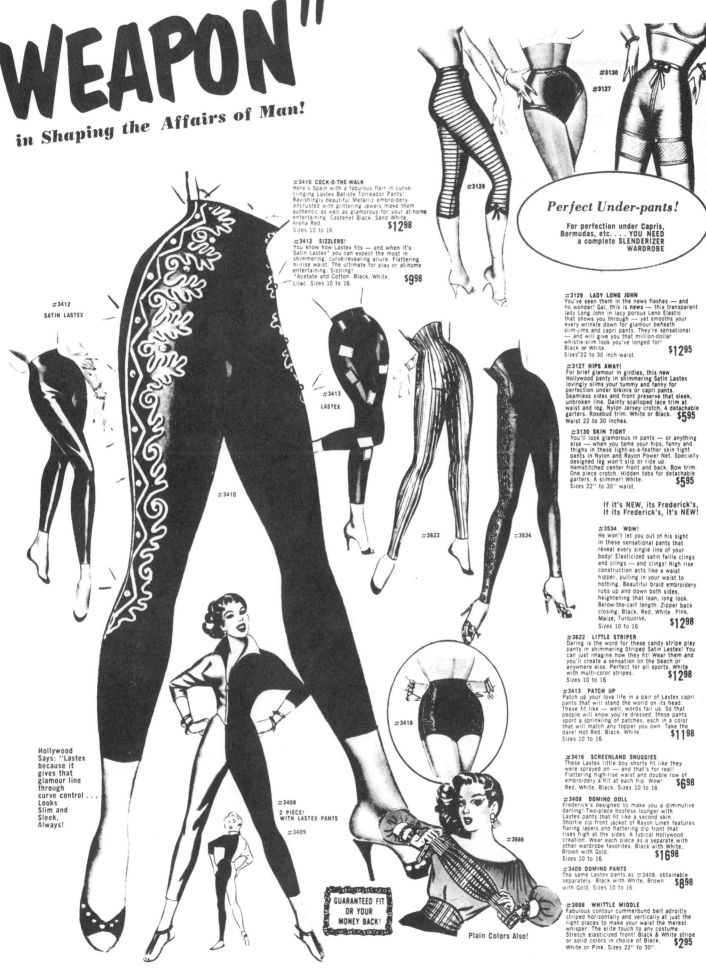

WEAPON"
in Shaping the Affairs of Man!

Perfect Under-pants!

For perfection under Capris, Bermudas, etc. . . . . YOU NEED a complete SLENDERIZER WARDROBE

#3410 COCK-O-THE-WALK
Here's Spain with a fabulous flair in curve-clinging Lastex Batiste Torreador Pants! Ravishingly beautiful Metallic embroidery encrusted with glittering jewels make them authentic as well as glamorous for your at-home entertaining. Castenet Black, Sand White, Arena Red. Sizes 10 to 16. **$12.98**

#3412 SIZZLERS!
You know how Lastex fits — and when it's Satin Lastex* you can expect the most in shimmering, curve-revealing allure. Flattering hi-rise waist. The ultimate for play or at-home entertaining. Sizzling! *Acetate and Cotton. Black, White, Lilac. Sizes 10 to 16. **$9.98**

#3412 SATIN LASTEX

#3413 LASTEX

#3410

#3129 LADY LONG JOHN
You've seen them in the news flashes — and no wonder! Gal, this is news — this transparent lady Long John in lacy porous Leno Elastic that shows you through — yet smooths your every wrinkle down for glamour beneath slim-jims and capri pants. They're sensational — and will give you that million-dollar whistle-slim look you've longed for! Black or White. Sizes 22 to 30 inch waist. **$12.95**

#3127 HIPS AWAY!
For brief glamour in girdles, this new Hollywood panty in shimmering Satin Lastex lovingly slims your tummy and fanny for perfection under bikinis or capri pants. Seamless sides and front preserve that sleek, unbroken line. Dainty scalloped lace trim at waist and leg. Nylon Jersey crotch, 4 detachable garters. Rosebud trim. White or Black. Waist 22 to 30 inches. **$5.95**

#3130 SKIN TIGHT
You'll look glamorous in pants — or anything else — when you tame your hips, fanny and thighs in these light-as-a-feather skin tight pants in Nylon and Rayon Power Net. Specially designed leg won't slip or ride up. Hemstitched center front and back. Bow trim. One piece crotch. Hidden tabs for detachable garters. A slimmer! White. Sizes 22" to 30" waist. **$5.95**

If it's NEW, its Frederick's, If its Frederick's, it's NEW!

#3534 WOW!
He won't let you out of his sight in these sensational pants that reveal every single line of your body! Elasticized satin faille clings and clings — and clings! High rise construction acts like a waist nipper, pulling in your waist to nothing. Beautiful braid embroidery runs up and down both sides, heightening that lean, long look. Below-the-calf length. Zipper back closing. Black, Red, White, Pink, Maize, Turquoise. Sizes 10 to 16. **$12.98**

#3622 LITTLE STRIPER
Daring is the word for these candy stripe play pants in shimmering Striped Satin Lastex! You can just imagine how they fit! Wear them and you'll create a sensation on the beach or anywhere else. Perfect for all sports. White with multi-color stripes. Sizes 10 to 16. **$12.98**

#3413 PATCH UP
Patch up your love life in a pair of Lastex capri pants that will stand the world on its head. These fit like — well, words fail us. So that people will know you're dressed, these pants sport a sprinkling of patches, each in a color that will match any topper you own. Take the dare! Hot Red, Black, White. Sizes 10 to 16. **$11.98**

#3416 SCREENLAND SNUGGIES
These Lastex little boy shorts fit like they were sprayed on — and that's for real! Flattering high-rise waist and double row of embroidery a'fit at each hip. Wow! Red, White, Black. Sizes 10 to 16. **$6.98**

#3408 DOMINO DOLL
Frederick's designed to make you a diminutive darling! Two-piece hostess lounger with Lastex pants that fit like a second skin. Shortie zip front jacket of Rayon Linen features flaring lapels and flattering dip front that rises high at the sides. A typical Hollywood creation. Wear each piece as a separate with other wardrobe favorites. Black with White, Brown with Gold. Sizes 10 to 16. **$16.98**

#3409 DOMINO PANTS
The same Lastex pants as #3408, obtainable separately. Black with White, Brown with Gold. Sizes 10 to 16. **$8.98**

#3666 WHITTLE MIDDLE
Fabulous contour cummerbund belt adroitly striped horizontally and vertically at just the right places to make your waist the merest whisper. The elite touch to any costume. Stretch elasticized front! Black & White stripe or solid colors in choice of Black, White or Pink. Sizes 22 to 30". **$2.95**

Hollywood Says: "Lastex because it gives that glamour line through curve control . . . Looks Slim and Sleek, Always!"

#3408 2 PIECE! WITH LASTEX PANTS #3409

#3416

#3666

GUARANTEED FIT OR YOUR MONEY BACK!

Plain Colors Also!

For you...
With Love
Fredericks of Hollywood

S **#8430 WESTERN WHIZ**
Whiz kid with feminine ideas? This is yours
. . . for your capri wardrobe. Cotton and
Nylon Stretch denim Capris with yoke back
design. Contrast stitching front and back.
Ranch Blue, Black, or Barn Red.
Sizes 8 to 16.   **$8.99**

T **#7025 GOLDEN CALF**
Glitter like his golden idol in shining
Acetate, Cotton, Rubber, Metallic Lurex.
Elasticized throughout to fit like a second
skin! Hi-rise waist, zipper back closing.
Gold, Black, Silver.
Sizes 8 to 16.   **$12.99**

U **#8374 OUT AND ABOUT**
Get out and be seen in these never-before
'Cotton Velveteen' hi rise capri pants,
imported for your pleasure. Black,
Hot Pink, or Turquoise. Sizes 8 to 18,
Junior sizes 7 to 17.   **$5.99**

V **#3412 SIZZLER!**
You know how Lastex fits—and when it's
Satin Lastex you can expect the most in
shimmering curve-revealing allure. Flatter-
ing hi-rise waist. Acetate, Cotton and
Rubber. Black, White, Gold.
Sizes 8 to 16.   **$9.99**

W **#8365 BETTERHALF**
Compliment yourself where it matters
most . . . Curvacious Wool and Nylon
stretch Flannel stirrup pants . . . and best
of all they can be worn with or without
stirrups. Black, Red or Green.
Sizes 8 to 18.   **$10.99**

X **#8024 CLASSICAL FIT**
Classic appeal—with the fabulous Frederick's
touch—Acetate Cotton lastex Capri pants
with high rise waist and to the ankles . . .
Black, White, Red and Turquoise.
Sizes 8 to 18.   **$5.99**

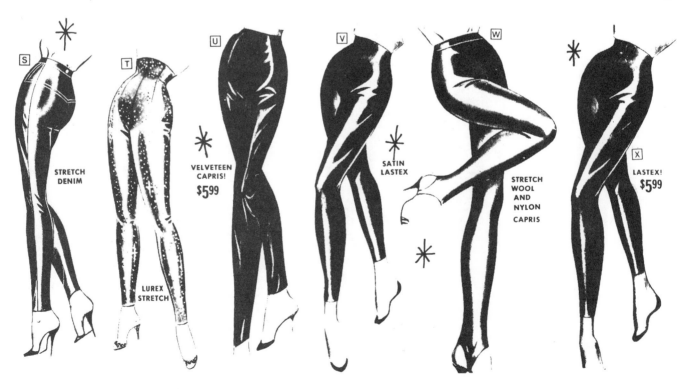

STRETCH
DENIM

LUREX
STRETCH

VELVETEEN
CAPRIS!
$5.99

SATIN
LASTEX

STRETCH
WOOL
AND
NYLON
CAPRIS

LASTEX!
$5.99

BUILT-IN PUSH-UP PADDED BRA

K #8014 LAME LOVELY
The halter that plunges to the lowest low . . . completely backless. Comes complete with its own in-up padded bra. Glittering Lame Gold or Silver. Sizes 32 to 36 A , B or C cup. **$10**

"Honestly, I've looked everywhere . . . but never have found fashions to compare with Frederick's. Wearing Frederick's clothes has made me oh, so popular!"

JULIE JERRETT
Top Hollywood Model

COPY OF $165 ORIGINAL

R #8435 SPELLBOUND
We challenge anyone to find such a dazzler for this price! Copied line for line from an expensive $165.00 sweater . . . our first-nighter cardigan in sugar-spun Orlon Acrylic, double-lined with filmy Nylon Chiffon and Nylon Lace. Magnificent full French Rabbit shawl collar, rhinestone closing. Black on Black, White on White, Brown on Beige. Sizes 36 to 42. **$25**

G #8279 MATE BAIT
Ahoy doll! . . . here's real mate bait . . . Frederick's fabulous French Fisherman blouse in Fortel, Dacron, Polyester and Cotton . . . Long sleeves are cuffed and button. Front plunges to a V with a high standing collar . . . adorable overblouse has two pockets. Powder Blue, Lime, White.   Sizes 6 to 16 **$8⁹⁹**

B #8396 LUXURY
Lurex metallic sheath skirt with lining fused right into the skirt! Eliminates sag, or loss of shape. For true holiday glama get the shirt #8395 to match. Acetate and Mylar Silver, Gold or Heavenly Blue. Sizes 8 to 16. **$9⁹⁹**

C #8423 BIG NIGHTS
Glamorous opening to important evenings . . . and a happy selection to play up your prettiest evening blouses or simple classics. Full floor length evening skirt in Rayon and Mylar Lurex, fully lined. Gold, Pink or Blue. Sizes 8 to 16. **$12⁹⁹**

E #7931 HIGH KICK
Nothing beats a pleat for figure flattery! a captivating skirt in Arnel Triacetate Jersey . . . under all your blouses and sweaters. White, Black, Aqua. Sizes 8 to 18 **$8⁹⁹**

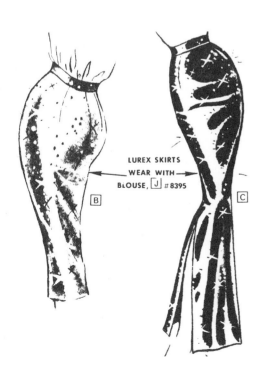

LUREX SKIRTS WEAR WITH BLOUSE, J #8395

B   C

E ARNEL **$8⁹⁹**

"Call me Mr, Fashion! I'm really hot this Spring! Have you seen my new see-through blouses? My Eyeball Bikinis? Deepest plunge necklines? Bras-on-the-half-shell? They're all in this catalog! **Don't miss a page!**"

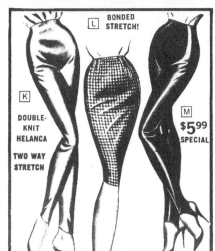

BONDED STRETCH!

L

K

M $5.99 SPECIAL

DOUBLE-KNIT HELANCA

TWO WAY STRETCH

$5.99

K **#8681 TALLY-HO**
Stirrups stretch these double-knit Helanca Nylon pull-ons to your curvacious dimensions. Two-way stretch capris hold their fit...never a wrinkle...never a bulge! Offered by Fredericks for the first time, in Black, Green Royal Blue.
Junior Sizes 5 to 15. $7.99

L **#8899 PERMA-SHAPED!**
The check that never bounces! Checked Stretch skirt of Cotton and Nylon is bonded to hold its shape and yours...permanently! No fear of sitzout here! Skirt zips up the back, with a cinched-in, hi-rise waistline. Black-and-White check.
Junior sizes 7 to 15. $5.99

M **#8840 THE FITTIN'EST**
Underscore your figure with the fittin'est stretch pants you're likely to see! Double-Knit Rayon and Nylon capris pull on, have a hug-tight elastic waistband. Stirrup straps hold them taut and trim. Black, Royal Blue, Green.
Junior sizes 7 to 17. $5.99

J **#8778 NEAT 'N NAUTICAL**
Wide white laces accent the bare midriff top, sleeveless and saucy in stretch cotton sailcloth. Contrasting white stitching on red, green or blue sailcloth. Sizes 6 to 16, junior sizes 5 to 15. $5.99

K **#8779 CAPTIVATING CAPRIS**
Hip-rider capris have fly-front lacings, contrasting white stitching on bold solid color stretch sailcloth to match the top. Sizes 6 to 16, junior sizes 5 to 15. $8.99

HOLLYWOOD APPROVED SCREEN STYLE

J

K

A **#8638 LURING TORSO**
To bare or not to bare...it's up to you! Cover up with a chiffon scarf. The bold bare the bosom...let the town talk! Band under the bust lifts the bosom, forms shoulder straps. All this in gleaming Stretch Acetate and Lurex! Bonded back! MEOW! Blue, or Bronze.
Sizes, Misses 8 to 16.
Juniors 7 to 15. $16.99

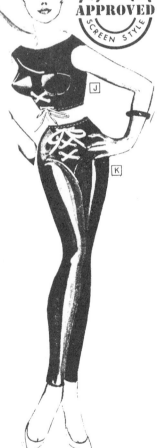

BABY LOOK AT YOU NOW!

A

LUREX!

Frederick says, "clothes make the woman!" Let every inch of you be more provocative in creations designed to make the most of YOU! "For every style for every mood, for every whim of every woman, we have the answer!"

SHIRRED MATTE
JERSEY BLOUSE

#8478 DOUBLE DATE
Hey doll! This is the perfect complement to your Helanca stretch capris . . . Frederick's all Nylon Elastron stretch coin dot sweater . . . Back zips for *easy off-again* . . . *on-again* style. Tremendous fitting beauty has turtleneck . . . and is sleeveless. Dots on White Background. Black, Navy, Red or Turquoise. Sizes 32 to 38. **$7⁹⁹**

#8475 MAD MOOD
If you're in the mood for the most madly marvelous capris ever . . . you'll love these Nylon Stretchlon Double Knit figure flatterers. Just pull on . . . *no zippers or waistband worries.* Fantastic figure fit. Turquoise, Black, Pink, Yellow. Sizes 8 to 16. **$10⁹⁹**

#8682 SHAMELESS!
Next-to-nothing sun topper balloons over your bosoms! Covers them, and very little else! Ruffled neck is elasticized all around. Wear it *on* the shoulders . . . *off* the shoulders . . . as a halter . . . completely sleeveless! WOW! In Turquoise, White, Black, or Pink Cotton. Sizes 8 to 16. **$2⁸⁸**
2 FOR $5⁵⁰

2 For $5⁵⁰

WEAR 5 WAYS!

LOW AND BE HELD!

$6⁹⁹

TREMENDOUS VALUE! D
$4⁹⁹

B

REVERSIBLE
ZIP FRONT
OR BACK

A

$5⁹⁹

IN
QUICK-DRY
ARNEL
$4⁹⁹

C

E

WAS
$5.99
NOW
$3⁹⁹

A **#8238 OFFICE ATTRACTION**
Be it the office . . . school . . . or just plain going everywhere . . . you'll have a million compliments in this Pima Cotton Blouse with wing collar. Outstanding styling: sleeves are tight with balloon effect . . . front line plunges. White or Black. Sizes 32 to 38. **$5⁹⁹**

B **#8243 BABY BLOUSE**
Baby . . . you'll never believe the attention you will attract in this Rayon and Acetate Crepe dream with ¾ sleeves. Elasticized waist makes the perfect fit. Snow White, Blue or Pink. Sizes 32 to 38. **$6⁹⁹**

C **#8863 FLATTERER**
A blouse to bless your bosom! Low square neckline adds a self-bow for flattery. Side gathers encourage an up-and-out profile. Sleeveless. Buttons up the back. In glorious Arnel Triacetate that washes . . . quick dries . . . needs hardly a touch of an iron. White. Sizes 32 to 38. **$4⁹⁹**

D **#8855 SQUARE TOP**
Be a Square! Top your pet pants and skirts with this deeply square-topped, frankly sexy overblouse! Ruffles all around the scooped-out neck and elbow sleeves. Buttons up the front. Immaculate Fortrel Rayon and Cotton fabric scarcely needs an iron. White. Sizes 30 to 38. **$4⁹⁹**

E **#8830 OVER-EXPOSED**
Leave your midriff bare for browning! Cotton double-knit Limbo Top is elasticized around the bottom to cup up under the bust. With zipper in back, it's a high turtleneck. Reversed, the neck's a deep, daring "V". White, striped in Black, Pink, Maize or Green. Sizes 6 to 16. **$3⁹⁹**

Fun MIXER

A #7030 **WESTERN WHAHOO**
These levi pants are sure to keep him home on the ranch . . . authentic Western styling done in a glamorous rayon and acetate lastex fabric that glistens like satin. Black, Lilac
Sizes 6 to 18. **$10⁹⁹**

E #7350 **SWITCHEROO**
It's a girl's privilege to change her mind! Abbreviated Arnel Triacetate Jersey Crop Top switches about to suit your whim. Zip it in front for a daring plunge . . . zip in back for a turtleneck. Elasticized bottom hugs the rib cage. Orange, White, Powder Blue, and Pink.
Sizes S-M-L. **$4⁹⁹**

F #7291 **SMOOTHIES**
Smooth new YOU in Stretch Matte Jersey Garrison pants! They're the Lithe and Lean LOOK for Summer! Cut fly-front and widely belted, they stretch for a fit that really zings! Acetate and nylon. White with leatherette belt to match Pink, Green or Navy Candy stripes.
Sizes 8 to 16. **$8⁵⁰**

E #7347 **CLASSIC BEAUTY**
Wear this versatile fortrel rayon and cotton Ivy-League look roll-up sleeves shirt with pants or skirt — never needs ironing . . . perfect traveling companion for a skirt worn in or out. Comes in lovely multi-color stripes of predominantly Pink, Blue or Lilac.
Sizes 32 to 38. **$4⁹⁹**

F #7348 **SOLID BEAUTY**
Solid color version of #7347 in White only. Sizes 32 to 38. **$4⁵⁰**

G #7293 **SWING LOW**
Low-priced hipsters you can afford to own in every color! Underslung Garrison Pants are man-tailored in Avril Rayon and Cotton for easy summer care. Two-ring belt . . . two button trim . . . fly front . . . cuffed pant bottoms. Green, Blue or Black.
Sizes 8 to 16. Only **$5⁵⁰**

reversible

E *stripe shirt*
F *solid shirt*

G *pants*

stretch matte jersey

A SATIN LASTEX!

A #8074 **GOING PLACES**
A jaunty jump-in that's real whistle-bait. Loves leisurely entertaining, and going places . . . outdoors of course. Zippered legs, tied waist. Arnel Triacetate jersey. Black or White.
Sizes 8 to 16. **$12⁹⁹**

C #7189 **THE LITTLE COLONEL**
Fellas will present arms when you parade in this! Mitey-military Jumpin has a dropped waistline, easy fit. V-neck . . . double breasted . . . ashine with bright Brass buttons! In stretch Dacron Polyester Cotton: Black, Coral, Vibrant Blue. Sizes 6 to 16; Junior sizes 5 to 15. **$15⁹⁹**

D #7155 **IRRESTIBLE**
He's so attracted! He's drawing closer! He can't resist YOU IN MARIBOU! Long-sleeved Rayon Acetate crepe blouse has a high front neckline . . . a back that's deep and bare. Fine fluffy Maribou outlines the neckline and cuffs. Fully lined. In Black or White. Sizes 30 to 36. **$17⁹⁹**

ZIP LEGS

HOLLYWOOD CAMPUS DANDY SUIT

MILITARY
PANTSUIT

B

B #7145 **ATTENTION!**
An All-Girl adaptation of military MOD-
ness! Fast-paced Pantsuit has a new
longer jacket . . . stand-up collar, epau-
lets, Brass buttons! Straight garrison
pants are long 'n leggy! All-Cotton,
pinstriped in Blue-and-White; Plum-
and-White. Sizes 6 to 16;
Junior sizes 5 to 15. **$19⁹⁹**

H #8735 **PINTOS**
Western cowboys ride the range in
pants exactly like these. (Longer, meb-
be!) Cotton Denim short shorts have
that snake-hips look. Authentically
saddle-stitched and nail studded. Zippered crotch closing. Big hip pockets
hold your old bandana! Ranch Blue.
In sizes
6 to 16. **$3⁹⁹**

SHORT SHORT
PINTOS

H

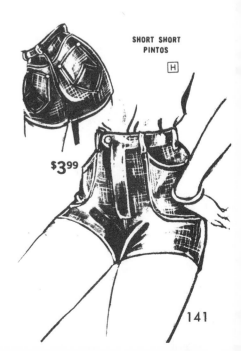

$3⁹⁹

for the frederick's
SPORTIN' LIFE

**FREDERICK'S IS HOLDING THE LINE
AGAINST INFLATION!** In spite of cost
of labor and materials going up, UP,
U-P! We can't promise to maintain
these low prices forever . . . so order
now while the bargains last!
Mr. Frederick

G #2—7598   LOVE FOR SALE
Catch his eye and capture his heart. "Her" turtleneck sweater also comes with stylish french cuffs in 100% double knit acetate. Has back zipper with free love symbol! White, Black or Blue. Sizes Small, Medium or Large.   **$12**

H #2—7597   PEACE OFFERING
Make him the most talked about man on the block. "His" newest of the new turtleneck sweaters has fashionable french cuffs. Comes with free peace symbol! 100% double knit acetate. White, Black, Blue. Sizes Small, Medium or Large.   **$12**

his and her

free peace symbol

DOUBLE
your pleasure
DUOS

free cuff links

#2—7401   LOVERLY
You'll look romantic in this simply loverly arnel triacetate jersey with its low scoop neck, dramatic long sleeves and figure-making empire tie. Have one in Black and another in White for many changes. Sizes 8 to 18.   **$12⁹⁹**

#2—7386   RETE PLEAT
Love that permanently pleated HUGE accordion neck! Hugs your neckline high . . . then folds back into a flattering cowl collar. Textured Acetate pullover has long sleeves . . . zips up the back. Matches #2—7384 pants perfectly! Red, Gold, Green. In sizes 34-40.   **$10⁹⁹**

#2—7563   LETTER GIRL
They'll want you on their team, when you wear this "H"-backed blouse! It's cotton gingham check in Pink, Yellow blue checks with white.   **$7**
Sizes 8 to 16.

#2—7590   SHIRT 'R SHIFT
Meditate on this . . . a two-in-one deal with man-appeal! You can wear it as a meditation shirt, or a swinging shift . . . looks fab either way! Great with easy-in buttons all down the front. White or Grey linen rayon. Sizes 10 to 16.   **$14**

142

LUREX
LASTEX
WAS ~~$35~~
NOW
$19⁹⁹

*hurry, while they last
at this price!*

HOLLYWOOD
APPROVED
SCREEN STYLE

#2—7652 GURU-VY
What would the Maharishi say
about this? Nehru-for-you capri set
with button down jacket and side-
zippered one-button pants, slim leg
style. Cotton twill. Gold, Red or
Black. Junior
sizes 5 to 15.   **$16**

#7487 SCINTILLATION
One-piece slimline Lastex is aglow with
Metallic Lurex to make your curves
twinkle. Enhancing bra's built in for
strapless interest, shirring's bosom-
beautifying. Gold, Silver, Black. **$19⁹⁹**
Sizes 8 to 16.

sheer

RIBBON
KNIT

LEATHERETTE

**SEPARATES
DOUBLE
YOUR
GLAMOUR**

#2—7832 SHEER SHIRT
It's a body shirt designed for sheer
flattery! In see-through cotton voile,
tailored with an angle on feminine
lines. White, Yellow, Blue.
Sizes 32 to 38.   **$9**

#8195 LOVE-LY GAL
What a blouse! Exciting ribbon knit . . .
elasticized peek-a-boo waist-band. Lace
trimmed beauty. Rayon, Acetate with Nylon
lining. Beauty Beige. Black-nite,
Jewel White. Sizes 10 to 18.   **$6⁹⁹**

#7684 EASY MIX.
Terrific topping for Frederick's other
leatherette lovelies! A plunge front
leatherette shirt to fall free or tuck tight.
Yolked in front and back for dash and flare
Black, White or Beige Vinyl
Leatherette.   **$8⁹⁹**
Sizes 32 to 38.

143

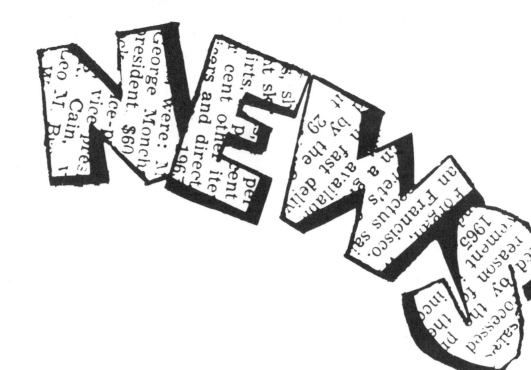

If you want to look just great all the time I'd suggest you shop from Frederick's catalog . . . I've always been delighted.

Irene Baxman

MODEL ACTRESS

Money couldn't buy the compliments I get on my Frederick's of Hollywood styles . . . I love them.

Marilyn Tindall

Top Hollywood Model

Fashions are always easy to find in the Frederick's catalog so I suggest you order today so you'll look your best. I always do.

Venita

MODEL ACTRESS

Thanks Frederick's . . . The best advice I can give aspiring starlets is to wear your clothes. Frankly I count on them for myself.

Nora Hayden

My Christmas wouldn't be complete without my Holiday wardrobe from Frederick's.

Marilyn Turner
Hollywood
Fashion Model

*You can always be sure of
first and second glances, when
you're wearing sportswear
with that Hollywood-look . . .*

J #2—7644 SNAKE-Y
Snakes are your best friends . . .
when they're made into our deep
plunge bell-leg jump in. Ties at
shoulders show you off . . . to him.
Back zipper. Fully-lined bust. Lurex.
Snakeskin print.
Sizes 6 to 16.   **$22**

C #2—7835 WIDE-LEG PANTS
Wild, wide-leg pants are wildest in a
border print. It's a rich-girl look
in rayon/silk. Back-zipped for our famous
fit. Lilac or Red.
Junior sizes 5 to 15.   **$10**

D #2—7705 PLEATS GALORE!
The kickiest idea in pants is a pair of
straight leg pants that flare out at the
knee with a hundred pleats! Great
walkin'. Fits to the waist and has back
zipper. Rayon-linen in Purple or
Mint Green.
Junior Sizes 5 to 15.
Misses Sizes 6 to 16.   **$15**

E #2—7842 WRAP PANT
Pants learn a new way to take a front
zip. The clever side wrap closing hides
the zipper, accents your hipline for
a hip-happy look. In carefree cotton.
Beige, Lime or Yellow.
Junior sizes 5 to 15.   **$11**

F #2—7836 STRIP POLKAS
Cute cut-out cut-ups in cotton. Polka
dotted pants with a strip showing on the
side for a great show of legs. Back
zipped. Black and White. Red
and White. Junior sizes 5 to 15.   **$13**

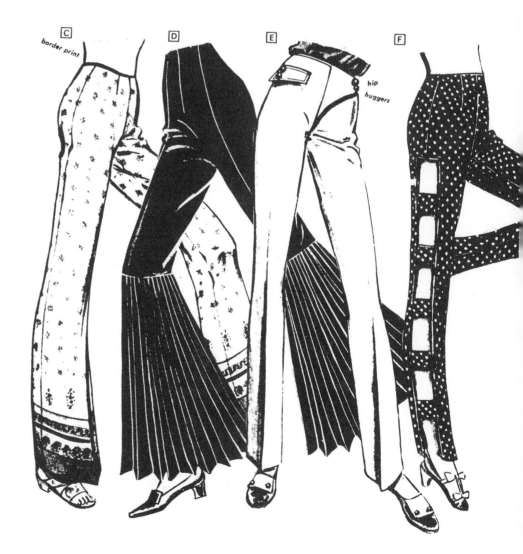

border print

hip huggers

Body lovin' RIBS

KNIT-TO-FIT YOUR EVERY CURVE

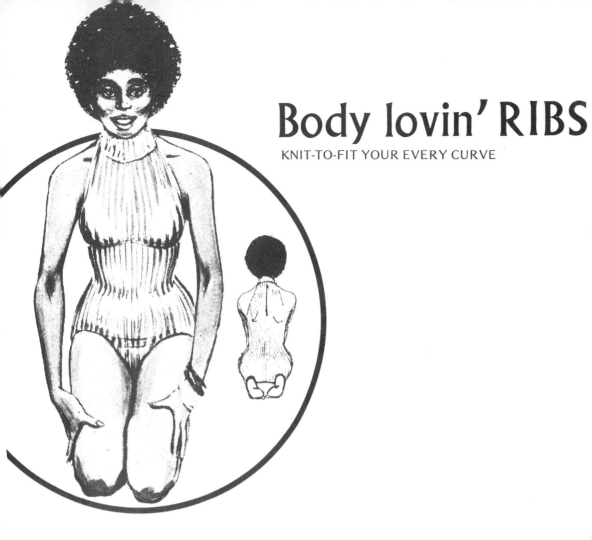

#6—1797 THE "BODY" BEAUT
Glorify your image in this one-piece,
rib knit, stretch nylon, body suit . . .
turtle neck style . . . hugs snug to
show every luscious line of you.
He'll love it — and you in it! No
bra; zip back. Hand washable, drip
dry. In Pale Lilac, or Pale Peach.
Sizes: Small (3-5), Medium (7-9),
Large (11-13). **$23**

fit 'n flare

knit jumpin

**#2—7190 DRAMATIC
ENTRANCE**
Designed to make the most of you,
this sensational jumpin plays up
the daring contrast of black and
white for all its worth. Back zipped
with turtleneck and fit and flare legs,
this is meant to be worn when you
really want attention! Chavacette
acetate knit in black/white. **$37**
Misses sizes 8 to 14.

zipper all
the way
down!
each
side

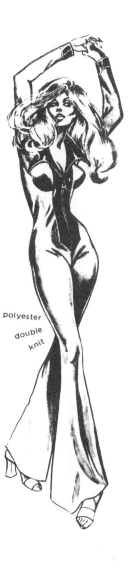

polyester
double
knit

#2—7191 DOUBLE SENSATION!
Two front zippers go right up
and down the front of this fantastic
flare-leg jumpin. Revealing as can be,
without actually showing what you
have, except in dramatic outline.
Flare legs and stand-up cowl neck.
Chauvacette acetate knit in purple
with gold zippers or black
with red zippers.
Misses sizes 8 to 16.
Junior sizes 7 to 15.   **$28**

#2—7471 LOOKING GOOD
Two-tone jumpin zips up (and down)
the front for easy in-and-out super-
smart 100% polyester knit. Collar,
front panel and cuffs on the ¾ sleeves
contrast with the body-huggin' jumpsuit
that features 21'' fit 'n flair legs.
Chinese Red with Navy Blue trim, or
Black with Chinese Red trim.
Junior Sizes 7 to 15.
Misses Sizes 8 to 16.

KNIT TRICKS
(neat tricks!)

147

DO
your own
THiNG!

B.P.*s do...
with frederick's
of course

(*beautiful people)

RING-A-DINGERS
Blow your mind with this 3-pc.
combo! Baby cotton cord vest and
pants are frantically fringed in
shredded suede cloth. Vest is all hung
up with bright gold chains . . .
hip-hugger pants fan out from the
knees. Matching sheer crepe
buccaneer shirt is open collared,
elastic-snug at the wrists!
Geronimo!

#2—7196   BUCCANEER BLOUSE
Vanilla colored wash-and-wear
pull-over. Misses Sizes: Small (6-8);
Medium (10-12); Large (14-16).
$10

#2—7197   VEST
In Brown. Junior Sizes: Small (5-7);
Medium (9-11); Large (13-15). **$11**

#2—7198   PANTS
Zipped front, with fore-and-aft belt
loops. In Brown or Taupe. **$17**
In Junior Sizes 5 to 15.

Frederick's Parade of Fashions
as Seen on
"The Johnny Carson
Tonight Show"
"The Virginia Graham Show"
"Ralph Story Special"
"The Steve Allen Show"

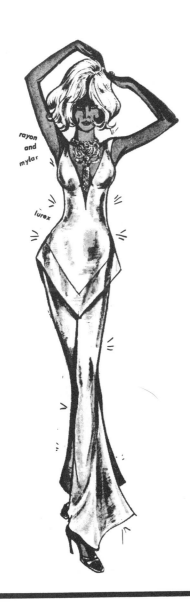

rayon
and
mylar

lurex

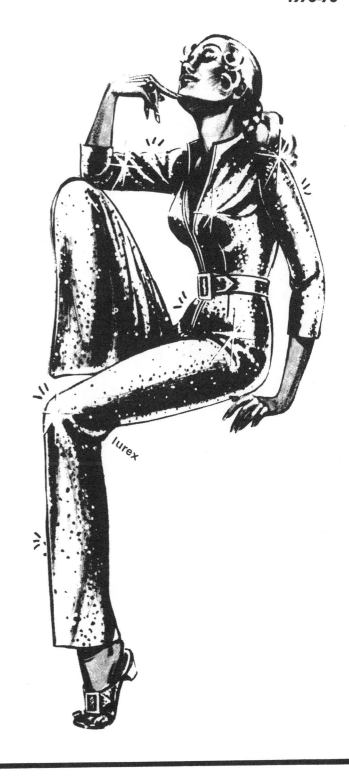

lurex

**#2505 LOOK OUT FOR
LUREX** . . . the look that fans the
spark of love into a 3-alarm fire!
Gleaming Lurex pants set is deeply,
revealingly V-necked. Tunic top
comes to deep points front and
back. Pull-on pants.
Ravishing in Silver or Gold Lurex.
Misses Sizes 6 to 16.   **$28**

#2—7062 HOT LINE
This sizzling Lurex Jumpin is almost
too hot to handle! Shimmering Rayon-
Mylar is Bonded to hug tight, stay
shapely. Long front zipper lets you
plunge the neckline low and open...
tighten it teasingly taut.
Silver or Gold.
Sizes 8 to 16   **$25**

$10

2 pc. lounge set

lurex

2-pc. fashions at a price!

Money Back Guarantee

A #3-4279　　　SHOW-OFF
Why hide your light under a barrel? Dare to be a terrific show-off in these cling-tight culottes of 100% Nylon. Halter neckline plunges to the waist. Wide-legged pants are fitted and flattering through the hips. In Black only.
Small (32), Medium (34-36), Large (38).　　**$10**

B #3-4281　　　JERSEY JIVE
Costs just pin money! Looks like a million dollars! 2-pc. Acetate Jersey lounge set has pull-on pants . . . a short-sleeved tunic top with elasticized neckline and waist. Love that fit, so clingin' and close.
Gold, Lilac or Pink.
Small (32), Medium (34-36), Large (38).　　**$10**

C #3-4278　　　CUT-UPS!
Captivating culotts, up-cupped and cut out V-neck plunge shows your double exposure...cut out sides bare the rib cage. Culotte pants are so wild and wonderful ...watch yourself swing with the action!
Blue with pink trim.
In 100% nylon　　**$15**
Misses sizes 8 to 16.

D #2-7213　　　PAMPAS PETS
Try the South American way! Acetate bonded for lasting fit, gaucho culottes are belted with plated chains . . . short bolero vest is banded in braid. Red-with-black orlon polyester vest; black-and-white checked culottes.
Junior sizes 5-13. 2-pcs.　　**$18**

F #3-4306 GOLDEN GODDESS
Evenings by firelight call for this glamorous long golden lurex robe. With demure but seductive mandarin collar, ¾ sleeve, snap front braided with gold trim. Glow alive in his eyes. In gold only, small 8-10, medium 12-14, large 16-18.　　**$30**

150

1970

deep
"v" plunge

cut-out

2 piece
set

D **#3—4307** **FLOWER CHILD**
Lovely to look at, and ripe for the
picking! It's like a lot of girl for little
money in Frederick's acetate crepe
culottes. Cap sleeves and plunge neckline top the wide—wide culotte pants.
Flower patterned as shown, or similar.
Misses sizes 8 to 16.
$15

E **#3—4275** **PINK LADY**
2-Pc. Pink Nylon lounge set . . . too
exciting to relax in! V-neck top
laces the bodice together just
barely. Bell-bottomed pants pull
on for perfect fit. Wash it like
a pair of hose! Sizes
Small (32), Medium
(34-36), Large (38).
$15

A #2—7398 OLE!
The bold Spanish way to bare a cold
Shoulder! Black lace and fringe-
dangles wrap around a sleeveless top
...fill in a pant leg that's slit high.
Provacative! Hot peppery! White
arnel/nylon knit body with Black
cotton lace trim.
In Junior sizes 5 to 13.   **$33**

B #2—7271   INVITATION
Remember, gal, you're asking for
it! Sexy peasant blouse has an
elasticized neckline just waiting to
be PULLED DOWN with the action! Wide shirred bodice . . .
push-up sleeves. Permanent press
polyester/avril blend. In White
only. Misses sizes
32 to 38.   **$7**

C #2—7265   FOR KICKS!
More than pants . . . they're
PANDEMONIUM! 30" wide legs
have 3-seamed inverted panels inset for a flare that's fantastic! Fit
tight-tight from the knee up, high-
rising to mold a full waist. Chavacette Acetate, in Black, Cloud
Blue or Hot Pink.
Junior sizes 5 to 13.   **$15**

D #2—7237
        POP EYE SHIRT
A booby trap in pop art! What it
is is a really GREAT PUT-ON . . .
a photo-funny shirt that makes it
hard to believe his eyes! 100%
cotton, in pop-eye pink or bunny
beige. Just pull it on and SHOW!
Small (6-8); Medium (10-12);
Large (14-16).   **$5**

lace
with
fringe

needs no
ironing

DO YOUR OWN THING

HOLLYWOOD
APPROVED
SCREEN STYLE

$5

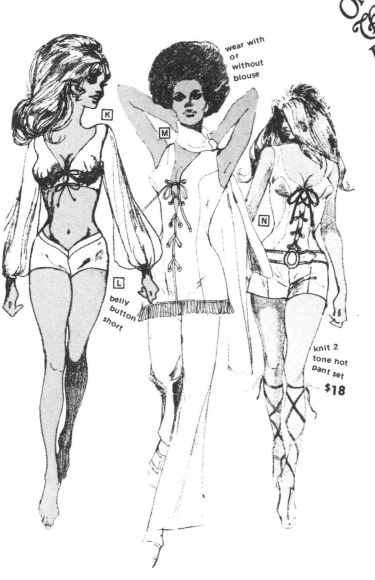

wear with
or
without
blouse

K

M

N

L

belly
button
short

knit 2
tone hot
pant set
$18

Oh,
Those
Peek-a-Boo
*Hot
Pants!*

K #2—7293 **TORRID TOP**
To tie or not to tie, that is the question.
Whether it is better to leave the top
open...or draw it together at V-neck and
midriff! You can wear it "Peek-a-
boo" front if you dare! Elastic
wrists push up or down. White, Pink,
Blue or Lilac Acetate Nylon.
Small (6 to 8), Medium (10 to 12),
Large (14 to 16).   **$10**

L #2—7270 **SHOW DOWN**
How short are short-shorts? Looka
here at these, babe . . . and then
you'll know! Short enough to dip
low down and bear the belly button. AND in nylon stretch Helanca
to knock em dead! Have White,
Purple or Black. Misses sizes
6 to 14; Junior sizes 5 to 13.   **$7**

M # 2—7353 **FRONTIER WHOOP—LA!**
Mod squaw's take-off of the Red Man's
fringed vest & pant. Bare beautifully
in the plunge V-neck, sleeveless,
laced front jacket or cover up modestly
with a mad blouse. Pant has 19" straight
leg. Rayon crepe stitch bonded knit
acetate in White or Blue. Misses sizes
8 to 16.   **$15**

N # 2—7352 **IN—CAT**
Wanna be the IN-CAT on his list of kittens?
Try the look of this 2-piece short set,
and he'll never have eyes for another.
Acetate and Nylon has a scooped-neck
top laced down the front to a low
dropped belt. Hot Pant Shorts. Red
or Blue, with White trim. Junior sizes
7 to 15.   **$18**

PATCHWORK POW
in genuine Suede Leather! A mini you'll love . . . he'll love . . . and all your friends will envy! Snaps up the front to a low scooped neck.. Has a high-rise Empire waist, an A-line shorty skirt. In patchwork pattern of Brown and Tan Suede. Junior sizes 5 to 13
B #1-2168 $35

PROVOKING
pants set is a copy of a high priced import! Knowing and naughty two-toner has a diamond-shaped insert in front. Mock turtleneck and matching pull-on fit 'n flare pants. Polyester knit in Brown-with-Ivory or Black-with-White. Misses sizes 8 to 16
C #1-2250 $28

SLIM IN
and shape up in this pants suit! Makes lavish use of contrast stitching for the skinniest, sultriest look! Long-sleeved pull-on has a wicked V neck. Pants pull-on to fit 'n flare. Chavacette Acetate knit in Wine with Blue stitching or Grey with Black. Junior sizes 5 to 13
D #1-2247 $26

genuine suede
B

C
copy of import

very slimming!
D

two-toner

contrast stitching

A Frederick's wardrobe just isn't complete without Frederick's great fashions

Mary

If He's LOOKIN'...You're SHOWIN'

THE '30s LOOK!

F

Everybody asks me where I get my marvelous clothes. I could be mean and not tell . . . but I'm really proud to say—Frederick's of Hollywood!

Debbie

wear as pant suit or mini dress

GANGSTER SUIT
. . . to set you right with the mob!
Pin-striped man-tailored Polyester knit has a wide-lapelled two-toned jacket, pull-on cuffed pants. To be worn with a wicked swagger! Scarf included. Black with White stripes.
Junior sizes 5 to 13
F #1–2248 $33   scarf included!

E #1–2925 **CHECK OUT TIME**
is anytime you're looking so SHARP in this! Super-swish jacket is double-breasted, double-buttoned, sashed at the waist and fully lined. Pants zip up the back for great hip-fit. In Red-and-White or Brown-and-White Acrylic knit. Terrific plaid! Terrific value!
Misses Sizes: 8 to 16   **$23**

F #1–2909 **WILD WAY**
to go panted. Or wear the top as a mini dress. Animal print shines and slinks on Acetate and Nylon. Low V-neck un-laces to your pleasure. Contour seamed to FIT, in wild life colors. Pullon fit 'n flare pants.
Misses sizes 8 to 16,   **$25**
Junior sizes 7 to 15.

PANT-HER

155

frederick's OF HOLLYWOOD

BELIEVES
A BODY-SHIRT
SHOULD

DO MORE
THAN COVER!

matching boots
D

C

BOOTS AND BODY MATES
Your most "together" fashion look!
Boots and body-shirts that MATCH!
CLINGY STRETCH-NYLON SHIRT
has a long front zipper for any kind a
plunge. Snap crotch. BOOTS
are 8-inch ankle high in calf-grained
Vinyl with soft foam inner-soles. Both
in Black with White.

C #3–4775 BODY-SHIRT $14
Bust sizes 32 to 38
D #3–4774 MATCHING BOOTS $13
Sizes 5 to 9½ inches
Medium widths only

LESS IS BEST
when it comes to body suits. This one in flat knit Nylon has got to be the briefest! Everything shows, just like a second layer of skin! Deep V'd halter neck ties in back. Bare back. Bare underarms. Snaps at the crotch. White, Black or Hot Red.
Sizes Small/Medium, Medium/Large.
C #3-4631 $8

TRICK TOP
A neck that's bound to be noticed! Tricky ribbed trimming wraps from neck to side. Wear it high low or opened for plunge. Nylon body top's a play suit . . . a wear-under pantser. Snaps at the crotch. Black or Hot Red, with White ribbing. In sizes Small/Medium, Medium/Large.
F #3-4614 $14

"PEANUTS"
New "Peanuts" styled shorts are really some little show downs! Hug the hips. Ride below the navel. Zip up the front with two small buttons. Polyester stretch knits, so you know they fit fantastically! In White, Yellow, Hot Pink.
Junior sizes 5 to 13
G #2-7588 $8

Shake up your PLAYMATES

A #1–2486 **MIDI-KNIT**
Here's a mighty pretty midi . . .
Chavacette Acetate knit long-sleeve
dress and pant duo. Empire style with
V-neck. Wear alone as a dress with
buttons open, as you dare, for leg
watchers, or over flare-out pull-on
pants. Purple or Black.
Junior Sizes 5 to 15.   **$28**

TOP PERFORMANCE
A top that shows you off coming and
going! Ruffles frame the plunge V-
front...ripple down the squared-off
cut-out back. Pants pull on to fit
'n flare. 2-pc. set in Red or Royal
Blue Chavacette Acetate knit. In
Misses sizes 6 to 14.
Junior sizes 5 to 13.
C #1–2225   **$36**

"I love Frederick's pantsets. They're made to fit and flatter GIRLS!!"

Cindy
Actress/Model

WHAT A FIT!
How close can a cling knit fit? THIS close. . . then flare into wide wild legs! Shiny Nylon Ciré cups the busts, cuffs the sleeves. Chavacette Acetate knit. Grey with Black Cire, Beige with Brown. Sizes: Misses 6 to 14; Junior 5 to 13.

A #1—2359 $42

SHINY
CIRE
TRIM

show
off
neckline
2 ways!

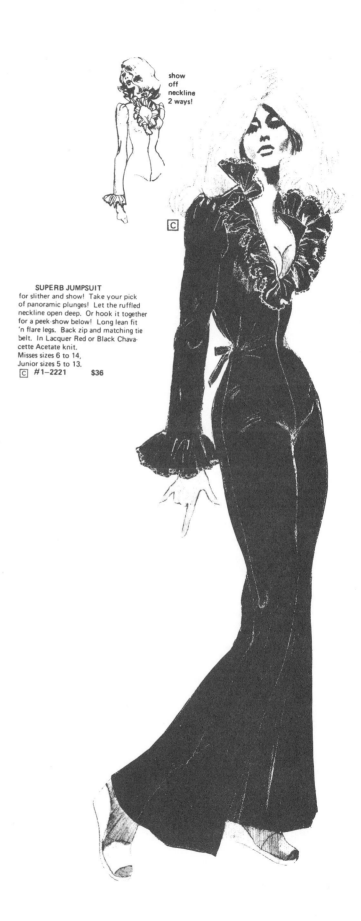

SUPERB JUMPSUIT
for slither and show! Take your pick of panoramic plunges! Let the ruffled neckline open deep. Or hook it together for a peek-show below! Long lean fit 'n flare legs. Back zip and matching tie belt. In Lacquer Red or Black Chavacette Acetate knit.
Misses sizes 6 to 14,
Junior sizes 5 to 13.

C #1—2221 $36

MATCH 'EM

pucker stretch D

K Ribbed-Knit Cotton

L Wear over Blouses 'n Turtlenecks

M Rib Cotton Knit

Bare Back Cotton Knit

J

PUCKER POWER
shows it like it is! Cotton top is elasti-cized with 5% rubber for bust control. Straps slide on or off shoulders. Wild wear with pants and shorts. In Yellow or Red. Small (5-7), Medium (9-11), Large (13).

   #2-7910 $8

COOL OFF
in the hottest thing going! Ruffled and ribbed mini midriff has straps that stay up or slant off the shoulders. Terrific in Bright Yellow, Pink or Blue Cotton. One size fits 5 to 11.
K #2-7909 $7

KITCHY-COO!
He'll love this soft and cuddly shrink top. Baby-ribbed and deeply V-necked, you'll wear it bare as is . . . or layer it with blouses. Light Blue or Coral Red Cotton knit.
Sm (5-7) Med (9-11) Lg (13)
L #2-7896 $7

TEENY TOPPER
The casual way for minimum cover! Cotton tie-back halter is ribbed knit for bust control. Red or Navy, trimmed in White.
Sm (5-7), Med (9-11), Lg (13)
M #2-7916 $6.50

TOP-LESS
Cotton knit pullover snugs the waist, tugs low as you like. Leaves shoulders and back sensationally bare! Halter neck gathers and ties behind. White, Red, Blue. Small (5-7), Medium (9-11), Large (13-15).
J #2-7855 $6.50

    CLASSY CHASSIS
A hot pants set to show what you're made of! Backless top ties at the neck and waist, flares in a peplum. Short cuffed hot pants. Red with White trim or Avocado Green with White trim. Polyester knit. Junior sizes 5 to 13.
   #1-2439 $22.00 VALUE!
     NOW $18

160

"I love Frederick's body shirts. They're made to fit and flatter GIRLS!"

Lynn
Model

DOUBLE KNIT

Dolman Sleeves

Sleek and Lithe!

Lattice sleeves

Special!

1973

BODY LOVIN'
body-shirt in super-fit Nylon Antron double knit. Great Dolman sleeves with bow-tied cuffs. High neck with zipped up back. Snap crotch. Black, Blue or Camel.
Sm (32), Med(34-36), Lg (38), X-Lg(40).
A #3—4133 $18

SECOND SKIN body-shirt
in sleek and sexy Antron double-knit Nylon! Seamed to cup-up under the bust. Wide lapel collar. Long sleeves. Snap crotch. In Black or Camel.
Sm(32), Med(34-36), Lg(38), X-Lg(40).
B #3—4132 $19

WITCHY
A shirtmaker that goes from PRIM to POW! Buttons up to the chin. UNbuttons waist-deep for the widest plunge! Always holds its taut shaping, for it's snapped in place at the crotch. Long cuffed sleeves. So great with long or short pants. Orange, White, Blue, Pink or Turquoise Nylon.
Sm (32), Med(34-36), Lg(38).
C #3—4609 $9

CUT OUT CAPER!
He'll love the peek show you put on in this daring long sleeved body-shirt. A low low V-neck and keyholes tempt and tease . . . and so do sexy cut-out sleeves! Snap crotch for super fit . 100% Nylon. In White, Lilac and Black.
Sm(32), Med(34-36), Lg (38).
D #3—4679 $16

ruffled bare back

A Top

Cotton Knit

B Pant

F

SWEET 'N SEXY
Be his young thing with this demurely ruffled pinafore top. But turn around and he'll find you've grown up with a back that's bare and decidedly sexy. Bow in back for a provocative un-tie. In Cotton knit check. Pink/White or Blue/White.
Small (5 to 7), Medium (9-11), Large (13).
A #2—7829 $10

NIFTY KNIT FIT
A Gingham Check thing with Frederick's famous fit 'n flare, pull-on pant has elasticized waist, full 30" flare to the legs. In Cotton Check Knit. Pink with White or Blue with White.
Small (5 to 7), Medium (9 to 11), Large (13).
B #2—7830 $13

A.W.O.L
Saucy sailor style jumpsuit might not pass regulations, but it's sure to get you a lot of passes. Low V, Empire styling lets you "bust out" beautifully. But the real secret's in back. Collar is flippy slit to make it completely backless. Zip back, Frederick's famous fit 'n flare pants. In 100% Chavacette Acetate Knit. Tiger Lily Orange or Bright Blue..
Junior sizes 5 to 13.
F #2-7838 $40

Torrid Torsos

WAVE RAVES

Style No. 9—"VELVET VENUS"
Waterproof rayon VELVET.
Wear Bikini-style or covered-up.
Black, Royal Blue, Nude-Beige.
Sizes: 10 to 16........ **$8.98**

TORRID TORSOS

#150

#161

#571

#571—"SUN STUNNER"
This sexy sunsuit has polka-dot
strapless boned sun-bra top.
Wrapped front-ties. Revealing
slit denim shorts with bow-tied
polka-dot cuffs. Ocean Blue
shorts with Red and White
polka-dot top.
Sizes 10 to 16 **$6.98**

#150—"SAILOR GIRL"
Wolf-whistles will follow you
in this darling "sailor" swimsuit! Does things for every
figure! Firm lastex batiste;
has slim molded torso with
middy effect; accordion-pleated
skirt. Hour-glass curves
for every girl! Buy it NOW!
Navy with White skirt.
Sizes 32 to 38. **$11.98**

#161—"DO YOU DARE"
Wait till they see you on the
beach in this daring Bikini!
It's so revealing AND it's an
exact copy of alluring suits
worn by so many famous beauties on
the French Riviera! Nylon Jersey
is extra-clinging, caresses
curves like a second skin!
Fully lined. Black or
White. Sizes 32 to 38. **$8.98**

"HOLLYWOOD TRACK SUIT"
Cute little one-piece cotton terry-cloth romper-suit that will make men run after you! Long zipper; ¾ sleeves. White, Sun Gold, Pacific Blue. Sizes: 10 to 20.
Style No. 12— $8⁹⁸

BARE AND BEAUTIFUL

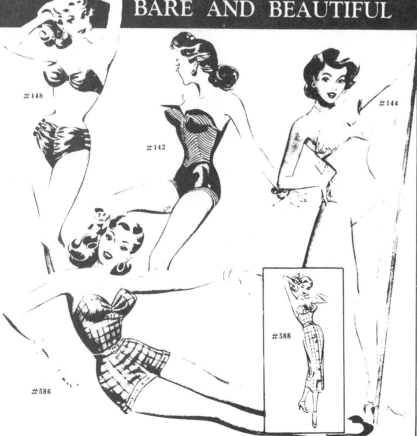

#148

#142

#144

#588

#586

#148—"DOUBLE DARE"
You'll be the belle of the beach in daring Bikini bathing briefs! Perfect bra-fit top is cut so low! Eye-catching side lacing. Lastex Batiste. In White, Coral, or Black.
Sizes 32 to 38. $5⁹⁸

#142—"HOUR GLASS"
Strapless Chevron Striped Lastex swimsuit. Cuffed petal bra top. New molded torso look gives you perfect rounded slenderness. Striped, cuffed skirtless briefs. Sea Blue, White or Black.
Sizes 32 to 38. $8⁹⁸

#144—"NEARLY NAKED"
A terry cloth treat! 2-piece bathing suit with cupped bra-top and removable halter ties. Elasticized shirring for fit. White or Lime.
Sizes 10 to 16. $4⁹⁸

#586—"SUN SPARKLER"
Sunsuit in new "ORO" fabric with boned bra-top, cuffed shorts, and zipper back. Molded to your pretty torso like wallpaper! $5⁴⁹

#588—"MATCH-UP" Skirt
Add button-front skirt for dates or street wear. Trimly tailored. $5⁴⁹

F OR C AMERA F ANS

Voila! Frederick's jewel-sparkled
Bikini #55 worn by Paris charmer
sunning herself on the Seine.

#870 "FIG LEAF" Dance-Set
Fabulous Nylon Lace Bra and Pants
The French have done it again!!
Straight from Paris—daring tiny
two-tone lace uplift bra and match-
ing Bikini panties have "Fig leaf"
applique. White, Red or Black
(All with Black Lace);
Sizes 32 to 38— **$798**

#863 "HANDLE WITH CARE"
2-piece Nylon Dance Set
For private eyes alone! Naughty
Frederick's creation teams a tiny
lace bra, trimmed with satin hands
AND filmy lace step-ins with a
satin crotch and daring satin trim.
Makes a really different gift for
any gal who's brave enough to wear
them! Black only.
Sizes 32 to 38— **$998**

#871 "BARE MINIMUM"
Filmy Nylon Lace Chemise
Is a Gift to Remember!
Any gal can wear diamonds if she
is lucky enough to own this tiny
sensation with diamond-shape inset of jersey. Buttoned step-in
crotch and bra-fit top. Sheer lace
barely veils a pretty torso. Red
or Black (with Black lace);
Sizes 32 to 38— **$898**

#863
NYLON LACE
$9.98

#870
NYLON LACE
$7.98

#871
NYLON LACE
$8.98

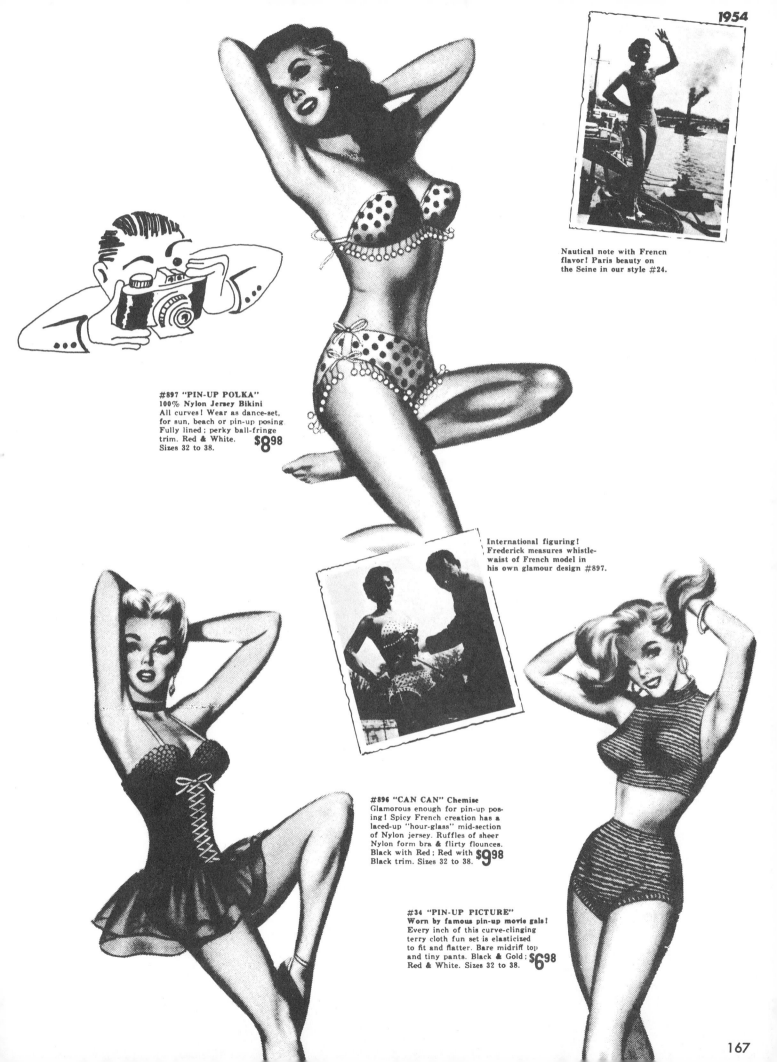

Nautical note with French
flavor! Paris beauty on
the Seine in our style #24.

#897 "PIN-UP POLKA"
100% Nylon Jersey Bikini
All curves! Wear as dance-set,
for sun, beach or pin-up posing
Fully lined; perky ball-fringe
trim. Red & White.
Sizes 32 to 38. **$8⁹⁸**

International figuring!
Frederick measures whistle-
waist of French model in
his own glamour design #897.

#896 "CAN CAN" Chemise
Glamorous enough for pin-up pos-
ing! Spicy French creation has a
laced-up "hour-glass" mid-section
of Nylon jersey. Ruffles of sheer
Nylon form bra & flirty flounces.
Black with Red; Red with **$9⁹⁸**
Black trim. Sizes 32 to 38.

#34 "PIN-UP PICTURE"
Worn by famous pin-up movie gals!
Every inch of this curve-clinging
terry cloth fun set is elasticized
to fit and flatter. Bare midriff top
and tiny pants. Black & Gold; **$6⁹⁸**
Red & White. Sizes 32 to 38.

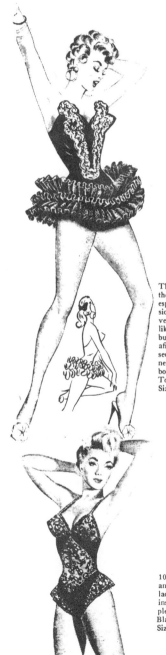

Sunset Strip

FIRE BRAND
The newest of Frederick's theatrical costumes designed especially for models and professional stage use. Imported rayon velveteen with high cut leg fits like it was born on you. Boned bust section l as exotic twisting V afire with hundreds of jewels and sequins. Fabulous yards of nylon net ruching in can-can style at bottom. Panther Black or Torch Red.
Sizes 10 to 16. **$29⁹⁸**

LACE SCANDAL
100% Nylon Chemise. Bra-fit top and buttoned step-in crotch on a lace creation with diamond-shape inset of jersey. Perfect gift to please any gal! Black or Red (with Black lace).
Sizes 32 to 38. **$8⁹⁸**

Frederick's is the store, where I get all my film-star fashions! In my career, leotards and tights are my daily costume . . . and Frederick's is my headquarters!

JEANNE BRETT, HOLLYWOOD STARLET

BACK STAGE BEAU
Created by Frederick on demand from show people! Theatrical costume weds rhinestone-dusted rayon velveteen midsection with patent leather effect bows exquisitely cut out at sides to reveal bare skin from leg to bust! Boned top is cuffed front and back with bow between busts. Twin bows on each hip, too. Really first-run theater sensation. Raven Black.
Sizes 10 to 16. **$24⁹⁸**

Spectaculars

HOLLYWOOD BACKSTAGE
Second skin leotards that love the chorus line, ballet, skating or model posing. Full-fashioned, one-piece sleeveless scoop neck. Made of HELANCA stretch, demanded by professionals! Fever Red, Panther Black, Snow White. **$5.95**
Sizes 8 to 16

Being glamorous is very important to my profession . . . and when I need leotards and tights I go to Frederick's where they are NEW, and DIFFERENT!

ELLEN FARREN, RECORDING ARTIST

SNARE
Nylon Helanca miracle yarn fits like a second skin, hugs curves. 1-piece runproof leotard is worn by top models, dancers. Black, White. **$5.98**
Sizes 10 to 18.

TOE DANCER
A handful of froth in Helanca stretch nylon tights. Your other skin from waist to toe. Washable! Sun Tan, Theater Black. Sizes Average, Long, Extra Long. **$8.98**

#1133
Curvaceous June Svedin ("Miss Washington") says, "Frederick's Styles Are All Show Stoppers..."

#40

Frederick says, "clothes make the woman!" For fashions designed with **you** in mind, take a tip from Frederick. "For every style for every mood, for every whim of every woman, we have the answer!"

Cheesecake Charmers

"The best looking life guard at the beach saw me in my white terry cloth sun suit. My Frederick's sun suit was **a real life saver,** as the handsome life guard is now my husband.
☆Toddie Young
Los Angeles, Calif.

KAREN SCOTT
International star of London, Paris and Hollywood. "In Paris it's Dior, here it is definitely Frederick's"

LINDA LOMBARD
Popular name-band vocalist and star of Broadway, TV, and the nationwide night club circuit, wears Frederick's No. 184 for glamour photos which show the beauty that won for her Warner Bros. title of "MISS 3-D". Linda says "Thanks, Frederick, for your **truly feminine** creations."

BEACH HOLI-DATERS

Terry Turns

WAVE WITCHERY
If it weren't for the woven Paisley Print in this exotic all-elastic suit, it would look like the skin you were born in! It fits every curve with dangerous and daring beauty. Off-shoulder neck and Maillot legs are simple slashing accents in solid tone Elastic with a crocheted look. Floating inner bra does the **most** to glamourize your bosom.
Black, Red, Blue.
Sizes 30 to 36
$14⁹⁸

LINDA LOMBARD
Popular name-band vocalist and star of Broadway, TV, and the nationwide night club circuit, wears Frederick's No. 184 for glamour photos which show the beauty that won for her Warner Bros. title of "MISS 3-D". Linda says "Thanks, Frederick, for your **truly feminine** creations."

TERRY TAKE OFF
No muss, no fuss—when you slip into this newest terry cloth creation. It's a shortie jump-in wrap around with no buttons to slow you up. Quick as a wink, it goes over your bathing suit at the beach, or over just you around the house. Lapels, sleeveless style, ties in back. Beach White, Sea Aqua.
Sizes 10 to 18
$6⁹⁸

TRIPLE THREAT
Darling terry cloth jump-in, perfect for playing, lounging or entertaining. Long zipper front, 2 side pockets and breast pocket with gay heraldic shield design. Washable, of course. Confetti White, Lemon Yellow, Copen Blue.
Sizes 8 to 18
$8⁹⁸

TWIN STARS
Bikini two-piece terry cloth sensation. Snug bra top has adjustable halter; brief pants are shirred at sides with elastic to really fit. Perfect for pin-ups, exercise or sun-bathing. Lime-Gold, White, Lilac.
Sizes 32 to 38
$4⁹⁸

FREDERICK SAYS,
"The Hollywood Look is The Look He'll Love!"

#1327

#1330

#1329

Sunset Strip

#1327 SHOCK WAVE
Raves will roll in like waves when you wear Hollywood's newest, most sensational shocker in glittering Metallic Lurex! Wicked little pants feature self drape climaxing in ring right over your tummy. One-shoulder top accentuates bosom glamour. Both bra and top fully lined, and elasticized for fabulous fit. White or Black Lurex.
Sizes 32 to 38 **$13⁹⁸**

#1330 TOU-TOU TEMPTRESS
This exclusive Tou-Tou creation is a **must** if you want to be the most glamorously dressed mermaid of 1957! Every line is created to flatter and excite! Lastex midriff clings like a second skin in startling contrast to striped Cotton Satin bust and double can-can flounce with its flirty fish tail back dip. Boned bust has hidden floating bra, lightly padded. Low back. It's a thrilling glamour creation — and one of Frederick's finest. Black or White both with contrast stripe.
Sizes 10 to 16 **$19⁹⁸**

#1329 PRIZE CATCH!
Here's a luscious surf sensation that will net you the most handsome man on the beach! Utterly new Wool honey-comb knit over Cotton gives it a startling "nothing on" effect that will make him look twice. Boned bust section is lightly shell padded. Don't buy this — **unless** you want to attract attention! White over Black or White over Fleshtone **$22⁹⁸**
Sizes 10 to 16

"... I really go crazy when I see all Frederick's lovely fashions ... you don't have to travel to Paris to be chic."

Michele Santini French Model and Actress

B #9532 BAUBLES
Frederick's fun and fanciful navel cover-ups for shy bikini wearers. Self adhering buttons, delightfully decorated with a flashing mirror, brilliant jewels, or a pert ladybug. They stay on in water, too. Just press on — lift off — use over and over. Set of 3. **$3**

NEW NAVEL COVERS!

B

SPARKLING METALLIC LUREX!
B

C #1949 SEA SPARKLE
This is one of the most sparkling sensational swimsuits we've ever had ... What a dream in Nylon and Metallic Lurex ... Halter front plunges to a daring, new low ... Bustline keeps in shape with permanent cups ... and deep v hook has two hooks and eyes for the lass with modest moments. Black, Glittering Gold. Sizes 32 to 38. **$25⁹⁹**

B #1507 GLAMOUR-GLOW
Clothe your body beautiful in glittering Mylar Acetate Metallic and Rubber lastex to display every line like a goddess. Built-in bra for comfort and extra special fit. Gold Glow or Shimmering Silver. Sizes 32 to 38. **$19⁹⁹**

F

HELANCA

G

$3⁹⁹

Mr. Frederick understands exactly how to design swimsuits that make you look your most womanly. He says: "Every Frederick's swimsuit is model-tested to make sure you get the most flattering fit possible."

F #1748 ALMOST SINFUL
A real "Second Glance" suit! And, after the second glance, all eyes will stay riveted on you. *Tiny drawstrings control the leg coverage.* Cut very bared of back, with a deep Sweetheart neckline. 100% Nylon Helanca in Kabuki Red, Royal Aqua, or Jet Black. Sizes 32 to 38. **$10⁹⁹**

G #1510 CHECK CHICK
Tiniest next to nothing bikini in checked cotton. Flattering bra puts YOU on top. Bikini pants with Naughty derriere bow tie. Black, Turquoise, Pink, all with White. Sizes 30 to 38. **$3⁹⁹**

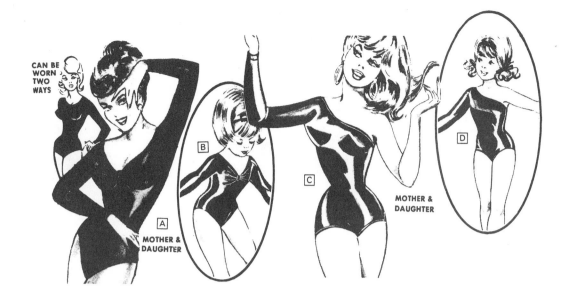

CAN BE WORN TWO WAYS

A

MOTHER & DAUGHTER

B

C

MOTHER & DAUGHTER

D

A **COSMONAUT**
You're a fast rising star in full fashion stretch Nylon leotards, styled with a Hollywood flair...plumetting front, adjustable 'V' neckline, high cut French legs...you've admired on your favorite T.V. and movie stars. Long sleeves, Velvet ribbon trim. Black only. **$5.99** Sizes 8 to 18.

B **LITTLE LADY**
Your little girl will be positively entrancing in this fabulous leotard that's made to match yours. It has an adjustable scoop-neck and it's made of comfortable stretch nylon. Black only. Sizes 4 to 14.
$4.99

C **PRIMA BALLERINA**
A dramatic leotard any ballerina would be proud to wear. It's a stunning one-shoulder step-in of form fitting stretch nylon. Black only. **$5.99** Sizes 8 to 18.

D **BABY BALLERINA**
Any little girl would look perfectly ador-able in this cute one-shoulder leotard that's just like mother's. It's wonderful for dancing school or recitals and it's made of comfortable stretch nylon. Black only. **$4.99** Sizes 4 to 14.
Little girls version of #4525

glamour DANCE-ABLES!

METALLIC MAGIC
All the Magic glamour of Lame Metallic stretch fabric plus the styling you love in a leotard. It has a scoop neck, long sleeves and daring French cut legs. Silver or Gold. **$12.99** Sizes 8 to 18.

frederick's
OF HOLLYWOOD

#1921   GO GO-WEST
Go West, young woman, for a bare bikini that's **wild, wonderful and wholly Frederick's!** Cotton and Nylon STRETCH DENIM is saddle-stitched into briefest levi pants . . . cowboy-belted, back zippered. Bra's terrific strapless or halter-styled! Turquoise, Ranch Blue or Wheat.
Sizes 30 to 36.   **$8**⁹⁹

STRETCH DENIM
WILD WEST BIKINI

#1935   FAKELY NUDE
Not as Nude as it looks . . . but he'll have to get up close to tell the difference! Swimsuit is all Black Net over Nude Arnel Triacetate Stretch Jersey. Wide diamond cutouts let the REAL YOU shine through! Built-in cups. Black Net over Nude Beige.
Sizes 30 to 38.   **$11**⁹⁹

#1949   BEACH BEAUTY
Beautiful and beautifying is this sensational imported deepwired V-neck one piece swim suit. Utterly figure flattering, it is completely backless, trimmed all around with self-ruching. Black or Mandairn Orange.
Sizes 32 to 38.   **$15**⁹⁹

BE A SUMMER SIREN

SWISHABLE FRINGE

Ⓐ   **#1917   FRINGE FROLIC**
Fabulous Frederick's bikini swim suit of Arnel triacetate jersey sports swishy 3 inch fringe on the up-lift bra top and Hollywood bikini pants. Bra is underwired for maximum support. Tiny but absolutely terrific in Black or White. Sizes 30 to 36.   **$14**⁹⁹

Hollywood Model and Screen Star

Nicole Jacques

You bet I'm a Frederick's of Hollywood fan . . . because I know I can order clothes that do so much to brighten every occasion.

#1941   EVE, BABY!
Adam will see a lot of YOU in this . . . and look no further! Wear this All-Cotton checkered bikini strapless or halter-styled. Underwired bra is brief, and all-bosom! Snug-fit pants, with shirred sides. White, checked in Black, Turquoise or Pink.   **$6**⁹⁹
In sizes 32 to 38.

174

#3—4148
CUT—OUT CAPER
Here's a baby doll set that's openly irresistible! Bits of you are meant to peek through the cut—out design. The rest is sheer Nylon, and completely see—through. Black, Red or Hot Pink, with Black lace trim. One size fits all. **$9**

#3—4427 TICKLE-OO
Feathers ring around the rosy cut-out nipples! Erotica for memorable nights, in a baby doll gown of sheerest Nylon lace. An elastic band nips in the middle. Matching tiny panties. Maribou feathers: Red with Black, or All Black. Sizes Small (32), Medium (34-36), Large (38). **$10**

#1944 EXPOSE
Beautiful way to expose the most of you, for a maximum tan. This is Frederick's briefest bikini ever, in all nylon velour with tie closings — contoured to fit only the bare essentials. Have one in each color. Black, Hot Pink or Lilac. Sizes 30 to 36. **$10⁹⁹**

These fashions are designed primarily for theatrical producers and professional performers . . . though a fun-loving gal may wish to add them to her personal wardrobe.

pastie set

#4682 GLITTER GIRL
Hundreds of sequins glitter and glow on this saucy set of bosom pasties and matching G-string bikini panty. One size fits all. Gold. **$8⁹⁹**

#3—4400 SENU—SATIONS!
A show Biz approach to fun on the home front! Over-the-nipples pasties have long twitchy tassles for easy twirl. Elastic bikinis are frantically fringed, sequin-trimmed. In Nylon and Rayon: Black, with Red fringe and tassles. One size fits Small Medium and Large. Two piece set. **$9**

#4828 BACK BEAUTY
Plungiest plunge in dreamland! Bedtime Baby Doll . . . almost TOTALLY FRONTLESS . . . dives deeper than the waistline. Lavish Lace ruffles the neck and bottom. Baby-brief Bikini crotchless pants have wide front ruffles. In Black or Hot Pink, both with Black Lace trim. Small, Medium, Large. **$6⁹⁹**

#4845 THE BIG CATCH
Angling can be rewarding and you'll feel like the big catch in this all new 3 piece 100% nylon fishnet. Cute little Red bows trim bra, bikini pantie and hose. Order this angler's dream by bra size. Black only. **$10⁹⁹**

✳ **Mr. Frederick says:**

We invite inquiries for quantity purchase discounts from bona fide TV and theatrical producers, nightclub owners, foreign and domestic motion picture studios, booking agents, and independent producers. **Please be sure** to use stationery bearing **company letter-head.**

SHEER

theatricals

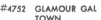

#4752 GLAMOUR GAL TOWN
Be tantalizing in this terrifically low, low cut back shorty gown of 100% sheer Nylon with lavish lace trim and bow. Matching split crotch bikinis also lace trimmed. Another Frederick's first! Black with Black Lace, Red with Black Lace. Sizes 32 to 38. **$7⁹⁹**

BRAND NEW!

C #6–1833 HOLD IT
The way to get a hold over him just might be this bikini . . . with its secret hold bra cup. Stays on with no hooks, buttons, zippers . . . just press, and presto it holds to your body with Velcro. Blue or black cotton with white dots.
Sizes: Small, medium, large. **$26**

HAVE A BEACH –
BALL

the SECRET!!!
H.B.P.
means HOLLYWOOD BEAUTY PROFILE

★ wig
★ eye lashes
★ bosom
★ waist
★ tummy
★ hips
★ calfs
★ ankles

Here's a *living* example of what H.B.P. means. Look at these two photos! . . . one, flat as a pancake . . . the other sensational, with H.B.P. She wasn't born that way . . NOBODY IS. She got help from Frederick's, with our miraculous head-to-toe Hollywood additions and subtractions! All the things that gave her that fabulous Hollywood Beauty Profile, yours for the asking, right in this catalogue! *AND YOU CAN HAVE IT TOO!* Go back and *read* every page *carefully!* Choose the items that will add where *you* need *more,* subtract where *you* need *less,* and glamorize what *you* have . . . for *your own* personal H.B.P. H.B.P. TURNS YOU ON, INSTEAD OF *UPSIDE-DOWN*
CAN YOU GUESS WHICH ONE HAS H.B.P.? COULD HE?

Mr. Frederick's says,

PROMISE HIM ANYTHING . . .

BUT GIVE HIM H.B.P.*

#7250 TAME THAT TERRY!
Wild Leopard tamed in terrific Terryl Cotton print terrycloth wraparound is great over wet bathing suits . . . to slip into after a shower. As a lounge-about sarong. Easy in . . . easy off. Animal print, bound in White. Sizes: Small. Medium and Large. **$5⁹⁹**

#7249 LAGOON LOUNGER
Wear this beauty over your suit to a quiet lagoon and you'll be in great style. This animal print trim terry wrap goes equally easily to the beach or bath. White with Animal Print Trim and Ties. Sizes: Small, Med., and Large. **$13⁹⁹**

#1961 ITALIAN RIVIERA
This smashing success bikini is imported from Italy by Frederick's just for you. The underwired cup bra top has elastic back and hooks so it can be worn halter style or strapless. Bikini bottom has elastic French cut sides. A must item for your summer of fun. Comes in multi-color print as shown. Sizes 32 to 38. **$8⁹⁹**

#2—1702 JUNGLE MUSIC
Jazz up the jungle in a one-piece animal print swimsuit. Brings out the male animal in no time. Deep V neckline has loops to tie or leave open as you dare! 100% nylon in natural leopard print. Misses sizes 8 to 16. **$26**

#2—1700 MAKE WAVES
Waves of nude-lined swirls create an exciting one-piece swim suit that makes a splash on any beach. Sweetheart neckline buttons down to the waist (mermaids unloop buttons for glowing nature look). Back plunges to waist where secret back panel holds you in firmly. Nylon and Lycra in Black or White (with nude lining). Misses sizes 8 to 16. **$26**

#2—1701 MAN BAIT
We went fishin' for the best man bait: lots of fishnet is the answer! We combined the two into a one-piece suit with a fishnet sweep to the navel and bikini bottom-look. Fishnet COMPLETELY surround you on the sides and the entire back! Built-in bra Nylon and spandex in Black or Brown. Misses sizes 8 to 16. **$28**

#4—5027 SHOWS OFF
For the gal who likes a little something under her see-through tops. This utterly transparent skin-smooth stretch bra has completely seamless cups. Hides very little . . . but what it shows off! Tantalizing with lace and chiffon fashions . . . terrific under a sweater! Nude-toned, in nylon lycra spandex. Available in Sizes: 32-36 A cups; 32-38 B and C cups. **$5 50**

#6-1866   ZIP CODE
The question is: how low to go? Giant White zipper will UNZIP all the way! Ribbed Ottoman knit swimsuit is skirted in front, ow-low backed. Molded-in bra provides great shaping. Sharp in Navy, smooth in Dark Brown Nylon doubleknit.
Misses Sizes: 32 (10), 34 (12), 36 (14), 38 (16).   **$18**

This is gonna be my Summer to blaze in the sun . . . with all that meets the naked eye!

Bernetta

#6-1894 BABY BARE
bikini. Dares, wickedly! Bares, bewitchingly! Fits to be seen with a hand knit look! Cross-over bra for a tie back and halter. Elasticized waist on bikini pants. Acrylic ribbed knit, in Moss Green or Sunny Yellow. Misses sizes Small (6 to 8), Medium (10 to 12), Large (14 to 16).   **$18**

#6-1897 ANY WOMAN CAN
find figure flattery in this 1 pc. stretch ribbed Nylon Knit! Straps convert from halter to low-tied back. Cling-close ribbing pampers every curve for a fabulous, personal fit. Red or Brown, with contrasting braided trim. Misses sizes 8 to 14.   **$18**

#5—9142 GOLDEN GIRL
Everything's gold that glitters. Every
itsy-bit of it. Gold sequins hangs it all
together. "V's" the metallic and
sequin bra. Low-belts the narrow
loincloth bikinis with sequins. In
Gold or Silver metallic, with matching
Polyester and Aluminum sequins.
One size
fits all   **$30**

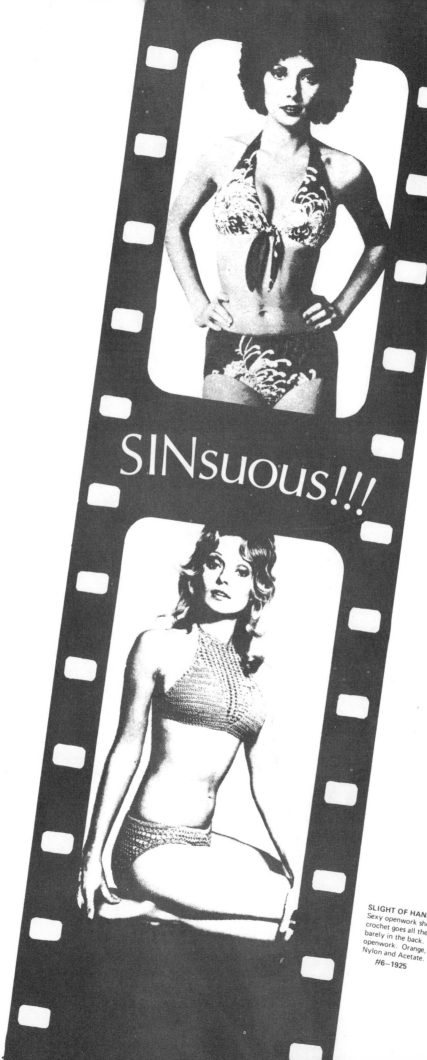

SINsuous!!!

TROPICAL PUNCH
It's a fake, that teasy tie in the bra front . . . what's the real thing is you and lotsa cleavage. Skinny semi-hiphugger pants. Tropical Lilac/Pink or Sand/Orange print. 100% Nylon. Colors Sand//Orange in sizes 7 and 9 only; or Tropical Lilac/Pink in sizes 7 to 13.
#6—1928

Was $18.00
NOW $15.88

SLIGHT OF HAND
Sexy openwork shows and tells plenty! Exclusive hand crochet goes all the way to your neck, narrows around barely in the back. Skinny back tie. Bikini panty with openwork. Orange, Powder Blue or Natural Beige Nylon and Acetate. Sm (5-7), Med (9-11), Lge (13).
#6—1925

$32.88

NO RISK . . . EVER!
TRY your Frederick's selection in the privacy of your own home, and if it isn't everything you've dreamed of, return it at once!

Mr. Frederick

BE COVERED BARELY and let the sun shine through! Wild and wonderful lace bikini has Nude insets to give you a tattoo tan he won't believe! Back-tied halter. White or Black Nylon. Lace is Nylon and Acetate. Small (5 to 7), Medium (9 to 11), Large (13). $17.88
#6—1956

HOLLYWOOD

HEART WARMERS

GORGEOUS *"Lustra Sheen"* GABARDINE *Gadabouts*

"WINNING WAYS" Suit
So feminine! New "soft look" 2-piece suit with full sleeves with slit cuffs, "Tiger-Lily" pockets. Self-belt has GOLD-colored lucky charm. FULLY LINED. Rayon Gabardine in Plum-Purple. Peacock Blue, Grey, Black. Sizes: 10 to 18.
Style No. 380—$22.98

only $22.98 EACH

"DANGEROUS CURVES"
"Flower petal" yoke of contrasting color; marvelous fit. FULLY LINED "cutaway" jacket, jewelled buttons. "Lustra-Sheen" GABARDINE in—
• Black with White Yoke
• Navy with Grey
• Autumn Wine with Grey
• Fall Green with Grey
Sizes: 10 to 20.
Style No. 384—$22.98

"TOP NEWS" Cape-Stole Suit and Matching Hat
Precious ALL-WOOL FLANNEL! Looks just like a jacket—but it's a high-style stole that you can drape any way you wish—so comfortable for gadding about. Matching skirt—wear them together or with other outfits. Sizes: 10 to 18. Glamour Grey only.
Style No. 382—$18.98
Matching Hat—Peaked brim is becoming! Sizes: Small. Med., Large. Grey.
Style No. 383—$4.98

Dressy LINED SUITS for All-Season Wear   Alluring Filmland Styles

"Entrancing" SUIT

"Swallow Tail" SUIT

Looks Lovely—Coming or going!

only $19.98

Sizes: 10 to 20.

FULLY LINED

Looks SO expensive with gorgeous black FUR-like trim. Softly draped lines ... full, full sleeves, molded bust. Rich rayon GABARDINE.
Dawn Grey, Black, Sun Gold, Sky Aqua
Style No. 276—

only $18.88

Perky double swallow-tail peplum turns eyes your way! "Butterfly" collar, dreamy fitted lines, FULLY LINED jacket. Rich sheen rayon GABARDINE.
Sizes: 10 to 20.
New Navy, Sun Gold, Black, French Grey.
Style No. 305—

GRAND VALUES

2-piece Suit-Dresses

"STEADY DATE"
Molds your figure into delicious curves! Flattering jacket has rippling fish-tail peplum, set-in belt, perky cuffs. Slim skirt. "4-Season" fine rayon suiting.
Sizes: 10 to 20.
Sun Gold, Foam Aqua, French Grey, Black.
Style No. 130
only $12.98

"HEART STEALER"
Most popular Hollywood style! New longer tunic-length jacket is SO becoming! Flowing collar, cuffs and skirt harmonize with striped jacket. Rich rayon suiting.
Sizes: 10 to 20.
Heavenly Aqua, Romantic Rose, Sun Gold, Paris Grey.
Style No. 131
only $14.98

OUR 7 STAR FEATURE...

"Glamour Queen" SUIT

only $19.98

★ Roll collar!

★ Draped bust!

★ Double row of buttons!

★ FULLY LINED!

★ Draped "pocket" detail!

Long torso jacket fits beautifully. Rich rayon sheen GABARDINE—for Four-season wear. AMAZING VALUE!

Black
Sun Gold
Sky Aqua
Dawn Grey

Sizes: 10 to 20

Style No. 320

★ Shirred hipline.

★ Slim skirt!

You've Seen it for $70

"FILM FAVORITE" Suit-Dress

2-piece style with pastel jacket and black skirt! Smart double peplum has "fish-tail" back with black scroll trim. Slim skirt. Hollywood-tailored of rayon gabardine.

Aqua, Cruise White, Rose or Glamour Grey.
All with BLACK Skirt
Sizes: 10 to 20

STYLE NO. 9   Only $11.98

$11.98

for Figure Flattery

• COPY OF A $70 CREATION

"Fashion News" SUIT

only $19.98

Coral Red, Navy Blue, Black, Dawn Grey

Style No. 321

FULLY LINED!

Newest Hollywood favorite—fully lined graceful, slit "Angel Wing" cape sleeves on a year-around suit! Molded bust, slim hipline. Gorgeous Rich-looking rayon sheen GABARDINE is wrinkle-free. Jacket FULLY LINED with rayon Satin. Sizes: 10 to 20

only $9.98

"BOLERO BELLE"—Darling two-piece bolero suit to wear day or night! Rich rayon GABARDINE with color contrast on flared collar, slit cuffs; two-tone buttons. For all-season wear! SIZES: 10 to 18, WHITE with BLACK; GREY with NAVY, GOLD with BROWN, BLACK with WHITE
STYLE NO. 79

"STORK DATE"

MATERNITY SUIT

Now—look pretty the Hollywood way while you're expecting. Adorable two-piece, cool comfortable suit of fine cotton in Navy with flower-fresh white collar, cuffs, pocket flaps. Fully adjustable skirt. Order your usual size. Sizes: 10 to 18.
Style No. 268....... $9.98

185

Glamorous "RAIN-or-SHINE" COATS

T.N.T.
Order To<u>day</u>
<u>Not</u> Tomorrow

$12.69

"TAFFETA TREASURE"
Water-Repellant Date Coat keeps you
dry—and beautiful, too! Dressy enough
for any outfit—wear it with or without
belt; full-circle skirt. Sizes: 10 to 20.
Silky TAFFETA in Grey, Black, Navy,
Purple.
Style No. 28—$12.69

GENUINE FUR!

Now! HOLLYWOOD ORIGINALS in MINK-DYED

$69.95 TAX FREE!

"FASHION STAR" COAT
MINK-dyed Coney! Luxurious,
full-cut, designed by master
furriers, exquisitely blended to
look like fabulous mink! Full
sleeves may be turned back
into cuffs; satin ascot-scarf is
detachable, gorgeous SATIN
lining is embroidered and gold-
trimmed. Sizes 10 to 20.

2 smart shades: Deep Mink
Blend (Rich Brown) or Silver-
Blue Mink Blend (Grey)
Style No. 135 . . . . only $69.95
(pictured) 38" long

Style No. 136
Full 44" length—$79.95

BOTH ABSOLUTELY TAX FREE!

"LAST WORD" SLING CAPE
Glamorous! Slip arms thru
slits, or wear casually over
shoulders—night or day! Full
cut; 25" long; satin lined. Gen-
uine Coney FUR in 3 shades—
Mink Blend (Brown); Silver
Mink Blend (Grey); Ermine
Blend (White).
Style No. 137

Sizes: 10 to 20. only $29.95

$29.95 TAX FREE!

IMPORTANT NOTICE:
A $10 deposit is required
on all C.O.D. fur orders.
Save postage and C.O.D.
fee by sending full pay-
ment with order.

Leopard Look
JACKET
Special—
only
$18⁸⁸

You'd swear it
was FUR!
Richly-patterned
fabric looks like
the real thing!
Gorgeous FULL
slit sleeves, fitted
lines . . . New!
FULLY LINED
in quilted
rayon satin.

"BACK TALK" Shorty-Coat
NEW length, NEW button-back, NEW pockets! FULLY LINED
rayon Gabardine coat that's smart enough to slip on over every-
thing you own. Back is as cute as the front! Real Red, Black,
Grey, Navy Blue. Sizes: 10 to 18.
Style No. 30—SPECIAL PRICE—$15.98

$15⁹⁸

"TWINKLE TOPPER"
Loads of sparkling, gilt nailheads glitter on the shoulders of
this divine little topper . . . back
and front. You'll catch his eye,
coming and going! Pert collar,
two slash pockets, gored "um-
brella" back. Fully lined in
rayon SATIN. Sizes: 10 to 18.
Petal Pink, Radiant Red, New
Navy, Dawn Grey, Honey Beige.
Style No. 23

only **$17⁹⁸**

Hollywood Glamour

STYLE 608

STYLE 606

STYLE 601

Velvet Trim

IMPORTANT: We ~~~ for a $10 deposit on all C.O.D. FUR order~

WE PAY $1 FOR FRIENDS' NAMES!
Send names and addresses of 10 of your friends who are NOT Frederick's customers. We will send you a $1 Friendship Certificate if they order. 1 to a customer!

STYLE 608—"DATE RIGHT" FULLY LINED SUIT
Exciting "leaf" inserts, padded hips, bound button holes, and a skin-slim skirt make this suit the most wanted date outfit of the season. Menswear Covert* Slate Blue, Green-Leaf, Glamour Grey. Sizes 10 to 18.

$22⁹⁸

STYLE 606—"CARESSABLE" FUR Cape-Stole
Smooth as mink, this ravishing dyed rabbit FUR is dressy enough for day-time or dance-time. The deep cape snuggles close to you and caresses you with its luxurious warmth. 2 pockets, tucked softly into the stole ends. White, Brown, Silver-Grey. Sizes 10 to 20.

$29⁹⁵

plus $5.99 Fed. Tax

STYLE 601—"DREAM DESIGN" VELVET-Trimmed Suit-Dress
Vivacious Velveteen collar in alluring black with lapels and buttons to match. Rayon GABARDINE. Slim 2-piece suit has dramatically draped hips and smart back interest. Black, Glamour Grey, Green. Sizes 10 to 20

$15⁹⁸

STYLE 603—"PARIS BOULEVARD"
100% WOOL yarn-dyed boucle' with simulated Persian Lamb Cavalier cuffs and becoming shawl collar. Trimly belted back; double breasted closing, 2 pockets. 33" long! Rich taffeta lining! Black, Red, Grey, Royal Blue. Sizes 8 to 16.

$39⁹⁵

(plus $1.50 Shipping)

STYLE 604—"SHOW TIME" Cape-Stole
"Persian Lamb" fabric* that will fool the experts! Exquisitely full cut with 2 pockets; satin-lined. Dressy for day or night. Jet Black. Sizes 10 to 20.

$24⁹⁵

*Rayon-and-Cotton

STYLE 609—"PARIS PASSION" Coat Sensation
Dazzling you, in this thrillingly beautiful new Wyandotte 100% WOOL suede, full length coat. "Stardust" buttons; delightfully daring slanted closing; taffeta lining! Full, full sleeves have soft folds that drape into deep cuffs. Nude-Beige, Electric Blue, Lipstick Red. Sizes 8 to 16.

$42⁹⁵

Wraps

STYLE
603

STYLE
604

STYLE
609

PLASTIC
RAIN
COAT

STYLE 607—
"CRYSTAL CLEAR" Rain-Coat
Clear "Plasti-Glow" Velon goes with
everything . . . fits over all clothing.
2 pockets, ventilated armhole, 3-way
belt; detachable hood; carrying case.
Sizes 10 to 18
$4⁴⁹

STYLE 607-B—Matching Booties
tie in bow; fit over any heel. Fit
Sizes 4 to 8½ shoe.
$2⁹⁹

CHECK THESE fashion musts
when you order from

frederick's

Frederick's, the home of famous, Glamorous Hollywood fashions.

While designing, Frederick drapes new fabric on one of his models.

#452 "DOUBLE DELIGHT
Completely Reversible 2-in-1 Coat
You'll adore its luxurious 100%
pure wool shag side—AND the
silky fur-like beauty of the
broadtail pile side, too! The
luxury you've dreamed of at a
tiny price! Deep shawl collar,
turn-back cuffs, two pockets.
Black with Gala Red;
Beige with Brown.
Sizes 8 to 16. JUST— **$34⁹⁵**

#621 "FUR FLATTERY"
Genuine Rabbit FUR cape with
stole-front of furry poodle-
cloth*. A must for dates! This
stunning glamour-wrap is perfect over daytime suits and
dresses, too! Luxurious, full
drape. Fully lined in Taffeta.
Persian Grey with Black FUR
or White with White FUR.
Sizes 10 to 20.
$27⁹⁵

#620 "MOONGLOW"
The Flattery of FUR!
This one fools the experts! You'll
be ready for a thrilling evening in
this FUR-like* luxury wrap that has
the look of fabulous Persian Lamb.
Silky Taffeta lining adds to the
luxurious effect of this once-in-a-
lifetime buy! Black; White.
Sizes 10 to 20. **$14⁹⁸**

#606 "CARESSABLE"
FUR Cape-Stole Fully lined
Make his eyes sparkle with pride
and admiration when you wear this
soft-as-mink, rich dyed rabbit
fur cape! Perfect for day or evening wear. Caressably soft. Two
pockets tucked softly into stole
ends. White, Mink Brown or
Silver-Grey.
Sizes 10 to 20. **$29⁹⁵**

FABULOUS *"Furs!"*

190

GIFT IDEAS FROM HOLLYWOOD

"STARRY EYED" Cape-Bolero
100% WOOL jersey . . . double fabric for body . . . perfect date-wrap. Wool-and-rayon fringe trim. Star-studded with loads of hand-sewn PEARLS.
Sizes: 10 to 20.
Red with Blue Trim;
Royal Blue with Red; All-White
Style No. 36
$13⁹⁸

"WESTERN STAR" Fringed Jacket in GENUINE SUEDE LEATHER! Soft as silk, beautifully fitted & trimly tailored; fringed pockets; fringed yoke back & front. Beige or Rust.
Sizes: 10 to 20. **Style No. 951.**
A real luxury for only
$29⁹⁵

GENUINE SUEDE

FOR BOYS OR GIRLS

STYLE 610—
"LITTLE DUDE"
SUEDE JACKET
For boys or girls! R... copper color fine sue... with fringed trim, b... and front. Sizes 2-4...
$15⁵⁰

STYLE 610-A. Sam...
jacket in sizes 8-10-1...
$18⁵⁰

Contest Winners!

Meet Veronica Stuecker,
No. 1 Lucky Moment contest winner from Detroit, Michigan, who spent a marvelous week at the famous Riviera Hotel at Las Vegas. She's also No. 1 glamour girl to her six small sons (ages 3 to 14) and her husband who loves her in that Frederick's look. Mrs. Stuecker wrote that *any* woman can hold her man, thanks to Frederick's fabulous Hollywood creations.

Second Prize—
Congratulations, also . . . to Jeanne Smith of Sequin, Texas, who won second prize of a beautiful lingerie wardrobe.

Third Prize—
Third prize gift certificate went to Mitchie Holcombe of West Asheville, North Carolina. Cheers to all these wonderful gals, and the Honorable Mentions, too!

Honorable Mention

Mrs. Belle B. Dixon	Miss Elizabeth V. Salvatore
Mrs. Joyce Korner	Mrs. Lennard Thomas
Mrs. Jayne Harris	Mrs. Carolyne Beverly
Mrs. A. J. Saviluoto	Mrs. Deloris Hunziker
Mrs. Valentine L. Starnes	Mrs. Ted Z. Held

Miss Dolores Goodhart

he loves you in a suit-dress

COPY of a $50 STYLE
#288

#241

#311

#334

SILK-with-rayon

LACE over
TAFFETA

#241 "IN DEMAND" 2-piece
You'll love the way this dressy acetate faille creation fits and flatters! Draped bust, pleated fishtail peplum, tapered skirt. Sizes 10 to 20. Grey, Black, Mint Green. **$15⁹⁸**

#288 "HOLLYWOOD STAR"
For beauties on a budget! Looks just like the ultra-smart original! Gored tunic-top with detachable white over-collar and hanky pocket; slim skirt. Linen-weave rayon. Navy, Mint Green, Sun-Gold. Sizes 10 to 20. **$16⁹⁸**

#329 "LACE SENSATION"
2-piece glamour creation—perfect for dates . . . dressy enough for a bride or bridesmaid! Lace over rayon & acetate Chromspun taffeta. Jacket has fitted midriff, draped bust, flared peplum. Slim skirt is back-zipped. New colors: Black over Red; Pink over Royal; Cocoa over Emerald Green. Sizes 10 to 20. Just— **$28⁹⁸**

#311 "DAY TO DATE" 2-piece
Wear it thru the day—and with your best beau at night! Silky rayon & acetate "Shantika" has a swirly peplum and smart 2-way collar; sheath skirt. Paris Grey, Lilac or New Navy. Sizes 10 to 20. **$18⁹⁸**

#334 "FASHION FAVORITE"
Slim-lined, luxurious looking, and priced SO low! Alluring fabric is SILK and rayon with a smart nubby texture. Shapely jacket has tiered hipline; the skirt is a slender sheath. Creamy Beige, Navy Blue, Melon Red. Sizes 10 to 20. Only— **$24⁹⁸**

FREDERICK'S STYLES
A HIT IN PARIS!!
Our popular Style #275 is shown here on a pretty French model, in front of famous Eiffel Tower.

Glamour Wraps

#269

WASHABLE
NYLON Fleece

#475 "SOFT TOUCH" Washable NYLON FLEECE Glamour-Wrap Ribbed miracle fabric looks and feels like wool—but it washes and dries in a flash! Kitten-soft, dressy! White, Aqua, Pink. Sizes 10 to 18. Special— **$7⁵⁰**

#269 "DATE GOING"
Frederick's own dream of a duster! Perfect dressy wrap for day or dates. Firm rayon faille with shawl collar and jewel trim on turn-back cuffs. Black, Navy, Beige. Sizes 10 to 18. SALE **$10⁹⁸**

#295 "GLAMOUR GAL"
Fabulous BUDGET FUR Cape Snowy Natural Ranch Rabbit (of United States origin) looks far more expensive! Luxurious, soft pelts; fully rayon-lined. Wear as cape or bolero. White Sizes 10 to 20. NOW— **$18⁹⁵**
*plus $1.90 Fed. Tax

192

frederick's OF HOLLYWOOD Ravishing Wraps

Glamour Coats

LET IT RAIN
Exclusive copy of European original! A favorite of the social set in France and Italy for its casual swank, and weather-wise protection. Double breasted trench coat, buckle belted, has huge pockets. So impeccably tailored you'll wear it in the sunshine as well as rain. Rayon and acetate gabardine, in White, Black or Beige. **$24⁹⁸** Sizes 10 to 20.

WEATHER VANE
New! Gadabout glamour-coat in water-repellent rayon "Gleam-Gabardine" with lustrous sheen. Full-cut, smart contour-belt has accent of soutache braid and gay sparkling rhinestones. Huge pockets and lapels. Midnite Black, Ice Blue, White Frost. **$19⁹⁸** Sizes 10 to 16.

FULLY LINED

STAR DUSTER
Cotton and rayon faille beauty features the newest mandarin type collar! Lavish cuffs on the three-quarter length sleeves and twinkly rhinestone buttons add excitement to this glamorous but practical coat. Wear anywhere, day or date time. Fully lined in rustling taffeta! Black, Turquoise, Beige. Sizes 10 to 18. **$14⁹⁸**

DAY OR DATETIME

OPENING NIGHT
Perfect to slip on over everything you own! Full cut, swingy date duster of firm, silky rayon faille with jeweled trim. Navy, Black, Beige-glow. Sizes 10 to 18. Just **$10⁹⁸**

WINTER WONDER
You'll be his hug bug in this ollegro and dynel orlon man-made fur. Can be worn as an exciting hood or cowl neck. Wrap around style with deep arm holes. Full generous sleeves and lined in Milium striped satin. Color Winter White, Pearl Grey, Cafe Au Lait. **$119⁵⁰** Sizes 8 to 16.

Same but in velvety 100% wool suede. Contrast color acetate taffeta lining. A terrific buy. Winter White, Night Black, Traffic Red, **$49⁹⁸** Sizes 7 to 15, 8 to 16.

Hollywood heart warmers..

#2280   FORGET-ME-NOT
Cuddly you in this snuggly soft-as-
fur shortie. Acrilan fibre fabric with
deep furry pile looks and feels like
luxurious fur (called "Sonata"). Cut
from an actual fur pattern to give
all the glamour of a genuine fur
jacket. Smart turned back cuffs, full
stand up lapels, 2 pockets. Richly
lined in lustrous satin finished
taffeta. A "go-everywhere" must for
your wardrobe. Honey Beige, Pearl-
Grey, Night Black. **$35.00**
Sizes 8 to 18.

#2196   AUTUMN AFFAIR
You're the most glamorous
woman of any season in this
Forstmann flannel 100% virgin
wool suit. Short jacket is all but
hidden by luxurious genuine fox
fur down to waistline. Magnificent
rhinestone clips at sides are
adjustable. Back is full above
waistband and lined in satin
milium. Black or Blue. **$119.50**
Sizes 10 to 18

#2197   MISS WONDERFUL
Miss Wonderful, elegant you in
this sensational new tunic suit.
Glamorous, genuine ranch mink
collar. Tunic features two rows
of stitching for added flattering
effect. Coat lined in Milium satin,
skirt lined half way down.
A Forstmann's woolen in swank
tunic length styling. Black
or Brown. **$119.50**
Sizes 10 to 18

194

#2536 TOP SECRET
This copy of a famous star's favorite topper
costs you only one-third the price at
Frederick's! Furry as can be, it's 90% Wool
and 10% Cashmere. Rabbit Fur collar looks
like mouton and detaches to make this a sport
jacket. The back is a triumph of Frenchy
tucking accented with bow. Stunning!
Champagne Beige, French Black,
Cinema Red. Sizes 8 to 16.   **$24⁹⁸**

#2307   TWINKLE STAR
Starring Hollywood's first love—
the hooded cocktail jacket! This one
snuggles against you in luxurious
100% wool suede, a'twinkle with
scattered bursts of jewels, pearls
and rhinestones. Face-flattering
hood may be worn as a cowl if you
wish. Fully lined in acetate taffeta.
All together a star duster you
can't be without. Black
or White.   **$34⁹⁸**
Sizes 8 to 18

195

"male tested".....

NORWEGIAN BLUE FOX!

#2106 SONIA
Elegant, exquisite Norwegian Blue Fox, dyed White... it's every girl's dream. Lovely shawl collar stole is fully Satin lined. What a perfect evening topping to wear with anything! (Plus 10% Fed. Tax.) **$75**

#2498 JUNGLE JEZEBEL
Here's one way to stalk your prey, clad like a famous film star in our jungle-like coat. Sumptuous roll collar snuggles up to your ears, double breasted, with flattering three quarter length sleeves. Luxurious Rayon Pile. Brown and Gold Jungle print. Sizes 8 to 16. **$29⁹⁹**

$10⁹⁹

#2947 THE CONTINENTAL
Travel first-class in this chic Continental summer suit. Dacron Polyester and Cotton fabric is SO wash-and-wear! Jacket has classic 3-button closing... comes with its own tuck-in checkered scarf. Slim side-zipper skirt. Pink, Blue or Beige. Junior sizes 5 to 13. **ONLY $10⁹⁹**

196

A #1—2235 MMMM-ARVELOUS
The long and the short of it! Under ankle-length coat, wear this short-as-sin matching mini in silk-soft brushed Orlon Styled down to the bare essentials . . . jewel-neck, sleeveless, and back zipper. 3'' vinyl belt matches coat. Off-White, in Junior Sizes 3 to 11. **$17**

B #1—2236 G-R-R-EAT COAT! 75
Ankle-length looks-like-leather vinyl coat wipes clean with a damp cloth. Comes and goes in all kinds of weather! Shapes in with a 3''-wide belt. Shawl collar and hem are soft-as-fur brushed Orlon Under it, wear #1—2235 dress! Brown with Off-White; Junior Sizes 3 to 11. **$45**

WONDERFUL
WRAP-UPS

C #1—2145 CAT'S MEOW!
Fancy the fun of a dress length Leopard! Frankly fake, but so luxurious! Coat is superbly styled with full sweeping lines, a convertible collar. 3-button front . . . ¾ sleeves. Rayon Acrylic pile print, fully Taffeta lined. Black and White Snow Leopard Misses Sizes 8 to 18. **$40**

D #1—2251 GET YOUR COAT!
Just for you — campus cutie . . . working gal's wonder. All weather cotton corduroy is laminated for warmth without weight! 100% water repellent. Huge 2-tone pockets are more than 12'' deep. Button trim, stand-up collar, flair back. Rayon lined. Beige trim on Camel or Brown. Misses Sizes 6 to 16. **$24**

FABULOUS FAKE
coat for a girl to go glamorous! Fake lush Reindeer fur is thickly edged with a curly Mongolian border. Such SWISH!! Wrap it and tie with leatherette belt. . . or let it hang open. Brown tones with White edging, in Cotton-backed Rayon. Misses sizes 10 to 16.
#1—7743 **$66**

GO WITHOUT FOOD
WITHOUT DRINK . . . BUT NEVER GO WITHOUT
GLAMOUR!

Flirtation Walk

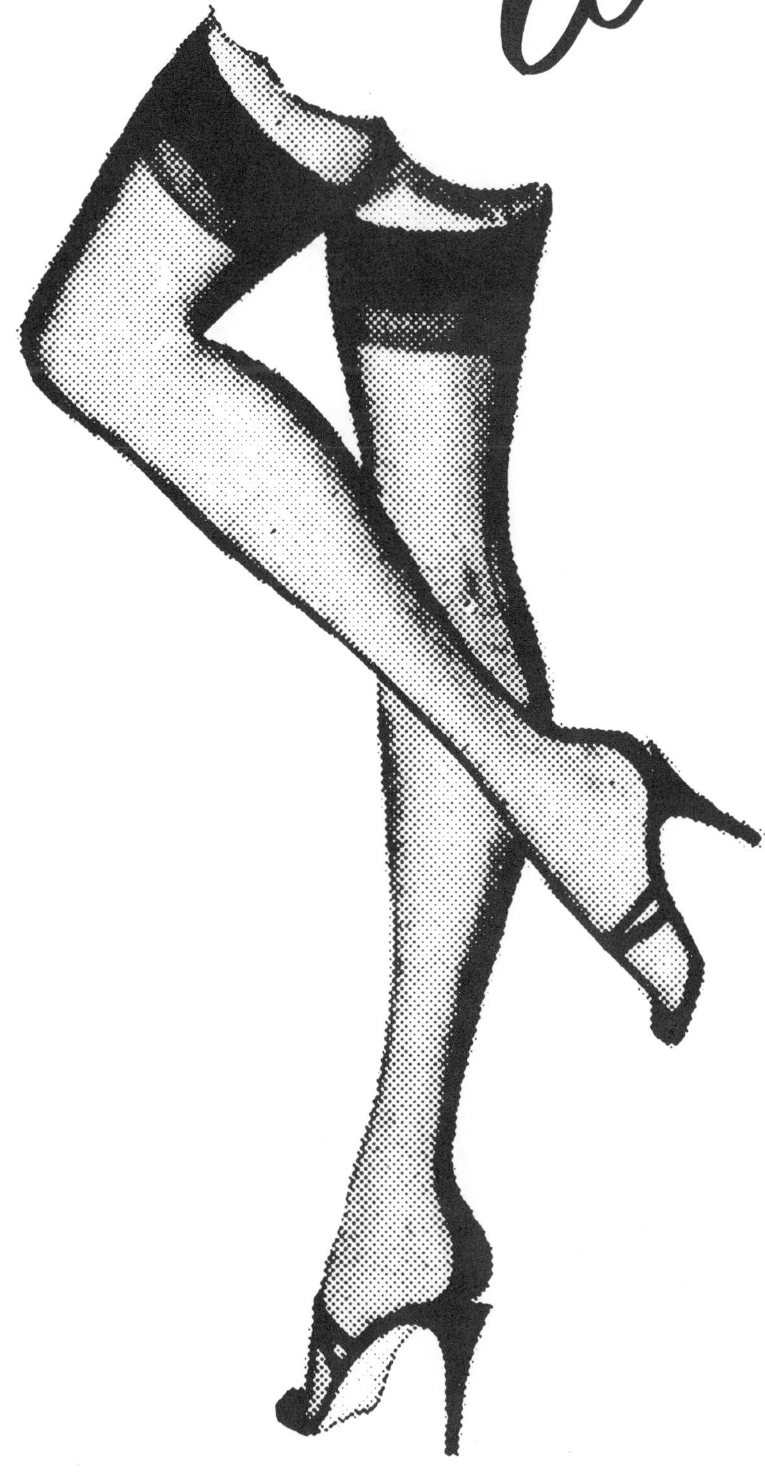

For YOU from Hollywood

GLAMOUR!

AMAZING VALUES!

EXCITING STYLES!

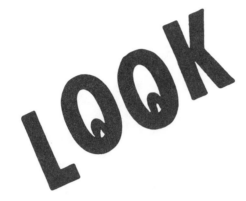 LOOK

STYLE 816—"LACE MARVEL"
Kant-run hose in SHEER
15 denier. (Guaranteed
runproof.) Black seams.
Taupe or Toast.
3 pairs **$4**⁵⁰

- 15-denier
- Super-Sheer
- Sizes: 8½, 9, 9½, 10, 10½
- Colors: Magnetic (Spicy Copper);
  Sweet Spice (Warm, deep beige);
  Moon-tide (Toast for all outfits).
  Style No. 15—

BOX of **3** pairs—
$6⁵⁰
(not sold singly)

STYLE 15—
Sheerest 66-gauge,
15 denier for
flattery. Taupe,
Copper, Beige.
3 pairs
$5⁷⁵

STYLE 915—"CUPID'S DART"
stockings to whisk you into
the world of love! Black heels,
seams, clocks. Sheer 15 denier.
Toast.
3 pairs **$4**⁶⁵

FREDERICK'S
ORIGINAL SHOES

Style No. 1006—"SARONG" Sandal
Side-draped, ankle-strap; open back;
sparkle trim. 3-inch heel.
Black or Purple Suede.... *$16⁹⁵*

Style No. 1005—"CINDERELLA" Sandal
Fabulous 4-inch heel on daring cut-out
creation with gleaming ankle-ties.
Black suede; Navy Kid Leather. *$16⁹⁵*

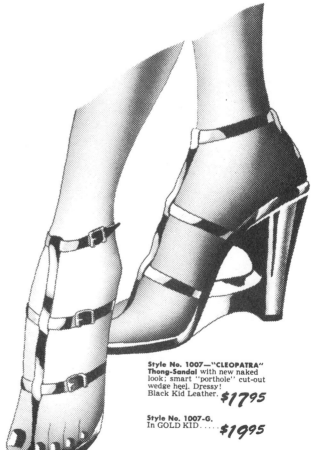

Style No. 1007—"CLEOPATRA"
Thong-Sandal with new naked
look; smart "porthole" cut-out
wedge heel. Dressy!
Black Kid Leather. *$17⁹⁵*

Style No. 1007-G.
In GOLD KID..... *$19⁹⁵*

NEW, SPARKLING CRYSTAL-CLEAR VINYLITE SHOES

"DOUBLE TREAT"
#1016 Hand tooled leather shoes combined with stylish suede. New Toast-Beige.

$17⁹⁵

#1085 "CRYSTAL CLEAR"
Dazzling Cinderella slipper in see-thru crystal Vinylite with exotic 4" clear Lucite heels, accented with stunning leaf design. Lucite bow at vamp. Truly fabulous!

$27⁹⁵

#1019—Perfect-match tooled leather and suede box bag. Beautifully lined in satin.

$12⁹⁵

CARVED LUCITE HEELS

#1082 "PEEP SHOW"
Crystal-clear vinylite combines with inky Black Suede in a smart ankle-strap sandal. Jewelled ring on V-cut vamp. Slim 4-inch heels. Neutral tones "go with" everything!

$15⁹⁵

#1083 "BUCKLE 'N' BAND"
Slim buckled band of suede trims vamp of this dress-up sling-back pump with open toe. 4-inch heels. Choose Tortoise Shell or Crystal Clear Vinylite with Black Suede.

$15⁹⁵

SPRING-O-LATOR NEWEST THING!

The magnetized hidden spring in the sole holds these stunning shoes firmly on your feet. They're a joy to wear . . . can't slip!

202

KEEP IN STEP WITH

Frederick's OF HOLLYWOOD

FOR THE NARROW FOOT!
#1051 "DOUBLE DRAMA"
Double "bracelet" straps; lattice work on exotic airy vamp. Extra-high 4-inch heels. Smart with all Frederick's clothes. Black Suede. Sizes 6½ to 8, Narrow. Sizes 5 to 9, Medium. **$15⁹⁵**

Jewel Heels

#1077 "DRAPED DRAMA"
Fashion drama afoot! New, draped vamp looks wonderful on 4-inch sky-high heel. Comfortable, stay-on Spring-O-Lator sole and sling strap back. In Black Suede or Red Calf. **$15⁹⁵**

#1075 "DATE BEAU"
Dazzle your date with gleaming jewel-encrusted, 4-inch extra-high heels! Triple stripping and bow-knot vamp; bracelet anklet. In Date Red Kid, Navy or Black Suede. **$19⁹⁵**

#1079 "TURF CLUB"
Genuine alligator ankle strap sandal! Sophisticated foot note for new fall fashions. Elastic inset at back assures comfort and fit! Extra-high, 4-inch heel. Brown Alligator. **$22⁹⁵**

#1076 "TWINKLE TOES"
Sparkling rainbow-toned glitter-cloth vamp accented with black suede. Skyscraper, 4-inch glitter cloth heel! Amazing stay-on Spring-O-Lator sole and sling strap back. **$16⁹⁵**

#1081 "SEE THROUGH"
Crystal-clear sparkling Vinylite plastic with 4-inch skyscraper clear Lucite heels. Draped vamp. Wonderful stay-on Spring-o-lator soles. Favorite of Hollywood stars! **$22⁹⁵**

#1084 "RAINBOW RIOT"
Bare-back beauty with 4-inch heels and Spring-o-lator soles that stay on when you walk or dance. Gleaming multi-color glitter cloth with Black accent. Peaked vamp. **$15⁹⁵**

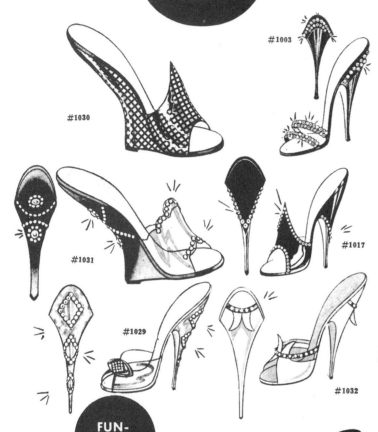

HOLLYWOOD HEELS

#1003

#1030

#1031

#1017

#1029

#1032

#1030 VAMPIRE PEAK
Flirty, Oriental metallic embossed suede with new vampire peak! Glamorous 4-inch rocket launcher wedge heels, and Spring-O-Lator soles keep them a part of you! Silver or Gold with Midnight Black. Sizes 5 to 8½B. **$24⁹⁵**

#1031 HOLLYWOOD AFOOT
Exquisite open toe, bare back, see-thru vinylite vamp! So flattering Oriental wedges, aglitter with rhinestone edging. Four-inch suede Oriental heel is Frederick's advance fashion in glamorous footwear! Jet Black only. Sizes 5 to 8½B. **$24⁹⁵**

#1029 DIAMOND HEEL
This newest open toe clear vinylite vamp is a real foot flatterer! Exquisite four-inch rocket heel in frosted lucite has diamond-shaped windows set in glittering rhinestones! You'll dazzle in these Spring-O-Lator soled darlings! Clear with White Kidsole. Sizes 5 to 8½B. **$22⁹⁵**

#1003 DAGGER DANCE
Barefoot boldness, broken only by two rows of glittering rhinestones across vamp, and at top of stiletto heel (suede). A daring flatterer with snug-to-you Spring-O-Lator sole. The very finest suede. Midnight Black only. Sizes 5 to 8½B. **$24⁹⁵**

#1017 DANGEROUS FOOTING
Danger's ahead for any man who sees you in this breathtaking foot flatterer! Spring-O-Lator cut-out toe, peaked vamp a-twinkle with rim-set rhinestones. Startling aluminum heel with rhinestones where peaked leather joins. Black patent leather. Sizes 5 to 8½B. **$24⁹⁵**

#1032 HEAVENLY DAZE
Surely heaven inspired this white kid, petal trimmed vamp. Lustrous rim set rhinestone trimmed gold band. Spring-O-Lator sole. Four-inch gold kid tower heel is exquisitely different with matching white petal trim and gold kid rhinestone band. Mystic White, Gold Trim. Sizes 5 to 8½B. **$19⁹⁵**

FUN-AFOOT

DANCING DATERS

#1073 FANCY FEET
New Riviera clog has white wood heel and platform sole. Flatters legs, adds inches to your height! Pretty button trim. Draped top in White kid or Black patent. Sizes 5 to 8½B. **$13⁹⁵**

#1024 RUN AROUND
Cute, casual clog has white straw vamp with gayest multi-color floral trim, fully leather lined for perfect comfort. Genuine imported Italian cork platform sole. Sizes 5-6-7-8B. **$13⁹⁵**

#1025 EYELASH JEWELS
Whisp of a bareback slipper in finest quality kid has eyelashed cut-out toe, individually jeweled, and huge jewels encircled with metallic embroidery setting vamp afire. Camellia White, Shell Pink. Sizes 5 to 8½B. **$17⁹⁵**

#1016 BEAU BAIT
Flirty little flared bows a-twinkle with rhinestones kiss the vamp and ankle strap of this fascinatingly styled sandal. It's sure-fire beau bait! Jet Black patent or Turquoise kid. Sizes 5 to 8½B. **$15⁹⁵**

Flats

#1071 "PRISONER OF LOVE"
Metallic kid thong sandal has eye-catching "ball and chain" trim. Elasticized instep strap, sling back, flat wedge heel. Silver or Gold. **$9.95**

#1072 "CLEOPATRA"
Kid sandal with side-swept strap over toes, criss-cross cord lacing, flat wedge heel. Comfortable! Adjustable buckle. Black, Desert White, Petal Pink. **$9.95**

#1070 "GLITTER KID"
Dressy moccasins in glove-soft kid fits just like a glove! It has a gleaming trim of metallic braid, glowing "jewels", king-size nailheads. SO comfortable! Leather heel. Black, White, Yellow. **$11.95**

#1088 "BRIDAL BLUSH"
Sling-back scuff of braided lacy Nylon net; elasticized to stay on. Frilly trim. Dazzle Red, White. Small, Medium, Large, Extra-Large. **$6.50**

#1087 "WEDDING BELLS"
Adora-bell rayon velvet leisure style has 5 golden bells and gold braid trim. Sunset Pink, Black, Blue. Small, Medium, Large, Extra-Large. **$7.50**

#1086 "GOLDEN GLAMOUR"
Elasticized gold mesh flat sandal with sling back and T-strap. Perfect for lounging. In Gold. Small, Medium, Large, Extra-Large. **$6.50**

Jewels on Your Toes

#1096 PIXIE TREASURE
Rhinestones, golden nailheads and lustrous pearls combine with silver filagree effect to ornament the pixie peak vamp of the alluring suede shoe. Fabulous ankle straps with embroidered tips. Tie in front. Black only. Sizes 5 to 8½B **$24.95**

#1033 MINK MOC
Soft-as-a-glove calf moccasins to wear indoors or outdoors, for lounging or play! Leather is shirred at sides and topped with real mink fur for that exotic touch! Champagne, Pink or Turquoise. Sizes 5-6-7-8B **$9.95**

Frederick of Hollywood checks the Italian and French Style Scene to bring **YOU** the latest in Continental Fashion Influences as well as his internationally famous Star Styled Hollywood Creations.

HOLLYWOOD

Italian Influence Bare Backs

#1146   PEARL ILLUSION
Pretty feet? Well, **show them** — in this barefoot glamorizer of finest clear Vinyl and Jet Black Patent Leather. Special attraction is gigantic pearl on pert criss-cross bow. A brand new backless beauty for more heel-appeal (on **high** 4-inchers). Spring-O-Lator sole for can't-slip comfort. **$19.95**
Sizes 5 to 8½B

#1147   FANDANGO!
A showtime sandle with one — two — **three** lustful-luster vamp straps to glamourize your foot with barely-there bareness. Perfect fit **plus** comfort is assured by Elasticized upper strap. Just right for "best dress" occasions. High 4-inch heel. Navy Calf or Raven Black Patent. **$17.95**
Sizes 5 to 8½B

#1148   LOVER'S KNOT
Love that shoe! Highest tapered heel Spring-O-Lator features clever "Lover's Knot" that trims two vamp strips at center. Shockingly bare, bare back and open toe flattery for all occasions. Enticing colors — Pink Lustre Calf, Champagne Lustre Calf, or Black Patent Leather. **$17.95**
Sizes 5 to 8½B

#1062   DEVIL DANCE
Criss-cross bands and daring new peaked effect make spring shoe news. 4-inch extra-high heels. Patented Spring-O-Lator sole to hold them on. A Filmland style! Black Patent*, Deep Purple Suede, White Calf. **$16.95**
Sizes 5 to 8½B

#1141   ANKLE ACCENT
Tri-tone tricks for your trim ankles demand **complete attention!** Clever little strap winds attractively around ankle and hides in instep. 4-inch heels. Smart three color combination goes with anything — and anywhere! Red, White & Blue or Pearl Grey, White & Black. **$17.95**
Sizes 5 to 8½B

#1140   FANFARE
Attention-getting Spring-O-Lator with flirty scalloped fan-tail at tip of open toe vamp and top of backless heel, bejewelled with six glistening White pearls. Delicate, but mighty, 5-inch heel. Truly "different." Cool Black Patent Leather or White Pearlized Broadtail. **$24.95**
Sizes 5 to 8½B

#1142   MANTILLA
Bareback beauty that fairly reeks of sophistication! Finest Imported Lace vamp and ultra-high tapered peak winks wickedly with rim-set rhinestone patterned in lavish clusters. 4-inch heels are cigarette slim. Vampire Black or Pearl White. **$24.95**
5 to 8½B

#1143   PARISIAN PACE
Sassy Spring-O-Lator sets the pace by combining Italian closed toe elegance and bareback boldness in chic finest Black Patent Leather. Spotlight-sparkle nailheads form double row to highlight vamp edge. Taper-slim 4-inch heel. **$22.95**
Sizes 5 to 8½B

#1144
Same exquisite vamp and heel styling as #1143 but without trim. In lustrous Black Patent only. **$19.95**
Sizes 5 to 8½B

Budget Beauties

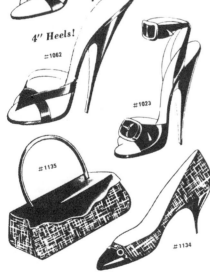

#1023   PARIS WALK
Twin metallic buckles on double strap sandals. 4-inch skysweeper heels. In Regal Red or Navy Calf; Jet Black Suede. **$16.95**
Sizes 5 to 8½B

#1134   ON THE TOWN
"Smooth" is the word for this sophisticated Spectator Pump of smart Silk Shantung and finest quality Leather. Tiniest buckle trims front vamp. A day-time or date-time must. Terrific with matching bag. Terrifically low price! Blue with Navy, Tan with Brown or Grey with Black. **$13.95**
Sizes 5 to 8½B

#1135   MATCH MATE
Bag of same smart Leather with Shantung trim on sides. Matches #1134. Expertly styled for arm accessory glamour. Finest Faille lining. A top item for quality and style. Blue with Navy, Tan with Brown or Grey with Black. Including Fed. Tax **$12.95**

#1066   CLASSY LASSIE
Exquisite D'Orsay vamp dress shoe copied from high priced Italian original. Suede toe contrasts with superb quality kid. Four inch sky-line heel. A strictly "class" costume accessory for those who insist on high styling. Black with Black or Red Suede Vamp. **$12.95**
Sizes 5 to 8½B

#1130   TOE TEASE
Such naughty feet! Showing off in front of everyone in their voguish "picture window" pumps! Crystal clear Vinyl vamp sets off slender strips of Leather across toes. Flattering slim-jim heel — unbelievably low price. Midnight Black Patent Leather, White Leather. **$13.95**
Sizes 5 to 8½B

FILM FOOTAGE

Sunset Strip Exclusive Sensations

#1003 DAGGER DANCE
Barefoot boldness, broken only by two rows of glittering rhinestones across vamp, and at top of stiletto heel (suede). A daring flatterer with snug-to-you Spring-O-Lator sole. The very finest suede. Midnight Black only.
Sizes 5 to 8½B   **$24⁹⁵**

#1120 FOOT LOOSE
Flirtatious Spring-O-Later in wonderfully **new** Polka-dot Printed Crepe. The perfect shoe for the very popular Polka-dot fashions this Spring. Excitingly draped vamp with an alluring little hat-shaped center-piece. Fabulous four-inch tower heel and bare back. White Crepe with Black Dot, or Navy with White Dot.
Sizes 5 to 8½B   **$19⁹⁵**

4" Heels!

#1114 STRAP VAMP
An open toe flirt with the newest look in foot glamour! Slim ankle strap as well as a fabulous cascade of slender straps across vamp are studded with glittering nail heads. Four-inch Jordan heel. In Gun Metal Patent with Silver Nail Heads, or Black Suede with Gold Nail Heads.   **$19⁹⁵**
Sizes 5 to 8½B

#1107 CURTAIN CALL
Witchery in gorgeous suede, aglow with sparkling rhinestones in exciting "curtain call" pattern at heel, side ankle straps and cut-out toe! High flown heel is beautifully tapered and a full 4½ inches high. An exotically different creation exquisite in every detail. Nothing like it anywhere. Black suede.
Sizes 5 to 8½B   **$24⁹⁵**

#1097 RHINESTONE RAVE
Stunning, foot-gripping Spring-O-Lator has crystal clear vinyl vamp adorned with luxurious black suede peak a-fire with dozens of glittering rim-set rhinestones — dramatically repeated on high-sweep, pointed back 4-inch slimmest of Hollywood heels. Black Suede and Vinyl.   **$24⁹⁵**
Sizes 5 to 8½B

#1129 TORREADOR TOES
Twinkle, twinkle little feet! Who can help but notice you — all aglow in jeweled splendor! Wear them anywhere, they're always "right." Temptin' colors and temptin' price, too. Ice Pink or Beige Leather, Black Patent Leather.
Sizes 5 to 8½B   Only   **$8⁹⁵**

Full Fashioned

#19 MIDNIGHT MESH
Full fashioned, open-worked sheer mesh lace in dramatic pattern for leg-lovely glamour. No heel reinforcement to deface alluring slim ankle lines. Perfect with backless shoes. Fully reinforced heel to toe, does not show. Midnight Black or Peach Beige.
Sizes 8½ to 11.
Box of **3** pairs   **$5⁹⁵**

Famed Helanca Stretch-Nylon with stay-up elastic tops

#6 SHEER MAGIC
New Helanca nylons fit like second skin and need no garters! Taupe. One foot size fits all. Short, medium, long.
3 pairs only   **$5⁰⁰**

The Leopard Look . . .

#1109 JUNGLE MAD
You're mad, mad, maddeningly provocative in these slinky charmers. All purry-soft leopard-printed fur, purr-fectly fabulous on your foot. Perky peaked vamp. 4-inch high dagger heel. Can't slip Spring-O-Lator sole.   **$19⁹⁵**
Sizes 5 to 8½B.

Play Footsies

#1136 CAT'S WHISKERS
Flirty little ceramic pussy-cat shows off its whiskers on vamp of clear Vinyl and Imported Natural Straw. Winking Nailheads trim lustrous Wooden clog sole. Purr-fect for so-casual glamour!
5 to 8½B   **$14⁹⁵**

#1061 LEOPARD-KINS
Adorable flattie of genuine leopard skin adds spice to any of your costumes. Superb quality leather sole. For making friends, these are purr-fectly alluring — and so-o-o flattering!   **$13⁹⁵**
Sizes 5 to 8½B

#1025 EYELASH JEWELS
Wisp of a bareback slipper in finest quality kid has eyelash cut-out toe, individually jeweled and huge jewels encircled with metallic embroidery setting vamp afire. Camellia White, Shell Pink   **$17⁹⁵**
Sizes 5 to 8½B

#1139 5-INCH CATWALK
A Frederick's First — And a New High! Pussy-footin' higher than ever before in these 5-inch sky-high heels! Softest Baby Leopard Print Fur from toe to heel will make you purr with delight! It's your 1957 hi-way to exciting glamour!   **$27⁹⁵**
Sizes 5 to 8½B

#1145
Same wonderful sky-high glamour as #1139 in snappy, lustrous Black Patent Leather.   **$22⁹⁵**
Sizes 5 to 8½B

5 INCH HEELS for the FIRST TIME!

For a More Glamorous You!

#1156   ROSANNA
Copy of $100.00 shoe.
A Rose Rhapsody plucked right from the garden and artfully styled into the most sensational slipper of this season or any season. Slimmest 5-inch heel is fashioned after the stem of a flower and garnished with two green leaves and one lush rose of stiffened Silk that actually cannot be told from real. Open toed vamp displays lover's knot in center. Choose either Midnight Black Suede with Passion Pink Rose or Stardust Red Kid with Ruby Red Rose. Why not both?
Sizes 5 to 8½ B.   **$29⁹⁵**

HOLLYWOOD *Footlights*

#18 ANKLE ALLURE
Lavish lace diamond design to dramatize your ankle and instep. Sheerest of nylon full fashioned witchery to grace your calf in this most unusual hosiery styling. Pale peach shade blends with natural flesh tones to let ankle lace stand out. Peach beige. Sizes 8½-11.
Box of **3** pairs $5⁹⁵

#18

#6   #19

Famed Helanca Stretch-Nylon with stay-up elastic tops

#6 SHEER MAGIC
New Helanca nylons fit like second skin and need no garters! Taupe. One foot size fits all. Short, medium, long.
3 pairs only $5⁰⁰

#19 MIDNIGHT MESH
Full fashioned, open-worked sheer mesh lace in dramatic pattern for leg-lovely glamour. No heel reinforcement to deface alluring slim ankle lines. Perfect with backless shoes. Fully reinforced heel to toe, does not show. Midnight Black or Peach Beige. Sizes 8½ to 11.
Box of **3** pairs $5⁹⁵

#1039 PLAY SUEDE
Your wardrobe won't be complete without this exquisite little flat sandal in suede that hugs you with bare-footed comfort. Petite bows and a daisy add an irresistible feminine flourish. Suede insole. Turquoise, Pink or Black. Sizes 5 to 8½B $4⁵⁰

#1059 HAREM SANDAL
Exotic Persia influenced this glamorous little satin slipper! Artificial flower on turn-up toe matches turn down cuff. Leather sole with so comfortable foam rubber inner sole. Perfect for hostessing at home.
Black only
Sizes 5 to 8½B $5⁹⁵

#1039

Play Glamour

#1059

#1124 GLAMOUR COMBO—Straight to you from Hollywood—a new two-tone clog with wooden heel and platform sole. The party-going favorite of famous stars! Sleek open-toe vamp sweeps upward to flirting peak trimmed with two gigantic rhinestones on a metal bracket. Huge nail heads add glamorous accent. Black Patent Leather with White Kid, or Black Suede with Gold Kid.
Sizes 5 to 8½ B only $14⁹⁵

#1126 STAR OF INDIA
Your foot will look **half** its size in this exotic East Indian-type creation with the new vanishing wedge platform sole! Black Suede vamp with Oriental peak is lavishly decorated with gleaming metallic braid and simulated pearls, imported from India. Black suede is dramatic contrast to natural high luster wooden platform. Cushioned inner-sole.
Sizes 5 to 8½B $18⁹⁵

#1127 TWINKLE TOES
Glamorous, lavishly brocaded Paisley patterned woven fabric in exquisite metallic cloth. Exotic jeweled button and tassel trim at tip of exciting peaked vamp trimmed in Silver Kid. Exotic disappearing Wedgie platform in gorgeous high lustre wood makes this a sheer dream in footwear.
Sizes 5 to 8½B $18⁹⁵

Teas'n and

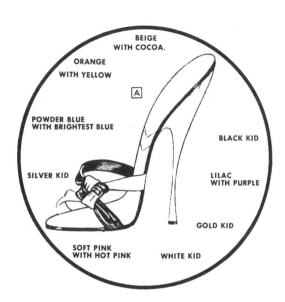

BEIGE WITH COCOA.

ORANGE WITH YELLOW

[A]

POWDER BLUE WITH BRIGHTEST BLUE

BLACK KID

SILVER KID

LILAC WITH PURPLE

GOLD KID

SOFT PINK WITH HOT PINK

WHITE KID

[A] #1147 RAINBOW KID
Here, at last, is the wispy spring-o-lator of your dreams. Rainbow colors them pastel, for sunny-season perfection. Flatter your feet in softest kid bands of two-tone magic, such light leather bands that hardly feel as though they're on! Sizes 4 to 10 Med. (Including half sizes.) **$19⁹⁹**

#1105 PANDORA'S PRIZE
Find the treasure . . . at Frederick's! Your favorite demi-Dorsay pump, restyled on its famous almost 5" heel, teaming up Black Frosted Calf with matching Crepe collar, Grey Frosted Calf with matching Crepe collar or dramatic Antique Green Calf with Green Crepe collar. Sizes 4 to 10, Medium. **$19⁹⁹**

#1042 SWISHY SHOE
Just watch that fringe swish and sway! They'll ask you "Where did they come from," and you'll tell them they're from Frederick's . . . in delightful Peau de Soie on almost 5" heel with flirty buttons and inches of flowing fringe. In Black only. Sizes 4 to 10 med. **$22⁹⁹**

ultra HiGH heels!

WHY 5 INCH HEELS ?

• they're downright flirty!

• they're whistle bait . . . attention getters

• they flatter your legs, improve your posture,

• they're all handmade, with selected lasts

#1145 FATAL FOOTSTEP
The sky's the limit in this glamourous pump with "almost 5"" heels. Goes any place with any dress, flatters your foot, round toe adds an extra measure of svelte sophistication to your outfit. Black Patent Leather. White Lustre Calf. Sizes 4 to 10 Medium. **$19⁹⁹**

210

Pleas'n!
new _HIGH_ in fabulous footwear!

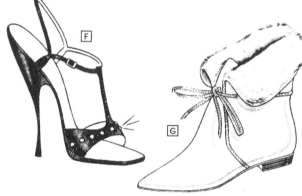

A **#1168 SILK STILTS**
Dance in them . . . prance in them . . . stand tippy-toe! Frederick's own Spring-O-Lators never let go! 5" heels raise you tall as a queen. These hand-turned beauties of regal Black silk are set ablaze with massive rhinestone buckles. Sizes 4 to 10 Medium. (Half sizes included) **$22⁹⁹**

B **#1171 CINDERELLA**
Catch a fella in Frederick's own hand-styled . . . hand-lasted . . . Glitter Cloth Spring-O-Lators! It's a hard shoe to miss, even on a crowded floor. Amazing 5" heel holds vamp miraculously close. Black, Gold or Silver Glitter Cloth. Sizes 4 to 10 Medium. (Including half sizes) **$19⁹⁹**

C **#1178 WIZARD WEDGE**
Behold the case of the disappearing heel! Cut-out in a way that's mystic and magical, it glitters to draw every eye. In Gold Monaco Cloth with Gold Kid vamp, Gold glitter heel . . . in Black Silk with Black Glitter heel. Sizes 4 to 10 Medium. (Including half sizes) **$19⁹⁹**

D **#1172 HIGH HATTIES**
Step happily ever after in Frederick's fabulous stitched Step-O-Lator! Stunning in Black Calf with Dark Gray stitching . . . in Gray Patent with Gray Suede . . . in White Brocade to be dyed-to-match. All with an almost 5" heel! Sizes 4 to 10 Medium. (Half sizes included) **$19⁹⁹**

E **#1169 SCANDAL SANDAL**
Wicked and wordly cling-close Spring-O-Lators rise on almost 5" heels. Flatter your feet . . . your legs . . . your walk! In rich Black Suede with small Black nail heads . . . in Golden Topaz Luster Calf with nailheads of brazen Gold. Sizes 4 to 10 Medium. (Including half sizes) **$19⁹⁹**

F **#1170 "T" TERRIFIC**
T-Straps with a difference! Teetery heels almost top 5" . . . vamp straps glitter with rhinestones and nailheads. Comfortable, too! In Black Silk or Gold Kid, they're fittin' for imprintin' at Grauman's Chinese Theater. Sizes 4 to 10 Medium. (Including half sizes) **$19⁹⁹**

G **#1180 WEATHER-BEATERS**
You're in from the ski slopes . . . lounging by the fire. Baby, it's cold outside! But snuggle your toes in these like-furlined booties . . . everything's warm and toastie! Lining is a nylon shearling wool. Cuffed boots come in White or Black Kid. Sizes 4 to 10 Medium. **$10⁹⁹**

H **#1175 BEAUTIFUL BOUNDERS**
Who wouldn't love these charming heels that lace-for-fun in the very best colors? Black Calf pumps have heels and back counters laced in Red Kid through Gold eyelets. Taupe Brown Calf laces Black through Gold. Top-All heels are nearly 5"! Sizes 4 to 10 Medium (Including half sizes) **$19⁹⁹**

J **#1120 BIG WHEEL**
Get into the swing of the big fashion! The feline favorite, the high boot with the collar cuff that can be turned up or down. Glamourous almost 4" heel. Great for all sport affairs. Gold Monaco Cloth, Black or Bone Calf. Sizes 4 to 10 Medium. (Including half sizes) **$19⁹⁹**

K **#1179 PUSS 'N BOOTS**
Dare to be catty! Rile your opposition with these mad-cat booties. Little-bitty heel . . . high-riding cuffs . . . ankle-slim lacings! Absolutely fantastic with your dressy capris, your lurex loungewear. In genuine Gold or Silver Kid. Sizes 4 to 10 Medium. **$14⁹⁹**

L **#1183 KICKAPOOS**
Your best foot's always forward in these high-rising booties. Newest fashion for casual wear . . . so great with pants and knee-skirts . . . you'll wear the cuffs turned up or down. Front laces. In soft supple leather: Black, Red, Olive-Green or Tan. Sizes 4 to 10 Medium. **$10⁹⁹**

M **#1181 KNEE-DEEPS**
Knee-high specials for that way-out look! Believe it or not, these boots originated in Paris! Pull them over tucked-in levis . . . try them with leotards or pipestem pants. Flat leather heels give miles of comfort. Black Kid. Sizes 5 to 10 Medium. **$12⁹⁹**

#6103 LEOPARD LURE
Live dangerously! Stalk your Tiger in these alluring Leopard-print Wooden Clogs. They'll cling to your foot . . . rise sky-high on guaranteed unbreakable heels. Toeless vamp is Leopard print on softest Calfskin. Sizes 4 to 10 Medium (half sizes included). **$22**

#6095 RECORD DATE
At your next record date, tap your toes in these striking multicolored striped fabric mules. Large bon-bon bow sets off almost 4 inch high heel. Sizes 4 to 10M including half sizes. **$20**

#8—6142 FALL FLATTERERS
Leg-watchers fancy these hard-to-find ankle straps . . . set on almost 5" heels! Choose from a variety of fabrics and colors: Black Silk, White dyeable Silk, fine Black Leather, Bone Ceylon Kid, Gold or Silver Kid. Take your pick . . . and step high in glamour! Sizes 4 to 10 Medium (including half-sizes). **$24**

#8—1146 GLAMOUR
Every woman's a living doll when she steps from her boudoir in these darling, flirtatious slippers. Marvelous Marabou on the vamp to lend allure to your evenings. Black on GENUINE SILVER KID; or White or Candy Pink on GENUINE GOLD KID. Sizes 4 to 10 Medium. (No half sizes) **$15**

#8—6161 MYSTIQUES
Behold the vanishing wedges with heels that disappear like magic! Perfectly balanced to fit and flatter, they'll intrigue every man, show off every leg. In black, white, bone or gold kidskin. Sizes 4 to 10 Medium (including half sizes) **$24**

#6101 MYSTIC WEDGE
Vamp him with your lovely leggy look! Behold these vanishing wedges with heels that disappear like magic! Perfectly balanced to fit and flatter, they'll cling to your foot draw every eye! Black, White or Bone Kidskin; glamorous Genuine 24K Gold Kid. Sizes 4 to 10 Medium (including half sizes). **$21**

#6125 HI-STYLE WEDGE
Have yourself a fashion fling and step into a pair of these foot flattering hi-style wedges! Daring new cut out disappearing wedge in Gold Alligator Leather, Silver Alligator Leather, White Tracey Kid and Black Tracey Kid. Animal Print. Sizes 4 to 8½ medium (½ sizes included). **$22**

#8—6196 CHAIN GANG
Chain him to your side . . . in this naughty, nifty ankle boot with its own chain! Fast-moving flat heels for real go-go girls! Black, bone, Sizes 5 to 10 Medium. (including half sizes) **$22**

#6136 THONG OF SPRING
You'll be his song in these beautiful gay song of spring thongs on mid high heel, soft kid skin with large buckle to set your legs apart from the crowd. In Black, White, Hot Pink, Shannon Green and Genuine Gold kid. Sizes 4 to 9 medium. No ½ sizes. **$15**

#8—6195 WOW!
They're the boots of the season mid-heel curved. White leather. Black, Bone, Antique Brown/Brown suede all over Silver or Gold Kid. Sizes 4-10 Medium. (including half sizes) **$30**

#8—6178 CUTIE-BOOTIE
Want to be the cutest thing on two feet? Wear these glamour boots and make the excitement scene! Close as skin in glittery gold or silver stretch vinyl Mid heel. Sizes 5 to 10 Medium. (including half sizes) **$25**

HOLLYWOOD APPROVED SCREEN STYLE

212

#1040 CUDDLE PUFF
See-thru Glass Slipper of crystal clear Lucite has 4" heel and puffs of fluffy Maribou. Exquisite mate for lingerie. Candy Pink. Sizes 4 to 9. **$17.99**

M #1037 FURRY FLUFF
Mmmmmm, to the boudoir with these darlings . . . in slippery satin with flirty Maribou on the vamp, to lend sparkle to your evenings! In Black, Ermine White or Powder Pink, with matching Maribou. Sizes 4 to 10 Med. (No half sizes.) **$8.99**

FROM HOLLYWOOD U.S.A. TO YOU!

HOLLYWOOD CALIF.

#1031 COWBOY KID
This boot for the girl who really likes to ride high in style . . . and comfort! The softy boot with the cowboy heel . . . that wears so well with those casuals Black Kid or Bone. Sizes 5 to 10 Med **$8.99**

#9068 COSSACK LOUNGE BOOTS
Relax in style as only the Europeans know how. Comfy knee-high boots are quilted satin for luxury and warmth, zip from heel to top in back and have a hot pink lining. Worn by the popular set in Hollywood. Black only. Size 5, 6, 7, 8, 9, or 10 **$11.99**

#1030 PIRATES PASSION
Shiver me timbers Doll . . . you'll be dancing in dazzling Gold and Silver . . . cause this Lurex boot is passion plus . . . Gold is trimmed with Gold Kid, Silver Lurex trimmed with Silver Kid. Sizes 5 to 10 Med. **$8.99**

#8—6150 CONQUISTADOR
You'll need a whip to beat them off, with these knee-high, 3 inch heel boots with the smoldering look in Catataan Black or Madrid White Calf, Silver or Gold Kid. Sizes 4 to 10 Medium (half sizes included). **$30**

#1029 TALE TEMPTRESS
You can bet your boot you'll get loads of compliments in your tall quilted boots of Gold Mylar . . . Fancy and fun for those casual moments. Gold only. Sizes 5 to 10 Med. **$6.99**

#1028 BEAUTY BOOTIES
Baby . . . you're kicking high in fashion with this Demi boot . . . trimmed with the elegance of Leopard. The boots the thing . . . this season in Black, Gold, Bone. Sizes 5 to 10 Med. **$6.99**

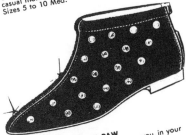

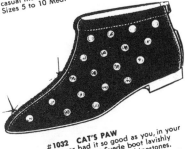

#8—6244 PANTSUIT PAIR
Add the perfect match to your pantsuits: our heavy almost 3" mid-heel boots with the "bulky" look. Ideal for wide-leg pants. Try them in Tan or White Leather; Black Patent; Genuine Gold or Silver with Hobnail design. Sizes 4 to 10, incl. ½ sizes. **$24**

#8—6241 STRAP-STYLE
Strap yourself into our harness pant boot with fashion's stacked mid heel. Perfect ankle high boots for all your harlow or wide-leg pants. Black ; Shetland Brown leather; White or bone leather. Sizes 4 to 10, incl. half sizes. **$25**

#1032 CAT'S PAW
A cat's never had it so good as you, in your lush and soft Velvet Suede boot lavishly embellished with sparkling Rhinestones. In Black only. Sizes 5 to 10 Med. **$9.99**

LOS ANGELES CALIFORNIA

213

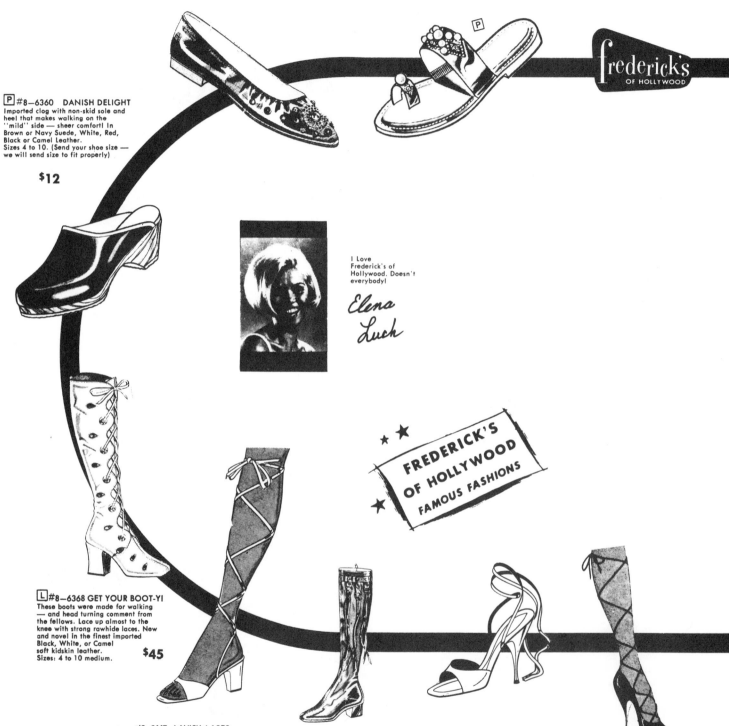

N #1339 GLITTERBUG
The new softee flat that glitters as it goes . . . in soft glove leather. Full air-foam cushioned inner sole. Multi-colored stones on vamp. Black, Bone or White 6.99 Genuine Gold kid.
Sizes 5 to 10. **$7⁹⁹**

P #1050 JEWELED GEMS . . .
Fit for a princess . . . these Frederick's classics, lavishly done with Rhinestones and pearls . . . You'll live regally in these high styled flat toe Gold or Black thongs . . . Sizes S, M, L. **$7⁹⁹**

P #8—6360 DANISH DELIGHT
Imported clog with non-skid sole and heel that makes walking on the ''mild'' side — sheer comfort! In Brown or Navy Suede, White, Red, Black or Camel Leather.
Sizes 4 to 10. (Send your shoe size — we will send size to fit properly)
$12

I Love Frederick's of Hollywood. Doesn't everybody!

Elena Luch

★ ★ **FREDERICK'S OF HOLLYWOOD FAMOUS FASHIONS** ★

L #8—6368 GET YOUR BOOT-Y!
These boots were made for walking — and head turning comment from the fellows. Lace up almost to the knee with strong rawhide laces. New and novel in the finest imported Black, White, or Camel soft kidskin leather.
Sizes: 4 to 10 medium. **$45**

#8—6447 LAVISH LACES
Long, long slim straps that can climb and wrap a sexy pattern on your legs, while you stand on flattering high-heel sandals. In Black leather, White, Gold or Silver kid. Sizes 4 to 10 medium, half sizes included. **$19**

#8—6384 TOUGH CHIC
For gals who like to get moving! Keep the action lively in these low-heeled boots with bold brass rings and free swingin' fringes. Groovey all the way from rough-it pants to with-it dress-ups. In Black or Brown suede, White kidskin, or genuine 24k. Gold or Silver kidskin. Medium widths, Sizes 4 to 10, ½ Sizes included. **$30**

#8—6446 ENTWINED
The heighth of allure are sporty sandals on chunky heels that get his eyes involved in your legs, too! Twine 'em up to your knees and tie a wicked bow there. In Black leather, White, Gold or Silver kid. Sizes 4 to 10 medium, including half sizes. **$19**

#8—6467 SEXY "ANN"
WOW! Wait until you're wearing these Man-Catchers! With the famous 5" heel. Silk laces that tie up for a long leggy look. Wear them with Colored or Black panty hose. In Black Suede with Black silk laces. Sizes 5 to 9 **$37**

frederick's OF HOLLYWOOD

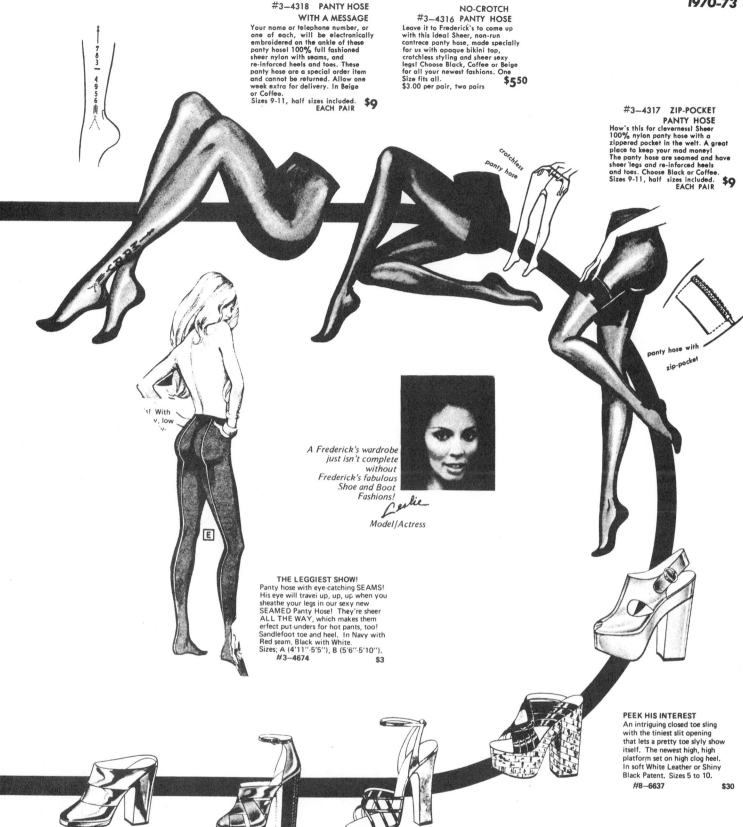

#3–4318 PANTY HOSE WITH A MESSAGE

Your name or telephone number, or one of each, will be electronically embroidered on the ankle of these panty hose! 100% full fashioned sheer nylon with seams, and re-inforced heels and toes. These panty hose are a special order item and cannot be returned. Allow one week extra for delivery. In Beige or Coffee.
Sizes 9-11, half sizes included. **$9**
EACH PAIR

NO-CROTCH #3–4316 PANTY HOSE

Leave it to Frederick's to come up with this ideal Sheer, non-run cantrece panty hose, made specially for us with opaque bikini top, crotchless styling and sheer sexy legs! Choose Black, Coffee or Beige for all your newest fashions. One Size fits all.
$3.00 per pair, two pairs **$5**50

#3—4317 ZIP-POCKET PANTY HOSE

How's this for cleverness! Sheer 100% nylon panty hose with a zippered pocket in the welt. A great place to keep your mad money! The panty hose are seamed and have sheer legs and re-inforced heels and toes. Choose Black or Coffee.
Sizes 9-11, half sizes included. **$9**
EACH PAIR

crochless panty hose

panty hose with zip-pocket

A Frederick's wardrobe just isn't complete without Frederick's fabulous Shoe and Boot Fashions!
Leslie
Model/Actress

THE LEGGIEST SHOW!

Panty hose with eye-catching SEAMS! His eye will travel up, up, up when you sheathe your legs in our sexy new SEAMED Panty Hose! They're sheer ALL THE WAY, which makes them perfect put-unders for hot pants, too! Sandlefoot toe and heel. In Navy with Red seam, Black with White.
Sizes; A (4'11"-5'5"), B (5'6"-5'10").
#3–4674 $3

PEEK HIS INTEREST

An intriguing closed toe sling with the tiniest slit opening that lets a pretty toe slyly show itself. The newest high, high platform set on high clog heel. In soft White Leather or Shiny Black Patent. Sizes 5 to 10.
#8–6637 $30

ROMAN ROAMERS

The best of Italian styling with Frederick's interpreting! Step in this high-riding, close-toe platformer and you'll know you put your best feet forward for fun! Almost 4-inch heel. Thin platform. White or Black patent, or Genuine gold leather.
Sizes 4 to 10 (no 9½).
#8-6640 $30

STACKED!

Almost 5" stacked heel with ¼" platform sets off braided front, closed back, sexy ankle strap.
In Camel Leather. Sizes 4 to 10.
#8–6554 $37

#8–6496 BIRDCAGE

An almost 5" blocky heel! NEW! Never before—the fabulous height of a 5" heel with the new clubby look. And the ever so popular ankle strap with delicate strippings over the foot. Comes in Black Suede, Hot Pink, Violet, Sand or Colico Yellow Suede, or White Pearlized Leather.
Sizes 4 to 10. $40

A REAL CORKER

The newest--the NOW-est! The highest cork platform and heel: Thin straps of patent leather are brought together with a diamond patterned buckle to set the whole "look" off. Deliciously light and comfortable. Patents in White with Bone, Bone with White, Black with Bone. Genuine Gold Kid with Bone.
Sizes 4 to 10 (no 9½).
#8–6642 $30

215

BEDROOM **E**YES

"ENTICING" Gown
Sheer as a cobweb,
lace-trimmed, ador-
able ruffled—and slit to
there! Sizes: 32 to 40.
Black-Beauty or Pink with
Black.
Style No. 724 $11⁹⁸

"BLACK BEAUTY" Sheer Gown
Stunning halter neck, molded
bust, and hip insets of
"see-through" lace. Rayon
sheer Ninon in Black, White.
Sizes: 32 to 40.
Style No. 118-A $7⁹⁸

"DREAM QUEEN" GOWN
Plunging neck, alluring
lines, lavish lace trim.
Sizes: 32 to 38.
Bridal White or Ice Blue
Rayon SATIN; Rayon
Crepe in Naughty Black.
Style No. 133
Special Price
only $5⁹⁸

"HONEYMOON" NEGLIGEE
Flowing sleeves, femin-
ine lines, and gorgeous
lace trim! Matches gown
perfectly.
Sizes: 32 to 38.
"Flower Petal" Rayon
SATIN in Bridal White,
Ice Blue. Rayon Crepe in
Naughty Black.
Style No. 132 $12⁹⁸
only

"JULIET" Nighty
Paris creation of sheerest 100%
NYLON with Nylon lace trim.
Naughty-Black or Flesh-Pink.
Sizes: 32 to 38.
Style No. 711 $13⁹⁸

218

"HAREM NIGHTS" GLAMOUR—JAMAS

- Two-Piece!
with DARING BARE MIDRIFF

only $8⁹⁸

EXCLUSIVE FREDERICK'S CREATION!

Look exotic, seductive while sleeping or lounging!

Gleaming rayon satin with bell sleeves and flowing trouser legs of sheerest ninon*. Sizes 32 to 40. Black or White.
Style No. 116

HOLLYWOOD'S ANSWER to How "BARE" Can LINGERIE Get?

"Naughty Nightie"

Daring, adorable short nightgown that hugs every curve, flatters your pretty legs—makes Him swoon! Made of filmy 100% NYLON Tricot with sheer yoke and trim of lacy NYLON net. Sizes: 32 to 40. White, Pink, Bridal Blue.
Style No. 131—SALE PRICE

$6⁸⁸

Frederick's Original "TV" JAMAS

"TELEVISION" Pyjamas
Be a glamorous hostess in rayon SATIN lounging pyjamas! Embroidered trim. slit trousers. Sizes: 32 to 40. White Jacket with Black Trousers; All-Black.
Style No. 119 — only **$14.98**

"GOLD RUSH"
T.V.—Jamas with boned bra-top and slit flared peplum of GOLD-striped faille*; full trousers of solid color faille*. Wide GOLD belt. Cherry-Wine, Black, Peacock Blue (All with Gold Trim).
Style No. 712 **$17.98**

GOLD TRIM

"COVER GIRL"
Lounge in crisp faille* with full trousers, boned bra-top, rhinestone-trim on velvet choker and on wide sash.
$15.98
Ruby Red, Black.
Style No. 701

"Spanish Accent"

"NIGHT OWL"
Skirt-like trousers of SATIN* with FRENCH LACE halter top (fits like a dream!) Black with Black Lace over Nude-look lining.
Style No. 713 **$17.98**

There's a Rush for **24 KARAT GOLD**

SATIN!

"HULA - LA" BRA-JAMAS
Daring 2-piece SATIN* bra and slit trousers.
(Elastic hip-band holds them in place.)
BLACK only. Bust sizes: 32 to 40.

Style No. 710

$9.98

1950-51

"MAD ABOUT PLAID"
Dynamite! It looks sweet
but fits like a dream to
show your curves for "After
Dark" entertaining. Zipper
closing. Black or Royal
Blue Faille* top with PLAID
TAFFETA* swirl-skirt.
Sizes: 10 to 18.
Style No. 703—
SALE PRICE—$10.98

NEW! "Slave Girl" $11.98

"SLAVE GIRL"
Glama-Jamas
2-piece bare midriff style
of sexy Satin-and-Sheer.*
Full trousers swing from
fitted hipband; naughty
jacket! Sizes: 10 to 18.
All-Black; Nude-Pink with
Black.
Style No. 700—$11.98

NEW! Home-Loving FASHIONS

PICADOR PYJAMAS

Hollywood adores this
2-piece outfit! Blouse
has full sleeves, scroll
trim of 24-KARAT
GOLD, molded bust.
Exotic short trousers tie
below the knee, have
separate sash. Designed
to bring out curves in
gleaming runproof
dress-weight rayon
jersey. Wear them for
lounging, on the street,
too—and the blouse may
be worn with skirts!
Sizes: 10 to 18.
Red or Black.
Style 87—

$16.98

"TEMPTATION"
Another DARING "Oo-La-La" creation with a
French Flavor. Plunge neck, slit skirt negligee is
scalloped to accent its curvey lines. Rich SATIN*
with sheer and lace trim. Sizes: 32 to 40. Black or
Nude-Pink with Black.
Style No. 705—$15.98

$15.98

PASSION FASHIONS

**STYLE 765—"GLAMOUR-ALL"
QUILTED TV LOUNGER**
Newest mid-calf length one-piece
creation for lounging, TV
or cozy at-home entertaining.
Stunning QUILTED Acetate
Taffeta, with long zipper,
elasticized waist, corded belt.
(Collar and cuffs faced in plaid).
Black, Red, Kelly Green.
Sizes 10 to 18
$6.98

**STYLE 716—"SHEER
DYNAMITE"**
100% NYLON
Filmy brief beauty of rich
Nylon tricot with sheer yoke,
puff sleeves and front of
PERMANENT PLEATS.
Black, Rose, Ice Blue,
Gold-Glow.   *$8*98

**STYLE 762—"SECOND SKIN"
SATIN NEGLIGEE**
Worn by a top Hollywood star!
Slips on or off in seconds . . .
may be worn as gown or robe.
BLACK Crepe-back
Rayon Satin.   *$8*98
Sizes 32 to 40

**STYLE 751—"BLOOMA-
JAMAS"—NAUGHTY
NYLON SLEEPERS**
Short, sweet, cute as can be
to show a gal's pretty legs.
Hi-lo neck, lace trim, shirred
elastic waist. White or Black,
in 100% NYLON tricot.
Sizes 32 to 40   *$8*98

After Dark

It's quilted!

STYLE 775—"COURTING TIME"
SMART DATE-JAMAS
Picture a quiet evening at home . . . the hostess a vision of allure and charm in enticing, exotic lounging pyjamas. Boned, strapless bodice; full flared trousers . . . look like a skirt. Matching fringed sash can also be worn to cover shoulders. Rayon faille. Black, Lime, Red.
Sizes 10 to 18

$15⁹⁸

STYLE 766—"SILVER SIREN"
Stunning zippered housecoat in new silver-tone Oriental print on fine "Bermuda Crepe"*. Silver cord pipes collar, cuffs, lapels. Swirling, full skirt. Coral-Red, Peacock Blue.
Sizes 12 to 20.

$12⁷⁹

STYLE 760—"BREAKFAST for TWO"
QUILTED COFFEE-COAT
Adorable dress-length housecoat in QUILTED Rayon "Angel Crepe". Plunge neck, 2 cuffed pockets, set-in belt for a tiny waist. Bust-curving, figure-hugging, divinely full! Red, Blue Heaven, Gold.
Sizes 10 to 18

$12⁹⁸

"HEART THROB"
Sheer Nighty
Alluring bib-top of heart-shaped FRENCH LACE with just YOU beneath! Flowing, lace-edged slit skirt of sheerest rayon.
Bust sizes: 32 to 40.
All-Black or Flesh-Pink with Black.

STYLE 756—"DREAM KISSES"
PERMANENTLY PLEATED!
100% NYLON dream-gown that will make sleeping a pleasure! Molded bust, lace insets on swirling skirt. Looks like expensive French lingerie. Gold, Blue, Black.
Sizes 32 to 40

$15⁹⁸

DAZZLING IN RED!!

#805 "NAUGHTY NUDE"
100% NYLON
Startling 2-piece Nylon dream gown with Nylon lace halter-bra top. (Adjusts with velvet cord! Favorite of Hollywood's top glamour queens! Filmy full skirt flows from hip-hugging lace band. Boudoir Black or Flame Red. Sizes 32 to 40.

$11⁹⁸

#806 "MIDNIGHT MADNESS"
100% NYLON
Who could sleep in such a gorgeous draped French nightie! Sheer as stardust, lovingly draped with lace to mold your bust. Sides slit down to waist. Daring bare midriff. Sheer full skirt with flirty flounce. Black or Scarlet Flame. Sizes 32 to 40.

$10⁹⁸

#809 "READY AND WILLING"
100% NYLON Negligee
Exciting stocking sheer NYLON negligee glorifies every girl's figure. Alluring FRENCH LACE follows each curve! The last word in allure and glamour! Full, flowing skirt has daring slit! Rippling sleeves. Ideal gift! Black Magic, or Flame Red.
Sizes 32 to 40.

$17⁹⁸

#803 "SATIN SENSATION"
ZIPPER HOUSECOAT
Look like a dream in the most stunning Satin* creation Frederick himself could find to glamourize you! Poured-in fit from the luxuriously quilted yoke to the swirling quilted hem! Yards and yards of Satin add to its shimmering beauty. Boudoir Black, Flame Red or Electric Blue.   Sizes 10 to 18.

$13⁹⁸

#815 "MIDNIGHT SUPPER"
Stunning Lounging Threesome
Fully lined quilted cape-stole, smart blouse PLUS slim, tapered slacks . . . all of rich "Glamour Crepe"*. Exotic for at home entertaining, lounging or TV. Perfect for cozy huddles on those cool evenings. Stunning color combinations. Lime or Red (both with Black trousers and trim). Sizes 10 to 18.

$19⁹⁸

FREDERICK is FAMOUS

PERMANENTLY PLEATED SHEER NYLON

"MISS TARZAN"
Two-Piece Leopard Print Shorty Gown and "Baby Pants" Jungle allure in carefree combed cotton plisse that needs no ironing. The gown has ruffled trim and bow on one shoulder. Tiny bloomers to match. 2-way elasticized scoop neck. Leopard print. Sizes 32 to 38. **$5.98**

HOLLYWOOD'S FAVORITE TERRIFIC TWOSOMES — TWO-PIECE SHORTY SETS

"GIFT SENSATION"
Permanent Pleats, Back and Front Every Inch is Fabulous Nylon! Men! Here's a real buy in one of the most glamorous gowns we've ever offered at this price! It's sheer, lace-trimmed and has curve-molded pleated yoke, whirling pleated skirt. Pink, Black, Riot Red. Sizes 32 to 40. **$8.88**

"SLEEPY TIME" Set
Hollywood nightshirt in striped cotton is extra brief. Add bikini pants for lounging. Red & White; Blue and White. Sizes 32 to 38. **$6.98**

"ARABIAN NIGHTS"
Alluring New Camera-Jamas Frederick's exclusive design in Nylon with billowing 15 denier (stocking sheer) slit trousers PLUS bust-hugging, bow-tied bare midriff top. Perfect costume for camera fans—real Hollywood pin-up glamour. Sizes 32 to 38. All-Black or Red with Black. Amazing at only— **$12.98**

for GLAMOUROUS LINGERIE!!

"DELICIOUS"
Look pretty for that breakfast date in a princess-line housecoat! Print criskay cotton has raised "3-D" look. Long zipper closing; hanky pocket. Real buy! Turquoise Blue, Navy, Orange. Sizes 10 to 18. **$7⁹⁸**

"DREAMLAND"
100% NYLON SHORTY
You'll blush when you see how short this thrilling cloud-sheer Nylon gown really is! Ruffled net trims yoke, puff sleeves and frilly hem. Perky tie accents demure slit neckline. Black, Bridal Blue or Red. **$8⁹⁸**
Sizes 32 to 38.

"HEART APPEAL"
2-piece Nylon Glamour Gown
40 denier Nylon jersey forms a curvaceous Bikini sleep-suit with contrasting heart trim. Sheer 15 denier Nylon overskirt ties at waist, and is perfect for lounging or pin-up posing. It's heart-trimmed, too. Black or Real Red with contrast trim. **$12⁹⁸**
Sizes 32 to 38.

"SISSY SHIRT" Sheer
Nylon shorty gown with lace yoke and perky collar. Full skirt, yoke back. Pink, Baby Blue, White. Sizes 32 to 38. **$7⁹⁸**

#1015

#1015 CUDDLE PUFF
Same as style #1014, but with softest puffs of luxurious Maribou as glamorous boudoir mates to fur trimmed lingerie. Ermine White, Seal Black, Lipstick Red. Sizes 5-6-7-8B. **$14⁹⁵**

#1014 CINDERELLA
Your Prince Charming will be sure to love you in this see-thru "Glass Slipper" of crystal clear lucite with glamorous nylon ruffled vamp. A sheer dream! Panther Black or Sultry Pink. Sizes 5-6-7-8 B. **$14⁹⁵**

#1014

227

#764 GEISHA TWIN
Exquisite nylon jersey kimona matches #763, even to huge hand painted dragon on back. Full Oriental sleeves. Tantalizing slits in skirt. Same colors and sizes as #763. **$15⁹⁸**

#763 GEISHA GLAMOUR
Curve clinging nylon jersey gown has real hand-painted dragon above bust! Diamond inset at midriff and shirring spell bosom beauty. Deep V coming and going. Teakwood Black, Flame Red. Sizes 32 to 38. **$8⁹⁸**

#964 FLIRTY FUR
Real MARIBOU fur trims hem of this glamour shortie gown set! Wear ruffled elasticized neck on or off. Matching sheer nylon Bikini panty. Midnight Black or Fire Red. Sizes 32 to 38. **$10⁹⁸**

#974 DREAM WORLD
Dreamy gown for dreamy nights! Nylon sheer has deep plunge neckline lavish with lace that cascades all the way down front. Daringly shired bust and tempting little bows between. Full skirt is a vision of permanent pleats. Shell Pink, Sky Blue, Frost White. Sizes 32 to 40. **$8⁹⁸**

#975 DREAM WALTZ
Sensational waltz length gown as sheer as a whisper! On or off-the-shoulder neck has alluring scoop frosted with scalloped nylon lace. Inset midriff clings, then flares into open-front skirt revealing rows and rows of lace beneath. Luxurious tone on tone nylon sheer. Ice Blue over Pink. Pink over White. Sizes 32 to 40. **$10⁹⁸**

#890 TINY TWOSOME
Nylon Gown and Panty Set. A whirl of permanent pleats! Lavish lace trim; brief bikini matching panties. Black only. Sizes 32 to 38. **$9⁹⁸**

#973 BOUDOIR BRIEF
Copy of a French Original! Seductive tone on tone nylon tricot sheer nightgown in shortie style, bewitchingly trimmed in miles of self-ruching. Bow tied peter pan collar, appliqued rhinestone trim. Matching panties with ruching around legs. Charcoal over Pink, Lilac over Pink, Red over White. Sizes 10 to 18. **$9⁹⁸**

#955 GLAMOUR SLEEP
From a star's wardrobe. In shimmering rayon and acetate satin— the *new*, exotic, halter-neck gown, cut very low both front and back. Elastic midriff shirring hugs like a second skin! Ruffles at neck cascade to ties between bust. Buttoned in back at waist. Midnight Black, Lipstick Red. Sizes 32 to 40. **$8⁹⁸**

#964

MARIBOU FUR TRIM #974

#975

Boudoir Heart Throbs!

#955

#973

2-PIECE

#890

228

Dramatic

"BABY DRESS" Shorties

#909 "BRIDAL GLOW" Nylon Honeymoon Creation! Sheerest of sheer Nylon shorty gown has ruffled lace bust and lavish lace trim on the full skirt. Skirt is slit to elasticized waist to display matching Bikini pants. Double lace Halter straps add glamour. Blue with White lace; Red with Black; or All-Black. Sizes 32 to 38. **$10⁹⁸**

#873 "LOVE MATCH" Nylon Short Gown & Matching Panties Brief, sheer gown is star-studded with dazzling rhinestones. Airy net yoke; ruffled trim. Pocket-size panties to match. Black or Blue-Belle. Cute gift! Sizes 32 to 38. **$11⁹⁸**

#889 "PRETTY BABY" Twosome Permanently Pleated Nylon Gown and Matching Panties. Nighty has lacy yoke and hemline; elasticized scoop neck. Tiny lace-edged pants are a perfect match. Lovely gift! Red, Black, Blue Mist. Sizes 32 to 38. Only— **$8⁹⁸**

for brides

#710 "BREAKFAST DATE"
Look like a pampered darling in this quilted cotton challis dotted peignoir! Yoke-back; extra-full cut; perky pockets and bow at neck. Red or Blue dots on White. Sizes 10 to 18. **$10⁹⁸**

#710

#711

QUILTED NYLON

#711 "BRIDE'S BOUQUET"
QUILTED posy-print Nylon crepe dress-length housecoat has 2 pockets, zipper-front. Rosebud print on pastels. Sizes 10 to 18. **$14⁹⁸**

GLAMOROUS LINGERIE . . .
is one of Frederick's specialties. If you're a bride-to-be . . . if you're already married . . . or still hoping . . . you'll be thrilled with these styles!

HEADING FOR A WEDDING

#922

#731 $12.95

SATIN

#712

QUILTED

#709

EVERY INCH QUILTED!

#922 "FEMALE ANIMAL"
40 denier Nylon jersey wraps and ties to embrace a pretty shape! Exotic leopard print. One shoulder is bared for drama. Sizes 32 to 38. **$14⁹⁸**

#731 "COME CLOSER"
QUILTED acetate Taffeta New Dress-Length Coffee Coat
Exciting wraparound, full-cut skirt; big, peaked pocket; huge gold buttons. Flared revers on the plunging neckline. Looks so pretty when lounging or having coffee-for-two. Shocking Rose, Paris Blue, Lime-Green. Sizes 10 to 18. Sale— **$12⁹⁵**

#712 "HONEYMOON HOTEL"
Negligee. Draped and shaped to hug every curve! Glistening embossed acetate Satin. Shirred bust, snug midriff, tiny waist. Flattering! Bridal Blue, Candy Pink. Sizes 10 to 20. Just— **$14⁹⁸**

#709 "LEISURE LOVE"
Real value! Housecoat in quilted washable Bemberg rayon crepe. 27" front zipper; full-cut sweeping skirt. Peacock Blue, Gold, Raspberry. Sizes 10 to 18. **$13⁹⁸**

1955

**TWO-PIECE
SENSATION**

#2700 OPEN HOUSE
Fabulous new rayon satin hostess gown has open side-slash from bust to hem, secured only with ties at waist! Gorgeous nylon sheer flouncing at bust cuff, hem and low back. Slimmest of shoestring shoulder ties. A captivating hostess robe, unlike anything you'll see. Black, Red. Sizes 32 to 40. **$12⁹⁸**

#744 "HOLLYWOOD LOUNGER"
Slit-Skirt Negligee and Slacks
Hollywood stars have chosen it for their exotic wardrobes—now Frederick brings it to you. An unusual lounging costume to make strong men drool! Slashed-skirt tunic-length negligee over slim, tapered slacks. Black with Red pants or All-Black. Sizes 10 to 18. **$16⁹⁸**

#2700

"You're a Dream Waking!"

#720

#743

#891 "HEART INTEREST"
Filmy Nylon dream-gown with full floating skirt, cut-out midriff and two lace hearts at bustline. Twin ties of velvet form halter. Sizes 32 to 38. Red or Midnight Black. **$12⁹⁸**

#743 "FATAL CHARM"
Sheer rayon Georgette Negligee Full, floating butterfly sleeves are SO graceful! Alluring drape in every flattering inch! Gift inspiration, too! Black or Pink. Sizes: Short, Medium or Tall. It's just— **$13⁹⁸**

#720 "FILMLAND"
FREE Embroidered First Name Gleaming, clinging Nylon jersey wraps, ties and drapes to mold the body. First name embroidered free on collar. (No C.O.D.'s) Gold-glow, Black, Red. Sizes 10 to 20. Special— **$14⁹⁸**

231

5^{99}

5^{99}
PERMANENTLY
PLEATED

8^{99}

HAREM
PAJAMA!

A **#4332   HAREM SCAREM**
A provocative harem pajama covered
with sheerest of Nylon, to give you
new exotic appeal . . . lacy top;
Arabian night-inspired balloon trousers
have panties built right in!
Red or Black.
Sizes 32 to 38. 5^{99}

B **#3961   SHEER DELICES**
Pretty pleats run all around to flatter your
curves. Nylon jersey clings dramatically.
Plunge neck, elasticized waist, sheath
styling add allure.
Vampire Red or Black.
Sizes 32 to 38. 5^{99}

C **#4273   JULIA**
A gown that conjures up enchanted fables,
torrid Roman nites . . . anything less
wouldn't do it justice! In sheer, sheer
1-layer Nylon, sleeveless to reveal your
lovely arms . . . Black, Red or Blue. 8^{99}
Sizes 32 to 38.

Sheer Sensations

#4402   BOUDOIR BABY
In the bedroom or playing hostess, be
darling . . . in this Cotton Cordana full
length robe. Zip in and out for a quick
change. Picture-pretty in
Blue or Red. Sizes 10 to 20. 9^{99}

#4583   TEMPTING
maribou and sheer nylon two-piece
pajama. Marabou circles the ankles
and the neckline of this appealing
sleeveless shortie top. Sizes
32 to 38. Black or red. 12^{99}

SATIN

MARIBOU
TRIM!

#4542 ANGEL FACE
The "Blonde Bombshell" herself created this look! You, too, can be dynamite, poured into our full-length
Acetate-Satin nightdress. Scooped-out
front and back stay up with the frailest
spaghetti straps. Knee-high side slits.
Midnight Black, Powder Blue
or Pale Pink. Sizes 8 to 16. **$12⁹⁹**

#4510 CAT'S MEOW
A bit of whimsy for the boudoir. Sheer,
Nylon baby-doll, with bikini pants,
screen-printed with a saucy kitten—
then trimmed with a fluff of maribou.
Pink, White, or Aqua.
Sizes Small, Medium,
and Large. **$6⁹⁹**

TOPLESS
BABY DOLL!

$6⁹⁹

#4557 FREDERICK'S FUN
It would be Frederick's...naturally...
and you'll love this...naturally. Two
piece Baby doll for those who dare...
Can be worn nude top with aid of spaghetti strap...or above bustline...and
it's lace trimmed for fun.
Black, Red. Sizes 32 to 38. **$8⁹⁹**

#4636 CUT IT OUT!
Fascinating double cut-out waltz-length
gown. Apart from its open bodice, it's
really quite demure! Modest jewel neck
...full drape...little dip in back. But
then...those cut-up cut-outs! Sheer
Nylon, Lace edged. **Black**
or Red. Sizes 32 to 38. **$6⁹⁹**

It wouldn't be Christmas if my stocking weren't filled with exciting things from Frederick's.

Marilyn Manning Hollywood Actress

SHEER

#3—4912   HEY! LOOKEE!
Low plunged back and front is flounced with Lace. NEW zipper closing starts front and center, runs down, under, and up the back. Legs are cut up high like a French bikini. All Nylon, in Black, Lilac or Red. Sizes Small, Medium, Large.   **$8**

#4784   SHEIK'S CHOICE
These wild harem PJ's have halter bra of sheer nylon trimmed with lace which matches split leg harem pants. Black lace G-string pantie is attached to low, low cut harem pants. Colors   Hot Pink/Black, Black/Black. Sizes S-M-L.   **$6⁹⁹**

#4855   3 LITTLE ZIPPERS
Want to find that different gift? Here it is, the newest 2 piece harem pajamas any where! Sheer 100% nylon hip hugger pants fit snugly at ankles, have front zipper halter neck bra, has 2 zippers. Black or Pink. Sizes: Small, Med., Large.   **$8⁹⁹**

#4456   BUNNY-HUGGER
Wrap yourself in bunny soft luxury of this cuddly acetate and nylon fleece. Favorite waltz length robe has easy wrap tie and wide lapel collar, ¾ roll up sleeves. Red, Blue or Gold in sizes 8 to 16.   **$12⁹⁹**

zip zip-zip
2 pc. set

zip closing
front to back

deep plunge

WILD LIFE

from
Frederick's Pet Shop!

#2-7575   LEAPIN' ANIMAL
Get the jump on flattery! Jump into
this fabulous fake fur   and
watch him jump to attention!
Has a front zipper and wrap belt
for close fit. Legs are slit. Animal
Print in acrylic, face fabric with
all cotton backing for shape keeping.
Misses Sizes 8 to 16.
Junior sizes 7 to 15.   **$24**

#3933   PINK ELEPHANTS
Whee! Gay little pink elephants frolic with
twinkling rhinestone eyes on cloud-sheer
Nylon baby doll and bikini. Rayon satin bows
Black, Aqua, Red.
Sizes 32 to 38.   **$3⁹⁹**

$7⁹⁹  D

#4362   DOLL HOUSE
Make yours Maribou! Luxury fluff trim
tops bustline and back of chic baby doll
pajamas. Wide ribbon ties add demure
touch to racy Nylon bikini and top. Daring
Black, Hot Red or Wonder White.
Sizes 32 to 36.   **$7⁹⁹**

SIN-SATIONAL

zipper →

3-4377   NIGHT OFF
More fun than sleeping in the nude!
Sheerest sleep suit of 15 denier
Nylon unzips down and around from
front waist to back. Wholly access
ible! Cut outs bare the breasts.
Lilac or Red, with Black lace trim.
Small (32), Medium
(34 36), Large (38)   **$9**

235

BE BEAUTIFULLY, BARELY BED-READY!

CHINA DOLL

Be **MOOD** right for love in a Mandarin gown that sets a wicked night scene. Long Nylon nightie is slit up the front, is practically bare-backless Mandarin collar clasps the neck . . . lets a wide cleavage show below. Sexy in Royal Blue or Black. Bust sizes 32 to 38.   WAS $13.00

D #3–4742   **NOW $11.05**

EYE OPENER

Every man's a voyeur at heart! So encourage his peeking in this baby doll that's open all down the front. Bare-backed halter cups the busts in lace-over-Nylon. Matching Bikini panties beneath. Precious in Pink, Black or French Blue with White, or devilish in all Black. Bust sizes 32 to 38.   WAS $12.00

C #3–4740   **NOW $10.20**

CUNNING CAFTAN

Two piece Caftan set slits daringly up the front, V's low at the neck. Lace trim frames a lovely view of you. Nylon. In Sable Gold with Black Lace, Royal Blue with Beige Lace and Black with Beige Lace. In sizes, Small, Medium and Large.

E #3–4023 $15

HAREM HONEYS

A P.J. set that's bound to get you the number one spot in **his HIS** harem. Top ties at neck, opens then ties again under the bust. Pull on pants have elastic waist, ankles... and under-panties built in. In 100% Nylon Tricot. Purple, Coral or Yellow-Gold. Sizes 32 to 38.

F #3–4905 $17

#3–4459 DELICIOUS!

An elegant way to spend the night! Full-circle gown of pursest Nylon is cut with a slashed V-neckline, clever up-darts to point out bust flattery. Swirls wide and alluring, in delicious shades of Strawberry, Green, or Turquoise. Small (32), Medium (34-36), and Large (38).

$13

#3–4413 LOW TO SHOW

A plunge neck to end all plunges! Night gown V.s wide open to way below the waistline. Shows off a lot of a girl's best features. In White or Hot Pink Nylon Tricot, strikingly edged with Black. Small (32) Medium (34-36); and Large (38).

$12

PASSION

236

TURN HIM ON WITH AN
ANIMAL ACT!

sheer

#3—4017 SIMPLY SHEER
For dreamy star-lit nights charm him in our simply sheer nylon gown with scoop neckline. You can wrap it around close to your body and adjust the Empire waistline to you. Marvelous in Black or Lilac and White. Sizes Small 32, Medium 34 to 36, Large 38. **$9**

SHOW PIECE
A long gown designed to delight! Nylon-sheer in front where the show is! Opaque in back! Plunge V-neck gathers at the waist with a jeweled band. Too exciting for lights out! Black or Pink Nylon tricot. Small, Medium, Large.
#3—4021   **$12**

SMOCK TOP
sweet sleeper flatters and fondles the breasts! Off-the-shoulder sleeves have skinny spaghetti straps. Mint Green, Deep Blue or Hot Pink full-length Nylon tricot. Small, Medium, Large.
#3—4830   **$8**

GO NATIVE
Brings out the explorer in every man! Deep V-plunge slink has a halter neck with straps that crisscross over a bare back. Elasticized waist-line for easy on and off. In animal print as shown. Bust sizes 32 to 38.
#3—4643   **$12**

FASHIONS

"I want to be glumorous for HIM, too . . . . . . that's why I shop Frederick's for my loungewear."

Mary
MODEL

"Scarfanet"
IT'S NEW !

Holds hair in place, hides curlers and pin curls . . . may be worn dozens of ways! Perfect after swim, shower or home permanent. Glamorous enough to wear with your prettiest dresses! Rayon crepe in Black, Red, Blue, or Multi-color STRIPES. **Style No. 115 — ONLY** $1⁹⁵

"Hollywood Sparkle"

It's A Scarf—It's A Hat— **DRAPE IT A DOZEN WAYS!** Glamorous velvet halo with flowing attached scarf of gleaming metallic jersey— to wear with your dressiest clothes or simplest suit. Black or Snowflake White. (Fits all heads!)

SALE PRICE

only $2⁴⁹

Style No. 37

#27 "HOLDING HANDS"
Nylon over Elastic Mesh
Extra-long, glamorous gloves for evening and pin-up posing. Exotic diamond pattern for a peek-a-boo effect. Daring, unusual gift every gal will be thrilled with. Black only. One size fits all hands. Special— $2⁹⁵

GENUINE FUR

"Luxury Look" Muff and Hat Set only $6⁹⁸ **TAX INCLUDED**

Fluffy little bonnet-band to sit on your curls . . . adorable matching muff—both in real FUR! Black, Brown, Angel White, Grey. Style No. 35 —

"Caballero" SPORT SHIRTS

$5.98 EACH

Style No. 20

Style No. 21

Fine tailoring, twin pockets, long roll collar, as worn by Hollywood stars! Sizes:
Small—14", 14½" collar;
Medium—15" & 15½";
Large—16" & 16½";
Extra-Large—17" & 17½".

Style No. 20—Washable Rayon Fuji Prints with Blue, Red, Green Backgrounds. $5.98

Style No. 21—Woven, checked DAN RIVER gingham in bold multi-color checks. $5.98

TWO FINE FABRICS !

FREE CHEF CAP

#1403 HOT LIPS
Startle your friends in this shirt with bright red lipstick prints twining their way across the bosom and coming to abrupt halt at collar, just beneath your right ear! Washable Rayon Crepe. Short sleeves, Italian collar. White or Silver Grey.
Sizes S-M-L-XL.
$8.95

#1431 LORD AND MASTER
Real crazy (and real practical) Hollywood chef's outfit for mix-masters and stew artists. He'll spoil the broth better in this colorful crash apron, alive with gadgets: a whistle for service, an animated worm for early birds, a cork (for the hole in your head), a zipper propitiously placed. Free chef's cap imprinted "Genius." Limited supply, so rush order.
Red and Yellow Plaid Vest, on White.
One size for all.
$5.95

Hand-Painted Shorts for MEN Only

$4.98 EACH

THE THING

OLD SOLDIERS NEVER DIE

"THE THING"
Naughty! Wonderful gift for a he-man Hand-painted— "The Thing" & bare hussy. WHITE rayon.
Style No. 11

"OLD SOLDIERS NEVER DIE"
Daring design shows famous song, Good-Conduct Medal, nude cutie.
WHITE rayon.   Style No. 16

#1415 "CASUAL LIVING"
Pullover sensation in luxurious new jersey (80% Orlon ; 20% Wool). Comfortable warmth minus weight. Easy washing, too! Unusual sunburst piping in contrasting color. Two-way collar. Black with Grey ; Navy with White ; Brown with Gold.
Small, Medium, Large, Extra-Large.
$8.50

#1420 PETTY GIRL SHORTS
Perfect gift for he-men! Two pairs of rayon crepe boxer shorts, each with a different Petty Girl screened design. You'd swear they are hand-painted! In waist sizes 32 to 42. Choose them in Assorted Pastels.
2 pairs, only $3.50

#1485 NEWSPAPER SHORTS
A simple pair of Boxer shorts printed as a 1999 newspaper gives you a peek into the future with all the news that's fit to print — and some that ain't, if you read between the lines! If you're curious about life on Mars — or life in general — these are a must. A real conversation piece! In fine quality Cotton. Sizes 30" to 42" Waist.
2 pairs only $3.50

FOR MEN ONLY ! FREE GIFT

FREDERICK'S "Pocket-Pin-Up Package". MEN! You get FREE with any order, a clear, transparent plastic wallet-size pin-up album! Holds 10 glamorous photos (or your business and identification cards) PLUS a thrilling pin-up picture in full color, AND a handy reminder card with space for listing your favorite gal's measurements (not missing a single curve!). Order now! Get your FREE Pocket Pin-Up Package . . . they won't last long !!!

"Sleeping Partners"

SATIN* SHEETS and HAND-PAINTED MATCHING PILLOW-CASES ... FOR GIFTS!

- Give a gift of dazzling glamour... luxurious, intimate, romantic! Rich colorful SATIN sheets, and matching pillow-cases. For married friends, your own husband or wife ... for brides and grooms to-be! Fit for a millionaire!

- **THE SHEETS**—are 85" x 108" long ... full double-bed size. Like sleeping on a silky cloud of shimmering satin.

- **THE PILLOW-CASES** are a precious pair in matching shades, with "His" and "Hers" hand-painted on them.

- **THE FABRIC**—Hand-washable, easy-to-iron Acetate Satin. It's known for washing and wearing qualities.

STYLE 03

- **THE PRICE**—only *$31.95* includes 2 SHEETS, 2 PILLOW-CASES IN GIFT BOX

Jungle

#1901 JUNGLE TWINS
The same glamorous leopard print broadcloth in Mr. & Mrs. Pajamas with black heart-shaped pockets. Split set; top for her, pants for him. In men's and women's sizes Small, Medium, Large. Give both sizes. **$9⁹⁸**

#1901

#1900

#1900 JUNGLE SHEETS
Anyone will purr like a leopard kitten over these glamorous jungle sheets in exotic gold and black leopard print, with matching pillow cases. Luxurious broadcloth, side trimmed in solid black. Two sheets, each 86 x 108". Pillow cases, standard size. Beautifully gift boxed. **$24⁹⁸**

Adam and Eve

#1479

#1479 KING OF THE ISLES
Cut a handsome figure in this easy-on after-bath wraparound sarong. Fine quality cotton terry that snaps at the side and is adjustable. Handy pocket holds gadgets. Matching fabric, foam rubber cushion soled scuffs with contrast piping, complete the outfit. A grand, two fold idea for the price of one. White only.
Sizes S-M-L **$5⁹⁸**

#3733

#3733 QUEEN OF THE ISLES
Step from your bath into this curve-hugging wraparound sarong of woven cotton terry that glorifies your figure! Button adjustment at top and waistline cinches in your curves. Contrasting piping outlines your form. Easy-on, easy-off styling is a pleasure. A gift idea — especially terrific when paired with #1479 "King of the Isles" companion sarong for men.
White, Pink, Blue.
Sizes 10 to 18 **$3⁹⁸**

CUTE BRIDE & GROOM GIFT!

#865 "SHARE A PAIR" Pyjama Set for Guys and Gals. She gets the tops—he gets the trousers! Both in rich Acetate SATIN with heart pockets. Black, Red, White. Men's and Women's sizes: Small, Med., Large. Give both sizes. SET— **$9⁹⁸**

9569 DUAL COCKTAIL SHAKER
Be the host or hostess who adds something new to their Holiday parties! Use head for 2, 4 or 6 jiggers of liquor. Place mix in nudie body. Shake... remove "bar-bra" and two plugs... pour two drinks into two glasses at same time. Capture the approval of all your guests...and have a "shaker full of fun!" Plastic. **$2⁹⁵**

NEW 9 COCKTAIL SHAKER

GENUINE JUNGLE PRINT FAKE FUR **$3⁹⁹**

HERS PUSHES IN PUSHES UP HIS

G **#4720 JUNGLE GEM** in
Wonderfully wild bra and bikini in a fabulous fake fur jungle print sure to make a leopard change its spots with envy. Bra is push-up padded for alluring cleavage. Bikini brief has elastic side insets for that gone-native look. Bra sizes 32 to 36, A, B, C cup. Rayon and cotton jungle print. **$7⁹⁹**

H **#4721 JUNGLE MATE**
Fake fur jungle print man's brief to match #4720 has elastic open sides. Sizes to fit 26 to 36 inch waist. Rayon and cotton print fabric gives the appearance of lush fur in jungle colors. **$3⁹⁹**

SHEER NYLON BIKINI FOR MEN:

$2⁸⁸

#4768 ADAM BRIEFS
Sensational men's sheer Nylon slumber bikini briefs. Satin bound with elastic top - fly front. Really something! Comes in Black or Gold. Sizes 28 to 36 **$2⁸⁸**

APPLY IN-A-TWINK
improve your wink

#9381 HUMAN HAIR EYEBROWS
Frederick's new beauty idea eliminates plucking or tweezing eyebrows. Made of human hair for that natural brow-line to enhance your beauty. Shape as you wish. Intricately hand fashioned on transparent backing. Self-adhesive and so comfortable to wear. Includes special application fluid and instructions. Light or Dark Brown, Grey or Black. **$4²⁵**

#9535 FUR EYELASHES
Bring French glamour to your eyes with long, thick, exquisite fur lashes. Precisely created to adhere so gently but surely. Daringly deceptive for the most glamorous, expressive eyes in the world! Includes special application fluid and instructions. Black or Brown. **$3⁹⁹**

#9023 HUMAN HAIR EYELASHES
Long, luxurious eyelashes imported from Europe form a natural frame for your eyes . . . only you will know they aren't your own! Delicate strands of real hair meticulously fashioned. Pre-shaped, self-adhesive, mix beautifully with your own lashes. Includes special application fluid and instructions. Black or Brown. **$2⁵⁰**

#9096 JUST FOR FUN
Sport-time is fun-time! Our visor cap dynel wig was created for your play-time. Pop it on at the pool, by the lake, at the seashore, on the golf course, in the convertible or wherever sport clothes are worn. Excitingly different! Black, Dark or Light Brown, Auburn, Blonde or Platinum **$6⁹⁹**

Allison Hayes

"Cuter Than Cute . . ." in Frederick's #22

#22 OCTO-PUSS CAR CAP
Real flap of a car cap that's a heigh-ho for Mommie-o and Daddy-o! It's in fine washable Rayon Linen crowned with a flippity floppity octopus in gaily colored wool yarn. Sharp visor, adjustable back. Real crazy Hollywood cutie for guys and dolls! White, Navy or Powder. Sizes S, M, L for men or women **$8⁹⁸**

#3-4151 MISS MIXER
This go-go girl will mix well at any party! Put your drink in her attached holder, press the button and she'll really shake up a mean drink! Stirs up the drinks — and the drinkers, too! Battery operated, 15" tall, shaped and we do mean "shaped" in life-like vinyl. Take off the removable gold bikini top if you're daring — WOW! (Battery not included) **$13**

GLAMOUR COVER-UP

#9001   COIFFURE PETALS
It's your secret what's under this glamorous petal hat! Hides rollers, pin curls, straggly hair. Cool and light weight to be worn while shopping, dining, poolside, in the convertible or just to be lovelier at home . . . Nylon petals are crush proof and perfect for traveling! White, Hot Pink, Orange, Avocado.   **$6⁹⁹**

#9382   QUEEN OF EGYPT
Be first with the exotic Cleopatra look . . . add to your wardrobe of wigs with long, and full beauty bangs.
Black, Blonde, Brown.
Plus $1.00 Shipping Charges.   **$10**

#2095   MATI HARI
No respectable enchantress would be without this exotic evening turban. Soft Rayon Velvet hat shapes to the head with a face flattering drape. Fully Rayon Taffeta lined with size adjustments. Black, Regal Red or Kelly Green.   **$11⁹⁹**

ICE CUBE NUDIES FOR "FUN" PARTIES!

#9490   NAUGHTY BUT NICE
Gift to please the menfolk and get parties off to a jolly start! A set of two Nudie ice cube trays that turn out the prettiest damsels you've ever seen. Plastic. 2 trays ————   **$1⁹⁹**

#4841   MEN-TIONABLES!
Men's nylon stretch fish-net shirt with V-neck and short sleeves. Lightweight, comfortable for sleep or daytime underwear. Black, White.
Sizes Small, Med., Large.   **$5⁹⁵**

NEW! IMPORTED! BEAUTY SPOTS!

#9520   BEAUTY SPOTS
What these flirty circles and hearts did for Madame Pompadour, they can do for you! Eye catchers . . . beaux catchers . . . they're the rage of the continent. Amazing new Beauty Spots, *IMPORTED FROM EUROPE,* adhere to the face, stick tight under the most trying circumstances. Package contains 10 Round & 10 Heart-shaped spots.
Federal Tax Included   **$2⁷⁵**

#9440   BROWETTES FOR LOVELIER EYEBROWS
Yes . . . your eyebrows should be your loveliest, most expressive feature! Browettes Eyebrow Mask is a fabulous new discovery that makes it a cinch to apply alluring new eyebrow shapings . . . choose from seven different eyebrow contours to correct uneven natural lines . . . so simple you can do it while wearing glasses. Complete kit with instructions.   **$1⁷⁵**

BUST MASSAGER

#9056   BUST MASSAGER
Amazing new Hydro-Forme massager, scientifically designed to help increase the size of your bust and to give it ideal form. Massages and increases circulation with firm whirlpool action of water therapy, safe and easy to use.

A FLATTERING PROFILE CAN BE YOURS   **$15⁹⁵**

FLATTERING FANTASIES

#9125   JEWELLED HIGHLIGHTS
Add interesting eye appeal to exposed places! For the more daring with knee-high skirts . . . on the front or outside of knee. For subtle glances on the calf of the leg. For provocative winks . . . over the bosom with one-shoulder or strapless dresses. Adheres ever-so-gently. Can be worn again and again . . . even over nylons. Set contains two rhine-stone fantasies.   **$2⁰⁰**

GLAMOUR GIFTS!

Was

~~$45~~

shape
your
legs
with
pads

HOLLYWOOD APPROVED SCREEN STYLE

#5—9027 UNCOVER HIDDEN BEAUTY
Stroke on a velvety creme. Feel the deep-down tingling action. Fresh Face is working to lift out impurities . . . you actually see them when you peel away the masque. Refines and smooths skin. Beneficial for every age group . . . is radiant answer for problem skin. **$2⁹⁹**

Beauty is more than Skin Deep

fresh face

#9391 LOVELI-LEGS
After years of planning and scientific research, Frederick's proudly brings you a sculptured, contoured leg pad with feathered edges, invisible to everyone. Designed to correct almost any defect . . . this molded plastic pad, is as soft as flesh, can be adjusted to fill in any hollow, or simply add curves to a ''thin'' leg. Wear with MAGIC COVER-UPS, the hide-all glamorous stocking. Light or Dark leg pads. **$29⁹⁹**

#9392 MAGIC COVER-UPS
MAGIC hose that do a wonderful cover-up job! Wear over your LOVELI-LEG pads . . . wear to hide unsightly blemishes, scars, birthmarks or varicose veins. Gives extra support to gals on their legs all day. Short, Average, Tall. **$11⁹⁵**

#9134 NATURAL LOVELINESS
Ten minutes to glamour! Work or play, dress or dream while your hair is setting! The latest in hairstyling ease and beauty eliminates sleeping on uncomfortable rollers . . . gives you perfect hair glamour. Hair sets while you have breakfast, before a quick date or after a rain. You'll never go back to the old-fashioned way of setting hair again! Box contains six minute-set rollers with unbreakable clips. **$3**

sets hair in 10 minutes!

ladybird wig

#7—9036 LADY BIRD
First Lady of fashion in Frederick's newest hair style. Lustrous synthetic wig can be combed and restyled. Black, Brown or Blonde. FREE stand. **$8⁹⁹**

#7—9221 BEAUTY STRETCH
Our marvelous no-care stretch wig has a permanent set. Wash it . . . let it dry . . . the set stays in forever.
Off Black, Brown, Blonde

#7—9236 THE NATURAL
Today's newest idea in stretch wigs and the very latest look is the NATURAL LOOK! Created to blend with the new Afro fashions and jewelry this Dynel wig is permanently curled on a lightweight stretch foundation. Jet Black, Off Black, Dark Brown or Mixed Grey **$14⁸⁸**

BRAIDS ''MAID''!
Newest addition to your Hair Wardrobe. A great collection of braids! Fashioned with wire to form loops, scrolls, rings, bows! They're *wild* hair fashion accessories to blend or contrast with your own hair. Create an ''in'' style . . . or any style you want using your own hair or another hairpiece.

#7—9704 MAXI Braids—Fat braids 30 inches long **2 FOR $5**

#7—9705 BRAIDLET—6 braids linked together 12 inches long **$4**

WHAT TO DO WHEN THE WIG'S AWAY!

#3—4147 ORGY BUTTER
Voluptuous & sensual — Orgy Butter! A smoothing, soothing warm red ointment with a subtly sexual scent, rubs easily into your skin — lubricates, delights, brings new pleasures in a multitude of ways. 4 ozs. or fun. **$3**

#9410 THE BIG TWIST . . . Watch those clever skins twist their way . . . to meet at the top of your head . . . in that devastating ''hide-all'' design. Exotic Autumn Haze U.S. Mink. Federal Tax Included **$22**

#9411 GAY TOPPER . . . We've got you covered . . . in smart top fashion in this hide-all hat . . . that's great for all occasions, wonderful for covering up untidy-hair or even rollers! In Jungle Print or White furry pile **$4⁹⁹**

#9418 HAT MAGIC . . . Don't worry about wind and weather! Wear this magnificent Maribou hat. Hugs your head in Wool Jersey . . . hides fly away hair . . . just right for the day when your wig's away! Glamour shades of Black, Royal, Red or Brown **$8⁹⁹**

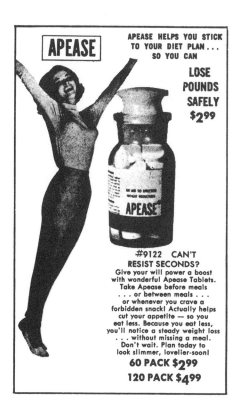

APEASE HELPS YOU STICK TO YOUR DIET PLAN... SO YOU CAN

LOSE POUNDS SAFELY $2.99

#9122 CAN'T RESIST SECONDS?
Give your will power a boost with wonderful Apease Tablets. Take Apease before meals ... or between meals ... or whenever you crave a forbidden snack! Actually helps cut your appetite — so you eat less. Because you eat less, you'll notice a steady weight loss ... without missing a meal. Don't wait. Plan today to look slimmer, lovelier-soon!

60 PACK $2.99
120 PACK $4.99

luxurious leopard satin sheets

SATIN SHEETS 'N PILLOW-CASES

FITTED SATIN SHEET SETS
Luxurious sleeping elegance you have always *dreamed* about. Become tantalizingly desirable under leopard satin sheets! Frederick's exclusive creation in the finest 100% Acetate Satin. Lint-free, allergy-free. Launder as any fine fabric or dry-clean. SAVE up to $11.00 by buying complete sets!

#5—9278 Double Bed Set — 90 x 108 **$48**   #5—9279 King Bed Set — 108 x 122 **$58**

GO WILD...GO ANIMAL

#5—9548 COZY UP TO A JUNGLE CAT!
Frankly fake, frankly fabulous throw. Actually it's blanket-weight cotton "fur" — great for snuggling up in. Toss it over a bed or sofa, drape it over a sports car seat, hang it up in den or dorm. It's a bigger-than-life 51" x 61", and completely washable. Black leopard spots against tawny beige with smaller ocelot spots on the reverse side. **$7**
ADD $1.40 SHIPPING CHARGE

FABULOUS FAKES
But only your safari-chief will know for sure! Go ahead, decorate dangerously with the lure of the Leopard, the zing of the Zebra, the excitement of the Pony! Lounge-inviting pillows are 15" square. Durable jungle-printed. **$5 EACH**
#5—9545 Leopard
#5—9546 Zebra
#5—9547 Pony
3 FOR $13.50

F #7—9745 FLIPPED OUT
A fall that flips into the many ways you want to dress your hair. Flip it on for a flipped-up fall. Flip it upside down for extra-long flirty gypsy curls. 14"-16" length ... MOST VERSATILE! ... in wash-and-brush easy-care mod-acrylic. Black, Off Black, Dark, Medium or Light Brown, Golden or Champagne Blonde. **$15**

Make your bedroom the Play RooM

RX FOR MARITAL HAPPINESS — guaranteed to increase intimate marital enjoyment & satisfaction. Specially designed inflatable vinyl pillow gives extra elevation with support — greater agility, freedom. Recommended by religious, medical, marriage counselors. 20" x 23" with washable zippered cover; 8-page manual.
#5—9544 Compat-A-Pillow. **$7**
ADD 85c SHIPPING CHARGE
#5—9561 Extra Compat-A-Cover **$1.89**

#5—9503 FRAGRANTLY FEMININE
Newest idea for the modern female ... a safe, gentle, refreshing deodorant douche of *exceptional fragrance!* Now you can eliminate the strong medicinal odor so old-fashioned in today's world. A truly unique experience in feminine hygiene. Available in Raspberry, Orange or Champagne **$5**

#5—9446 VICE SPICE
Ssh! This actually acts like you know what — without any harmful effects. When taken as directed, this distillation of genuinely imported spice will turn you on ... stimulate your partner ... make the going great! It's safe. It's very exciting! Try a 24-capsule package at **$5**

JOY JELL
Dee-licious! Let him savor the flavor of you ... your lips ... your skin! Joy Jell is a fruit-fragrant lubricant that glides on to soften, entice, eliminate dryness. Flavored to his favorite tastes: Strawberry, Orange, Grape or Pineapple.
#5—9448 Gift Set ... **$5** (All 4 Flavors)

#5—0516 OIL OF LOVE
A rare oil with an exotic fragrance —a path to sensual delight. Use it when you are with your beloved and you will set him aflame with desire. Smells delicious—gives a faint scent of lotus, warming to the body— even tastes good. **$5**

247

The Sensuous Woman
By "J"

The author of this book is not particularly pretty. Men never notice her in a crowd or whistle at her when she walks down the street. Yet some of the world's most exciting males consider her to be the perfect woman: beautiful; a modern Aphrodite; maddeningly exciting; the epitome of the sensuous woman.

A #5—9430 THE SENSUOUS WOMAN by "J" is already one of the country's most-talked-about books. Never before has there been such a candid, honest, well-written guide telling women how to satisfy themselves and their men. **$6**

Sent in plain wrapper.

#5—9471 SEX KNOW-HOW "THE ART AND SCIENCE OF LOVE" by Dr. Albert Ellis is that most wanted of all books on love-making: a handbook of marriage! More than 700,000 copies sold in the U.S. Published in 14 languages. Sophisticated and extremely liberal in attitude, its easy-to-read pages spell out the essentials of physical know-how. Details what you need to know for a really satisfying sexual relationship. **$795**
Sent in plain wrapper.

#5—9472 "SEX AND THE SINGLE MAN" by Dr. Albert Ellis sweeps aside sexual taboos to provide practical answers to single men's problems. Such as the pros and cons of abstinence, marriage. How to know love and what to do about it. How to pet and like it. What every man should know about bedmanship. How to pick a suitable wife. Unorthodox and unconventional, it abolishes Puritanism and vulgarity in favor of today's code of swinging ethics. Young, old, married, single . . . every man needs this book . . . every woman wishes he would read it! **$5**

mailed in a plain wrapper

#5—9470 NEED A MAN? At last a MAN tells WOMEN how to land a husband If you're single, widowed, divorced, "THE INTELLIGENT WOMAN'S GUIDE TO MAN-HUNTING" by Dr. Albert Ellis tells you everything you really need to know about men. Not the old-fashioned hogwash that has hurt your chances so far. Not your friends' well-intentioned advice. This book tells you what men look for in a woman and what they want of her. You learn how to please your man psychologically, physically and sexually . . . where to find eligible men, what to say to them, even how to pick them up. Discuss the sexual aspect of courtship too. A real must — have in your life! **$6**

mailed in a plain wrapper

SENSUAL WATER BED

#5—9598 WATER BED
Newest sensation for sensual, contoured sleep! Fun for play too! Just fill this heavy-duty vinyl inflatible bed with water, and the action begins. Every movement conforms to your body and desires. Firm, yet it moves with you... caresses with a wave-like motion. Nap, bounce or sun on it. Feel embraced by its sensual softness. The seams are sonic welded for even strength. Folds flat for fit in a carrying case. Great for poolside ...but best of all in the privacy of your bedroom. With terrycloth cover.

#5—9598 Water Bed	**$79**
#5—9615 Terrycloth Cover	**$20**

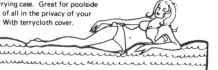

#5-9604 CHIN UP!
Give yourself a face lift in <u>one minute</u> flat ! Keep —or bring back — that firm young chin line with this easy 60 second air isometric exerciser. Bite down for 5 seconds, repeat. Exercises 14 face and neck muscles. No more double chins, jowls, sags and droops !

$4⁹⁵

Clinically tested and approved

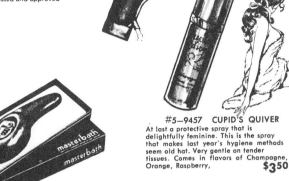

#5-9457 CUPID'S QUIVER
At last a protective spray that is delightfully feminine. This is the spray that makes last year's hygiene methods seem old hat. Very gentle on tender tissues. Comes in flavors of Champagne, Orange, Raspberry,

$3⁵⁰

#5-9429 FEMI-FRESHENERS
Give no offense ever . . . with this deliciously scented, delightfully delicate douche. You'll feel so ulta-feminine, refreshed, immaculately clean with the subtle fragrance that expresses the real YOU! So convenient! Each pre-measured packet mixes instantly to the proper strength in a quart of warm water. Choose scents of Raspberry, or Champagne. Box of 12.

$5

Mrs. Linda Rogers
Fowler, Indiana
A winner in our NEW WARDROBE CONTEST
Mrs. Rogers went from an up-and-down boyish build to ALL-GIRL proportions she'd always dreamed of ! She writes: "By using the Beauty Firm method and book on lovlier legs, I have increased my measurements from 33-23-33½" to 37½-21-37" in JUST 10 WEEKS!
WOW! Think how great THAT FIGURE will look in her new Frederick's fashions !

before *after*

#5-9690 MASTERBATH
The first hygeine cleanser for intimate areas. Makes such sweet scents! Patented feminine soap is anatomically shaped to penetrate and cleanse. Use oval-shaped end for regular bathing...Narrow end for hard to reach areas. Helps guard against offensive odors. Mildly deodorant, its gentle fragrance is intoxicatingly feminine.

$5

#5-9484 BUMPS & GRINDS
A hilarious drinking and stripping game any number can play. Starts with drinking and candlelight, but as Bumps and Grinds progress the first bashful blush is forgotten and more and more clothing is shed. When one player is down to his last piece of clothing, he blows out the candle and is declared THE WINNAH!

$6

ALMOST SINFUL!
(BUT SO-O NICE!)

#5-9624 GULP 'N GIGGLE
With a clear head, you can play for—ever! If limericks tickle your funny bone. . .and if you're a "gulper" not a "sipper" . . . your chances of winning are few. But think of the fun you'll have losing! A game any number can play. . .with or without partners.

$7

#5-9595   HER
Not since THE SENSUOUS WOMAN has a book created such excitement as HER! Written by "Anonymous," HER is a love story so candid you'd never dream it could appear in print! Together, a man and woman explore every nuance and variation, every torment and ecstasy in a sexual relationship too idyllic to end ...too hot to last. Order your copy, to be mailed in a plain wrapper.

$6

#5-9596 ZSA ZSA SAYS
"Before you marry, be sure you will like him as an ex-husband!" Hollywood's most glamorous femme fatale tells "<u>HOW TO CATCH A MAN, HOW TO KEEP A MAN, HOW TO GET RID OF A MAN!</u>" Book shares love secrets with husband-hunters, wives, widows, singles. It's must reading for every woman, written by a SEXPERT! Real revelation for every man!

$4⁵⁰

ZSA ZSA TELLS ALL!
* HOW TO CATCH A MAN....
* HOW TO KEEP A MAN...
* HOW TO GET RID OF A MAN!

FOR E-V-E-R-Y EVE!

#5—9426 BEAUTY FIRM

Have the beautiful <u>bustline</u> you've always dreamed of! Now it's so easy to get that fabulous figure <u>HE</u> admires. Special bust-developing device works to actually increase your bust-line measurements. See amazing results in just a few short weeks or your money back!

$6⁹⁹

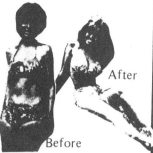

"It's simple but...highly effective! By using Frederick's Beauty Firm faithfully for a few minutes, I have increased my bust line from size 34½" to 37"!"

After

Before

Sherry Lynn Strieter
Downey, California

"I used Frederick's Beauty Firm for my bust and went from size 36 to 38!"

Before

After

Mrs. Thelma Junk
Remlap, Alabama

"To attain my new figure I used Frederick's Beauty Firm to increase my bust to 38½"!"

Before

After

Janet Smith
Longmont, Colorado

---

cordless vibrator for satisfying relaxation.

NEW

#7—9152 EXCITING NEW MASSAGER

Exciting and stimulating massager brings new found joys and pleasures for ultra satisfying relaxation. Deep, gentle penetrating massage gives soothing, beneficial relief from daily tensions. Women will find it invaluable for skin tone and complexion care.

7 inches long
Completely safe.
(Batteries not included.)

$2⁹⁹

#5—9665 GREAT VIBES!

A new deluxe massage vibrator that's NINE INCHES LONG! Great for getting to places you couldn't reach before. Cordless vibrator gives deep, gentle penetrating massage . . . the kind that works away aches and pains . . . makes you feel relaxed enough to purrr! Marvelous for improving skin tone, keeping you in the pink. And wait till you rub it up and down his tired and aching back. He'll LUV ya! Completely safe. ("C" batteries not included)

2 for $8⁵⁰
$4⁵⁰ each

NEW! Deluxe model 9" massager! Massages places you could never reach before!

Mrs. Richardine Richardson
Charleston, South Carolina
Won a FREE WARDROBE
in our contest!

Mrs. Richardson knew she had some weight to lose and some figuring to do. So she ordered herself a Frederick's Trim Cycle. The result: 28 pounds lost. Inches off hips, waist and bust. Down 4 dress sizes. She writes: "The Trim Cycle trims you all around: Firms the bust, pulls in the tummy, slenderizes the hips. Using it, you can eat what you want, but less. Have a little will power."
Right on, Mrs. Richardson! And right on is the way all the fabulous Frederick's clothes you've won will look on your right-nice new figure!

before   after

KNEE PADS ADD

to your pleasure! Let you do your thing without sore, chafed, aching or stiff knees! Made of soft and durable sponge rubber, they strap on. Are fully adjustable. Fit over or under clothing.
Set of two, only

#5—9184   only $2.98

make your own bed a vibra bed!

relaxes!   massages!

VIBRA BED

Convert your own bed into a VIBRA BED in seconds! Feel every part of your body come alive! Eases tensions! Soothes muscles! Brings tingling, vibrating sensations . . . a pleasure you BOTH can share! Maybe you've used a vibrating bed in a hotel or a motel. Now your own! Plugs into any outlet. Can also be used on a chair or sofa.

#5—9185 $9.95

WATER LIFT—OFF

Newest sensual sensation! A Frederick's first! Wait till you lie on this new water—filled pad! Specially contoured for lift-off, it rises and falls with a free—flowing motion. . .excites, supports, arouses. Recommended for its agility and freedom... guaranteed to bring a new level of enjoyment and satisfaction to your in-bed behavior.
Of extra—heavy vinyl, absolutely leak—proof.

#5—9632 $7

HYDRO-DYNAMIC BREAST CUP!

BEAUTY BUST PLAN

... to help build a beautiful bosom. BEAUTY BUST PLAN helps you bring your bosom to its most desirable development. Enclosed booklet explains the miracle of the female breast from first bud-like swelling to full sexual development. Teaches you breast care for a lifetime of health and beauty.

BEAUTY BUST PLAN:
- Assists in uplifting and sculpturing the bosom.
- Stimulates breast through Hydrotherapy (water treatment) Hydro-dynamic breast cup produces pleasurable mini-jets to increase circulation by water massage.
- Helps you achieve proper bust volume through diet
- Keeps skin nipples soft, supple, with special beauty cream.

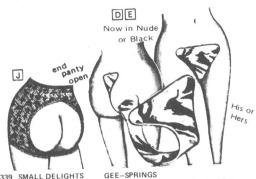

HELPS WITHOUT EXERCISE OR DIET!

#5—9237 $19.98
extra supply of creme

D E
Now in Nude or Black

J

end panty open

His or Hers

G   3-4339 SMALL DELIGHTS
Good things come in small packages! This all-nylon sleep-set makes three gorgeous packages or YOU! With maribou fluff for trim on each one, this elasticized bra and panty set is of sheer nylon with black lace edging. The rest is up to you! Assorted colors. One size fits Small, Medium and Large.

**$6⁵⁰EACH
2 for $11**

GEE—SPRINGS
HIS and HERS clip—on underwired Gee—Springs—a patented Frederick's exclusive! Wires fit comfortable, securely, covering everything that should be covered. Nylon animal—print fabric is removable for washing. There is also a little fun pocket for your "Mad Money!" Exciting mini coverage for maxi sunning! One size fits most.

D # 5—9499 HIS **$10**
E # 5—9491 HERS **$9**

THE BIGGEST
12-INCH VIBRATOR! One solid foot of pure joy! Thrills and massages. Reaches depths you never reached before! Arouses yet relaxes you to the point of PURRRING! For him, for her. Completely safe, with 2-speed high-low switch. Operates on 'C' batteries (not included).

#5—9327   2 for $9.50
$5 Each

12 Inches of Pure Joy!

---

the bed sheet that's sexy!

SHE SHEETS
A full-size NUDIE CUTIE printed on a no-iron white bed sheet! Breasts are 3-dimensional latex foam, removable for washing. You'll never be in bed and bored! Great gift idea! Flat sheets only.

#5—9188   Double size $16
#5—9190   King size $20

VICE SPICE
Ssh! This actually acts like you know what—without any harmful effects. When taken as directed, this distillation of genuinely imported spice will turn you on...stimulate your partner...make the going great! Try a 24-capsule package at

5—9446   2 for $9.50
$5 each

IRRESISTABLE
fruit-flavored nipple creams

NIPPLE CREAM
for nipples that bring out the full female of you! It's fabulous cream you massage in gently... helps keep the tips in the pink of condition! Deliciously flavored for lovers in Pink Grapefruit and Acreola Cherry. Gift-boxed. Set of two 1-ounce jars.

#5—9239 $5

EMOTION LOTION
For any part of the body you want to pamper! Gets warm when you rub it in. Gets HOT when you blow on it gently. Smells and tastes like fresh wild raspberries. YUM! An aid to groovy loving. Share some with someone special ... and seeeeeeeee!

#5—9117 $3.50

Look 10 years younger!

temporary wrinkle remover

before

after

 # 5—9531   TEMPORARY MAGIC
Lets you accomplish just what you had in mind when you use Temporary Wrinkle—Away. A drop or two of this miraculous liquid helps smoothe away wrinkles like magic and lessens puffiness under the eyes. Lines won't disappear forever, but they'll vanish for up to 8 hours, and that ought to be all the time you'll really need! Won't clog pores, rinses off with water. Contains no hormones or animal proteins. Big 1—ounce bottle.

**2 for $5⁷⁵
$3 each**

251

CUTAWAY CAPER
Double-breasted cutaway coat
lets him do his thing with zing!
In Polyester and Rayon weave.
White with Black trim or
Burgundy with Grey trim.
Coat: Small, Medium, Large, X-Large.
Pants: 28, 30, 32, 34, 36.
    #10—2187   2 pc $40

NEW
"Baggy"
Shirt!

STUD STUFF
A great control shirt that's loose 'n
easy through the shoulders . . . tight-
smocked through the waist and cuffs.
Button-front Acetate and Nylon in
White or Blue. Small, Medium, Large.
B #10—2856 $14

HAPPY PANTS
to go with Frederick's fabulous man-tops!
Great fit, slightly flared leg. Polyester
and Rayon weave. White or Blue.
Waist sizes 28, 30, 32, 34, 36.
D #10—2195 $18

THE HIGH WAY
to a high-waisted slimmed-in
sexy figure! Men's high-waisted
control brief shapes inches off
your waist, hips, lower back.
Lightweight . . . completely
comfortable . . . gives high back
support. Nylon Spandex body,
with a front Acetate/Cotton/
Rubber tummy panel. White.
Waist sizes Small (28 to 30),
Medium (32 to 34),
Large (36 to 38).
    #5—9299 $7.99

#3—4768 ADAM BRIEFS
Sensational men's sheer Nylon slumber
bikini briefs. Satin bound with elastic
top—fly front. Really something!
Comes in Black, Red and White.
Sizes 28-36.
    3 for $8⁵⁰
    $3⁰⁰ ea.

D # 5—9616 THE SENSUOUS MAN
by "M" is about to climb to the
top of this year's best—seller lists!
For the first time, a complete,
straight—from—the shoulder, well—
defined guide telling men how to
realize their full potential of love
life!   Postpaid **$6**

MAILED IN A <u>PLAIN BROWN</u> WRAPPER

hood attached

FUN FLARE
Pleated, flared sleeved shirt with fashionable long collar dresses him with pizazz! Acetate and Nylon weave. Black, Burgundy or White. Small, Medium, Large or Extra Large.

G #10—2188 $18

KOMFY KAFTAN
Grab your favorite sheik in this comfortable hooded caftan . . . and he'll feel like one. Laced up front, raglan openings for arms. Nylon Tricot in Purple, Black or Red. One size fits all.

#10—2194 $23

BODY TALK
A body shirt for him that molds to his muscles. Snap crotch for super fit. Floral pattern in stretch lace Nylon that lets you see that magnificent chest. Front zip, fashionable long collar. 100% stretch lace Nylon in Purple, White or Black. Small, Medium, Large or Extra Large.

#10—2193 $18

THE LEAST
he can wear for manly support. Padded Nylon jock strap comes in White or Black. One size fits all.

M #10—2867 $4

BOLD BIKINI
For the man who has everything! A mesh bikini brief with print pouch front. White or Black net with assorted Nylon prints. Small, Medium, Large, X-Large.

K #10—2180 $5.50

GET THE MESH-AGE
Men's mesh bikini brief only for very daring! Black or White Nylon mesh knit. Small, Medium, Large.

G #10—2182 $5

HANG IN THERE
in open fly-front shiny sexy Cire Nylon briefs. Surprises for the undressing! Elastic-topped pullons in Black or White. One size fits all.

H #10—2871 $5

#5—9125 "ANY WOMAN CAN" find love and sexual fulfillment! Single, widowed, divorced or married, the author of "EVERYTHING YOU ALWAYS WANTED TO KNOW!" tells it like it is for YOU! Dr. Reuben shows you how to attract a man's interest, how to make the man you want to marry want to marry you. And more! Does away with moral hypocrisy. Probes to psychological and emotional depths! Mailed in a plain brown wrapper. Add 75¢ for shipping and handling charges.

$7.95

BREAST PLATES to gild the lily! Fabulous new Gold® filagree breast plates are exciting to wear all bare on the bust or under a see-through shirt. Or over Frederick's body dresses! **Order for you!** One size will fit all!
#5—9255 (*imitation)

$12.50

12 "POSITIONS" WATCH! Do it, baby, all around the clock! Time tells you what position to take! Stainless steel watch case has a black-faced dial that marks the hours with the 12 classic "how-to's." Try one . . . try all! Black Suede-like band.
#5—9328

$15

Tell Time by the 12 Positions!

Just for Fun!

254

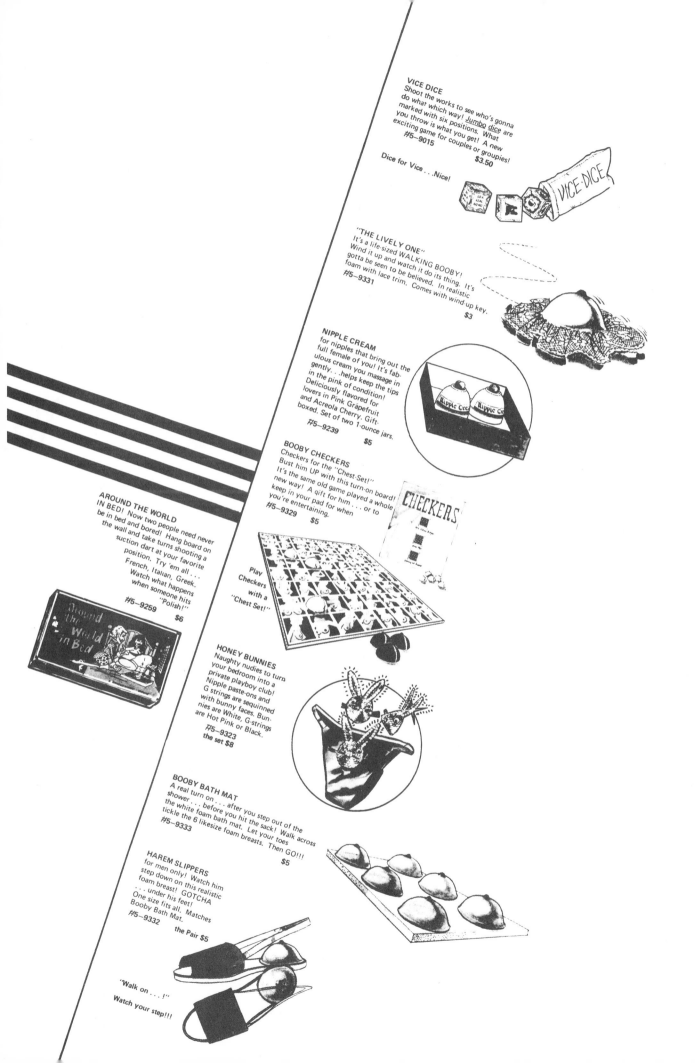

VICE DICE
Shoot the works to see who's gonna do what which way! Jumbo dice are marked with six positions. What you throw is what you get! A new exciting game for couples or groupies!
#5–9015 $3.50

Dice for Vice . . . Nice!

"THE LIVELY ONE"
It's a life-sized WALKING BOOBY! Wind it up and watch it do its thing. It's gotta be seen to be believed. In realistic foam with lace trim. Comes with wind-up key.
#5–9331 $3

NIPPLE CREAM
for nipples that bring out the full female of you! It's fabulous cream you massage in gently. . .helps keep the tips in the pink of condition! Deliciously flavored for lovers in Pink Grapefruit and Acreola Cherry. Gift-boxed. Set of two 1-ounce jars.
#5–9239 $5

BOOBY CHECKERS
Checkers for the "Chest-Set!" Bust him UP with this turn-on board! It's the same old game played a whole new way! A gift for him . . . or to keep in your pad for when you're entertaining.
#5–9329 $5

Play Checkers with a "Chest Set!"

AROUND THE WORLD
IN BED! Now two people need never be in bed and bored! Hang board on the wall and take turns shooting a suction dart at your favorite position. Try 'em all . . . French, Italian, Greek. Watch what happens when someone hits "Polish!"
#5–9259 $6

HONEY BUNNIES
Naughty nudies to turn your bedroom into a private playboy club! Nipple paste-ons and G strings are sequinned with bunny faces. Bunnies are White, G-strings are Hot Pink or Black.
#5–9323   the set $8

BOOBY BATH MAT
A real turn on . . . after you step out of the shower . . . before you hit the sack! Walk across the white foam bath mat. Let your toes tickle the 6 likesize foam breasts. Then GO!!!
#5–9333 $5

HAREM SLIPPERS
for men only! Watch him step down on this realistic foam breast! GOTCHA . . .under his feet! One size fits all. Matches Booby Bath Mat.
#5–9332   the Pair $5

"Walk on . . . !"

Watch your step!!!